The Wallflower

YAMATONADESHIKO SHICHIHENGE

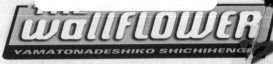

7

Tomoko Hayakawa

Translated and adapted by
David Ury

Lettered by
Dana Hayward

KODANSHA COMICS

Wall ower volume 7 is a work of fiction. Names, characters, places, and cidents are the products of the author's imagination or are used fictitiously. Any resemblance to actual events, locales, or persons, living or dead, is entirely coincidental.

A Kodansha Comics Trade Paperback Original.

Published in the United States by Kodansha Comics, an imprint of Kodansha USA Publishing, LLC., New York.

Publication rights for this English edition arranged through Kodansha Ltd., Tokyo.

First published in Japan in 2002 by Kodansha Ltd., Tokyo, as *Yamatonadeshiko Shichihenge*, volume 7.

ISBN 978-1-61262-320-7

Printed in Canada.

www.kodanshacomics.com

9 8 7 6 5 4 3 2 1

Translator/Adapter—David Ury
Lettering—Dana Hayward
Cover Design—David Stevenson

Contents

A Note from the Author

IT'S SIX FEET HIGH, AND IT'S HUGE!

MY...

...LIVING ROOM (JUST PART OF IT)

♥ Heh, heh, heh. It's the "Satan chair" or maybe the "devil chair." The thing in front is the "skeleton chair." I'd sure like to have a pentagon quilt hanging on the wall. ♥ . . . what am I . . . a witch or something? Well, that's my living room. It doesn't look like your ordinary house. But I wanna keep getting more of this stuff! ♥

—Tomoko Hayakawa

Honorifics Explained

Throughout the Kodansha Comics books, you will find Japanese honorifics left intact in the translations. For those not familiar with how the Japanese use honorifics and, more important, how they differ from American honorifics, we present this brief overview.

Politeness has always been a critical facet of Japanese culture. Ever since the feudal era, when Japan was a highly stratified society, use of honorifics—which can be defined as polite speech that indicates relationship or status—has played an essential role in the Japanese language. When addressing someone in Japanese, an honorific usually takes the form of a suffix attached to one's name (example: "Asuna-san"), is used as a title at the end of one's name, or appears in place of the name itself (example: "Negi-sensei," or simply "Sensei!").

Honorifics can be expressions of respect or endearment. In the context of manga and anime, honorifics give insight into the nature of the relationship between characters. Many English translations leave out these important honorifics and therefore distort the feel of the original Japanese. Because Japanese honorifics contain nuances that English honorifics lack, it is our policy at Kodansha Comics not to translate them. Here, instead, is a guide to some of the honorifics you may encounter in Kodansha Comics.

-san: This is the most common honorific and is equivalent to Mr., Miss, Ms., or Mrs. It is the all-purpose honorific and can be used in any situation where politeness is required.

-sama: This is one level higher than "-san" and is used to confer great respect.

-dono: This comes from the word "tono," which means "lord." It is an even higher level than "-sama" and confers utmost respect.

-kun: This suffix is used at the end of boys' names to express familiarity or endearment. It is also sometimes used by men among friends, or when addressing someone younger or of a lower station.

-chan: This is used to express endearment, mostly toward girls. It is also used for little boys, pets, and even among lovers. It gives a sense of childish cuteness.

Bozu: This is an informal way to refer to a boy, similar to the English terms "kid" and "squirt."

Sempai/
Senpai: This title suggests that the addressee is one's senior in a group or organization. It is most often used in a school setting, where underclassmen refer to their upperclassmen as "sempai." It can also be used in the workplace, such as when a newer employee addresses an employee who has seniority in the company.

Kohai: This is the opposite of "sempai" and is used toward underclassmen in school or newcomers in the workplace. It connotes that the addressee is of a lower station.

Sensei: Literally meaning "one who has come before," this title is used for teachers, doctors, or masters of any profession or art.

-[blank]: This is usually forgotten in these lists, but it is perhaps the most significant difference between Japanese and English. The lack of honorific means that the speaker has permission to address the person in a very intimate way. Usually, only family, spouses, or very close friends have this kind of permission. Known as *yobisute*, it can be gratifying when someone who has earned the intimacy starts to call one by one's name without an honorific. But when that intimacy hasn't been earned, it can be very insulting.

THE wallFLOWER

YAMATONADESHIKO SHICHIHENGE

ヤマトナデシコ七変化♡

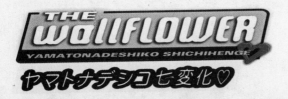

CONTENTS

THE wallflower
YAMATONADESHIKO SHICHIHENGE

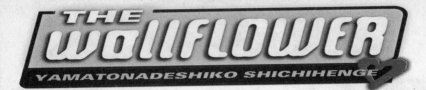

Chapter 27
Oui Monsieur

♥ BOOK 7 ♥

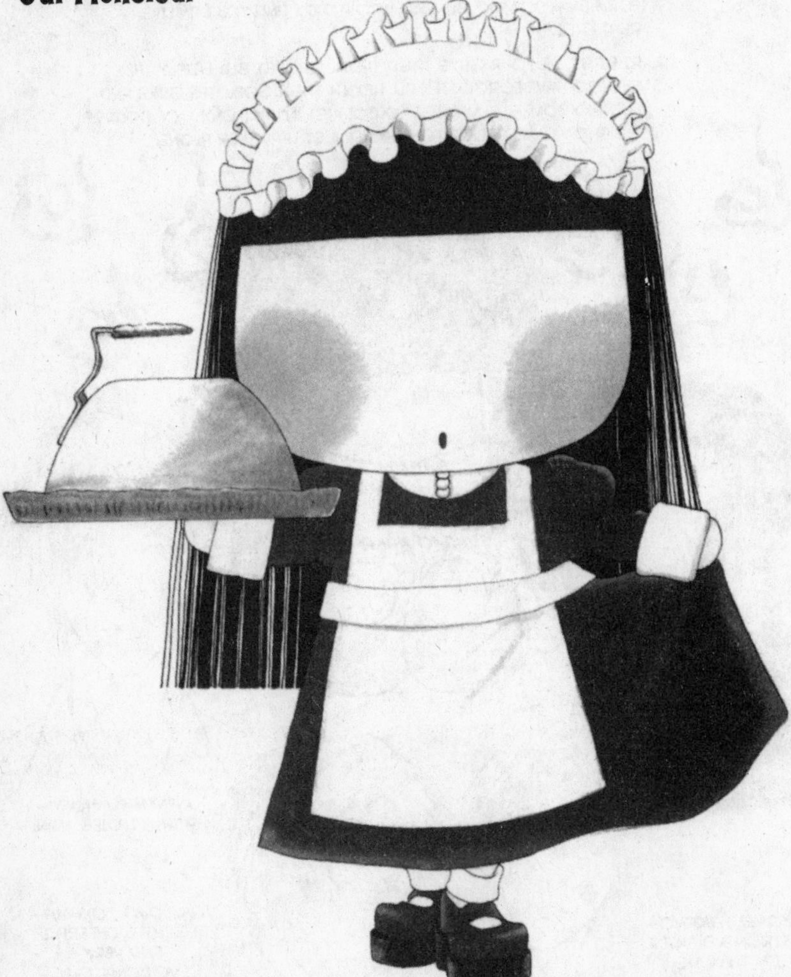

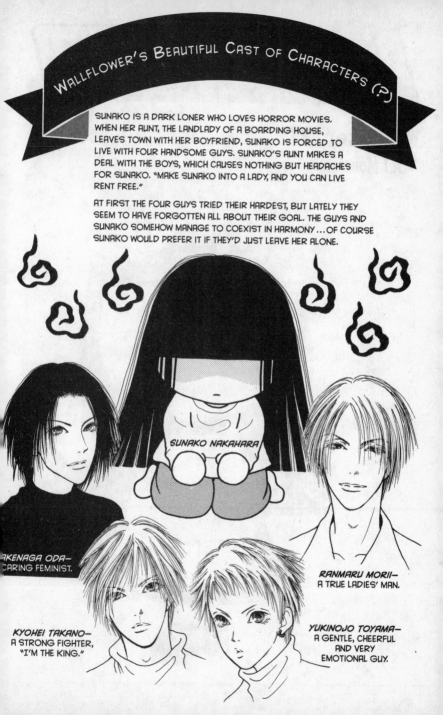

Wallflower's Beautiful Cast of Characters (?)

SUNAKO IS A DARK LONER WHO LOVES HORROR MOVIES. WHEN HER AUNT, THE LANDLADY OF A BOARDING HOUSE, LEAVES TOWN WITH HER BOYFRIEND, SUNAKO IS FORCED TO LIVE WITH FOUR HANDSOME GUYS. SUNAKO'S AUNT MAKES A DEAL WITH THE BOYS, WHICH CAUSES NOTHING BUT HEADACHES FOR SUNAKO. "MAKE SUNAKO INTO A LADY, AND YOU CAN LIVE RENT FREE."

AT FIRST THE FOUR GUYS TRIED THEIR HARDEST, BUT LATELY THEY SEEM TO HAVE FORGOTTEN ALL ABOUT THEIR GOAL. THE GUYS AND SUNAKO SOMEHOW MANAGE TO COEXIST IN HARMONY... OF COURSE SUNAKO WOULD PREFER IT IF THEY'D JUST LEAVE HER ALONE.

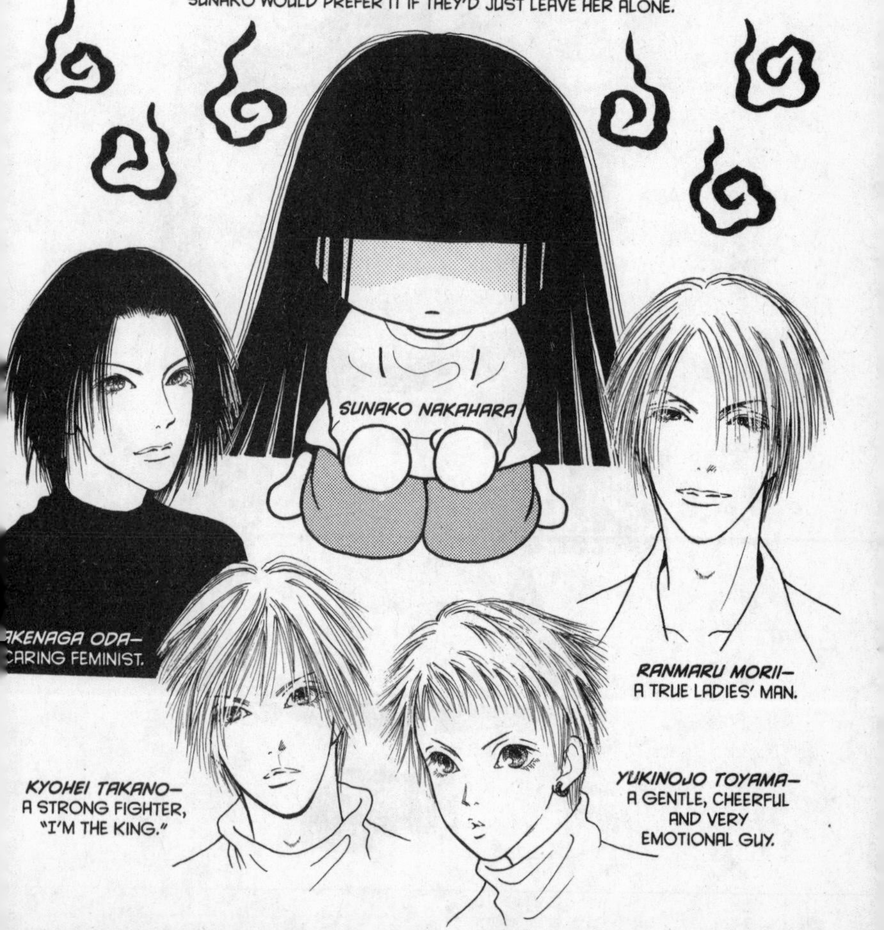
SUNAKO NAKAHARA
AKENAGA ODA—
CARING FEMINIST.
RANMARU MORII—
A TRUE LADIES' MAN.
KYOHEI TAKANO—
A STRONG FIGHTER, "I'M THE KING."
YUKINOJO TOYAMA—
A GENTLE, CHEERFUL AND VERY EMOTIONAL GUY.

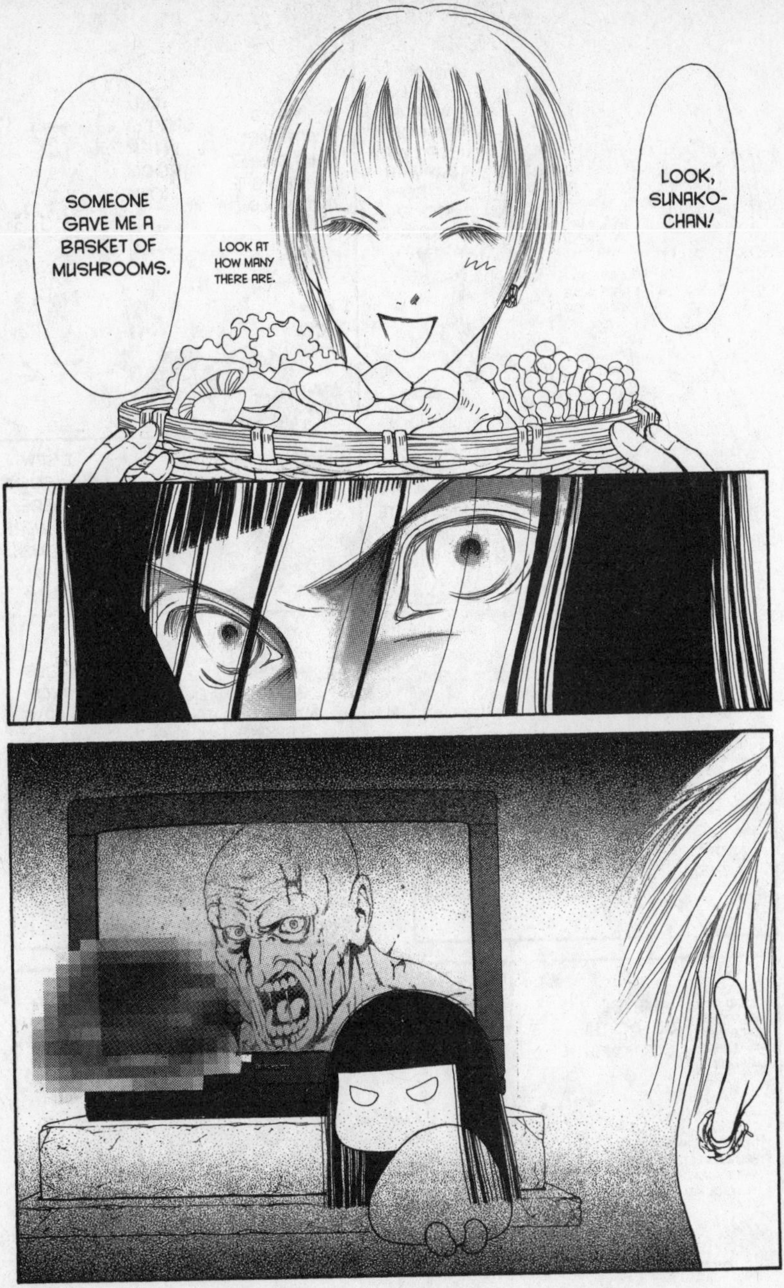
LOOK, SUNAKO-CHAN!
LOOK AT HOW MANY THERE ARE.
SOMEONE GAVE ME A BASKET OF MUSHROOMS.

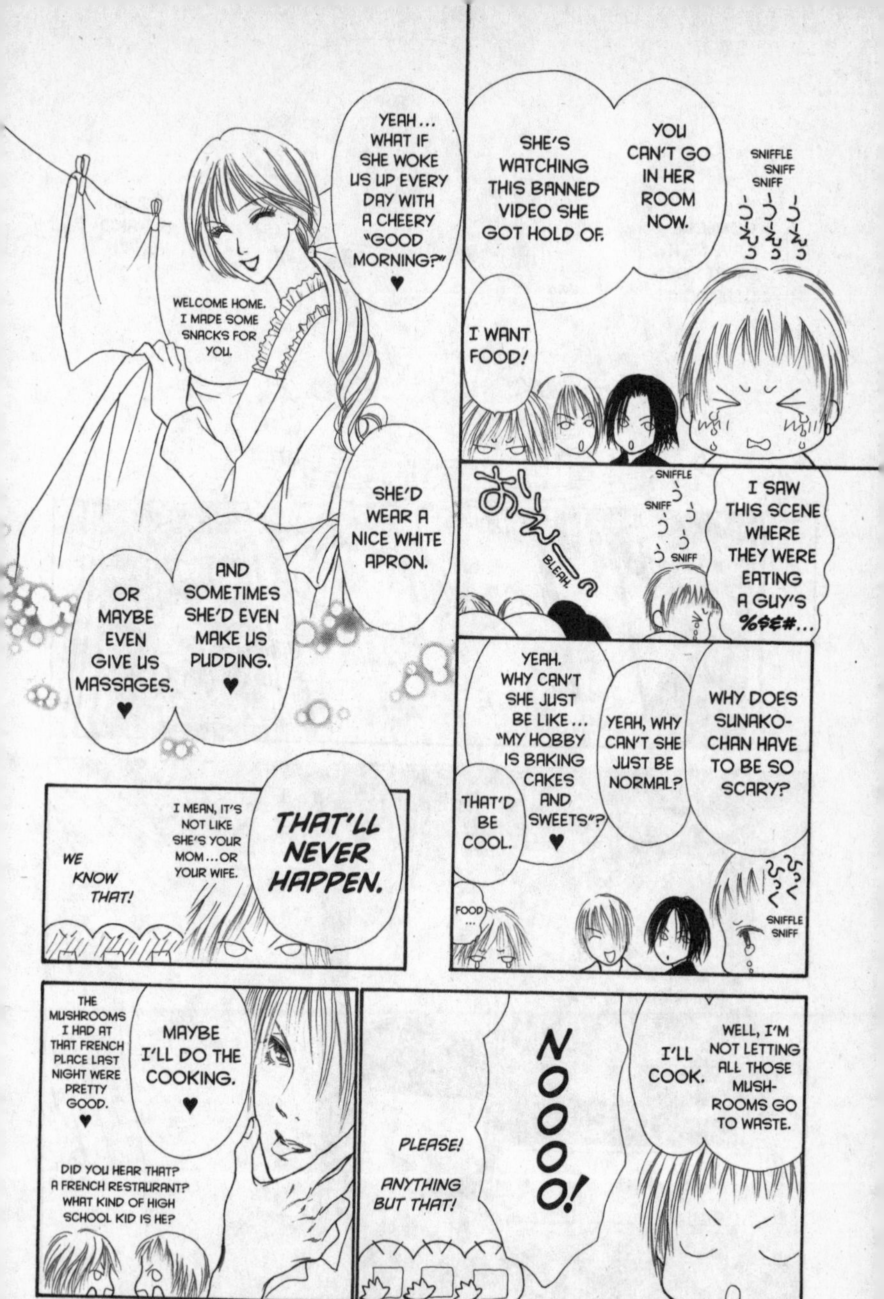
SNIFFLE SNIFF SNIFF
YOU CAN'T GO IN HER ROOM NOW.
SHE'S WATCHING THIS BANNED VIDEO SHE GOT HOLD OF.
I WANT FOOD!
I SAW THIS SCENE WHERE THEY WERE EATING A GUY'S %$£#...
SNIFFLE SNIFF SNIFF
BLEAH.
WHY DOES SUNAKO-CHAN HAVE TO BE SO SCARY?
YEAH, WHY CAN'T SHE JUST BE NORMAL?
YEAH. WHY CAN'T SHE JUST BE LIKE... "MY HOBBY IS BAKING CAKES AND SWEETS"? ♥
THAT'D BE COOL.
SNIFFLE SNIFF
FOOD...
YEAH... WHAT IF SHE WOKE US UP EVERY DAY WITH A CHEERY "GOOD MORNING?" ♥
WELCOME HOME. I MADE SOME SNACKS FOR YOU.
SHE'D WEAR A NICE WHITE APRON.
AND SOMETIMES SHE'D EVEN MAKE US PUDDING. ♥
OR MAYBE EVEN GIVE US MASSAGES. ♥
THAT'LL NEVER HAPPEN.
I MEAN, IT'S NOT LIKE SHE'S YOUR MOM...OR YOUR WIFE.
WE KNOW THAT!
WELL, I'M NOT LETTING ALL THOSE MUSH-ROOMS GO TO WASTE.
I'LL COOK.
NOOOO!
PLEASE! ANYTHING BUT THAT!
MAYBE I'LL DO THE COOKING. ♥
THE MUSHROOMS I HAD AT THAT FRENCH PLACE LAST NIGHT WERE PRETTY GOOD. ♥
DID YOU HEAR THAT? A FRENCH RESTAURANT? WHAT KIND OF HIGH SCHOOL KID IS HE?

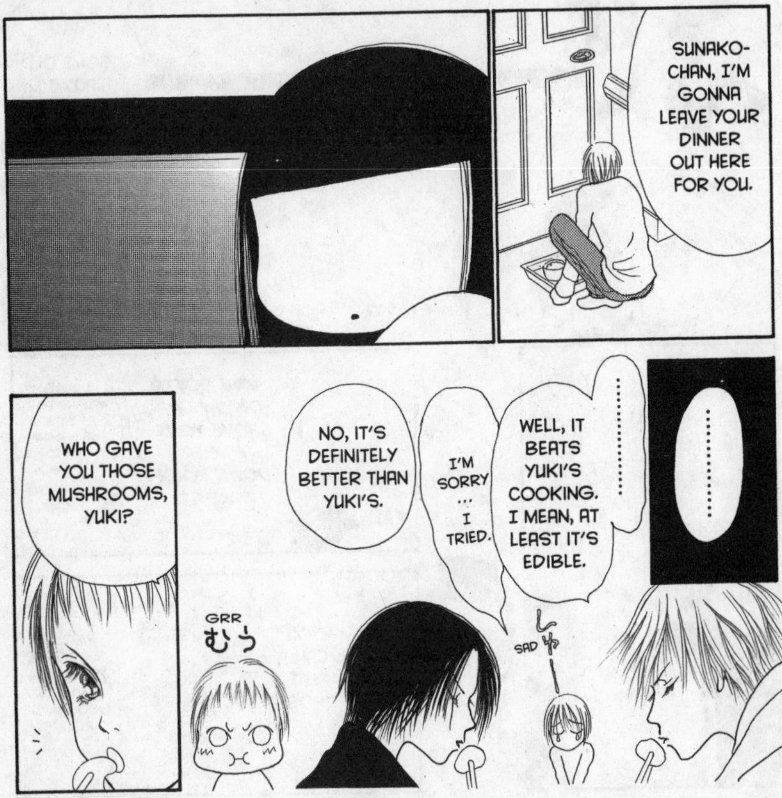
SUNAKO-CHAN, I'M GONNA LEAVE YOUR DINNER OUT HERE FOR YOU.
......
......
WELL, IT BEATS YUKI'S COOKING. I MEAN, AT LEAST IT'S EDIBLE.
SAD
I'M SORRY... I TRIED.
NO, IT'S DEFINITELY BETTER THAN YUKI'S.
GRR
むう
WHO GAVE YOU THOSE MUSHROOMS, YUKI?

BEHIND THE SCENES

IT WAS REALLY A PAIN DRAWING SUNAKO. I MEAN, IT TOOK TWICE AS LONG AS IT USUALLY DOES. SHOULDN'T THE MAIN CHARACTER BE EASIER TO DRAW? BUT IT WAS FUN DRAWING RANMARU IN COSPLAY. ♥ ... THAT TOOK A LONG TIME, TOO.

THE GENIUS ATSUKO NANBA SAVED THE DAY.

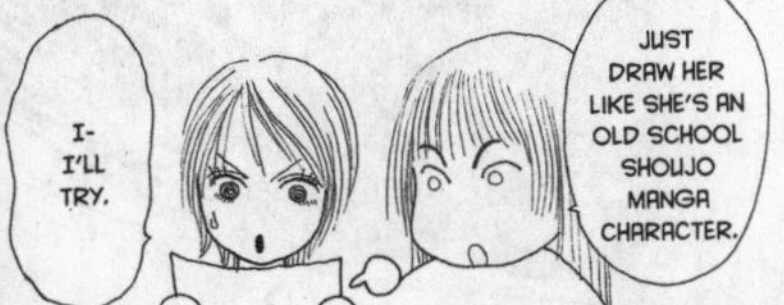
JUST DRAW HER LIKE SHE'S AN OLD SCHOOL SHOUJO MANGA CHARACTER.
I- I'LL TRY.

AND SHE DID A FABULOUS JOB! SHE DREW TWO PANELS ... SEE IF YOU CAN FIND THEM.

MY DEADLINE WAS THE SAME DAY AS THE BAROKKU CONCERT AT TOKYO KOUSEI HALL ... I STAYED UP ALL NIGHT, AND DANCED LIKE CRAZY.

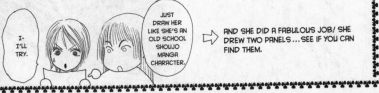

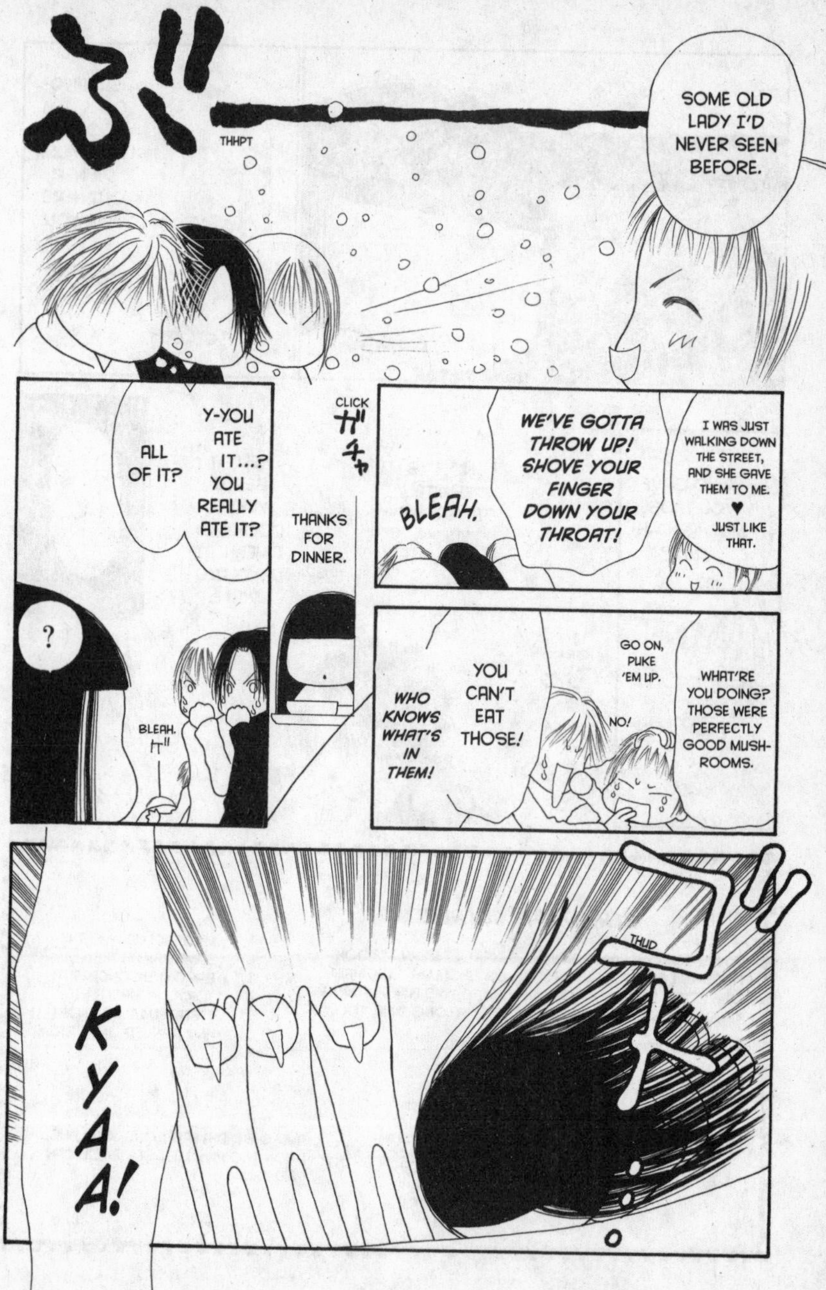

SOME OLD LADY I'D NEVER SEEN BEFORE.
THHPT
I WAS JUST WALKING DOWN THE STREET, AND SHE GAVE THEM TO ME. ♥ JUST LIKE THAT.
WE'VE GOTTA THROW UP! SHOVE YOUR FINGER DOWN YOUR THROAT!
BLEAH.
WHAT'RE YOU DOING? THOSE WERE PERFECTLY GOOD MUSHROOMS.
GO ON, PUKE 'EM UP.
NO!
YOU CAN'T EAT THOSE!
WHO KNOWS WHAT'S IN THEM!
CLICK
ガチャ
THANKS FOR DINNER.
Y-YOU ATE IT...? YOU REALLY ATE IT?
ALL OF IT?
?
BLEAH.
THUD
KYAA!

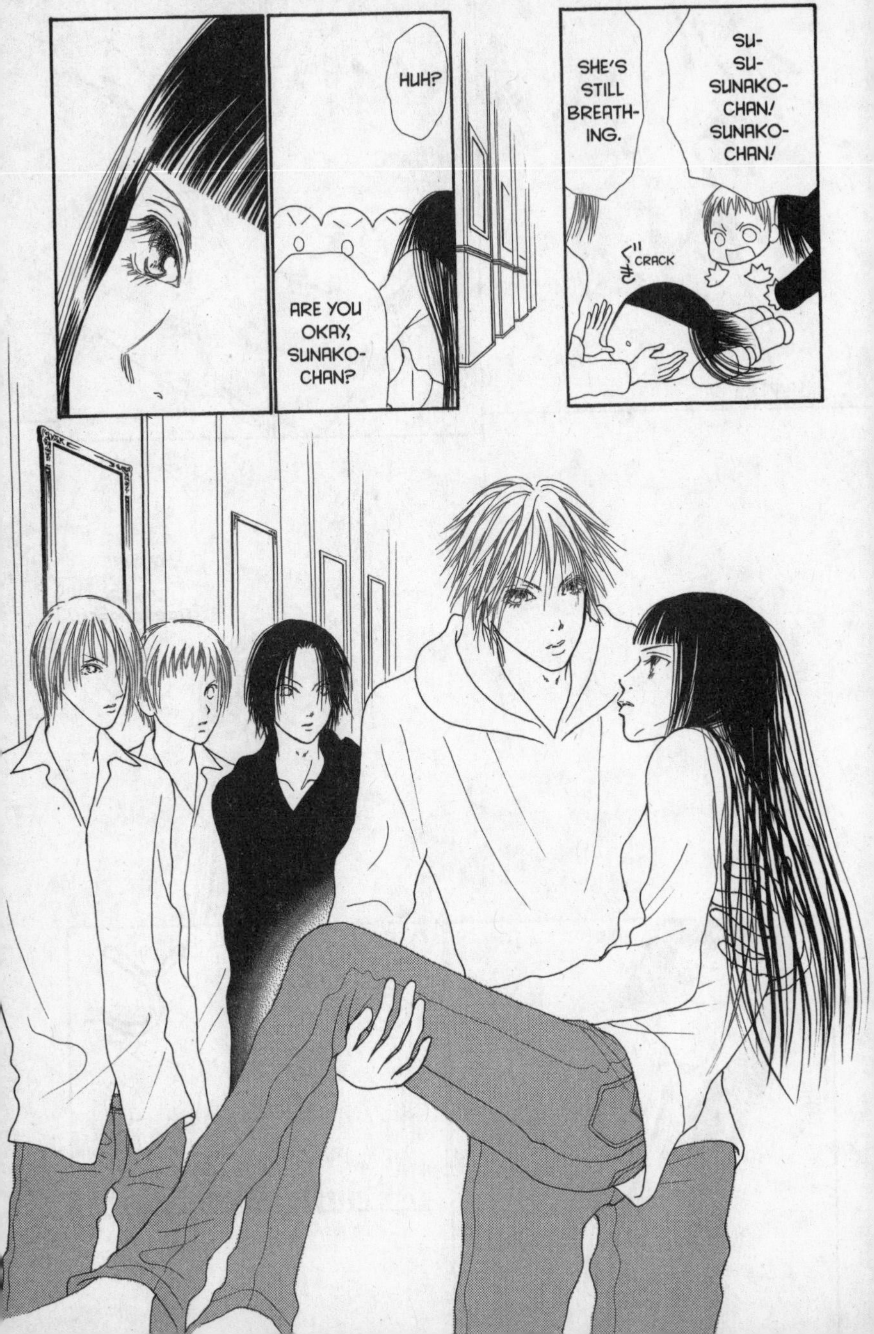
SU-SU-SUNAKO-CHAN! SUNAKO-CHAN!
SHE'S STILL BREATHING.
ぐき CRACK
HUH?
ARE YOU OKAY, SUNAKO-CHAN?

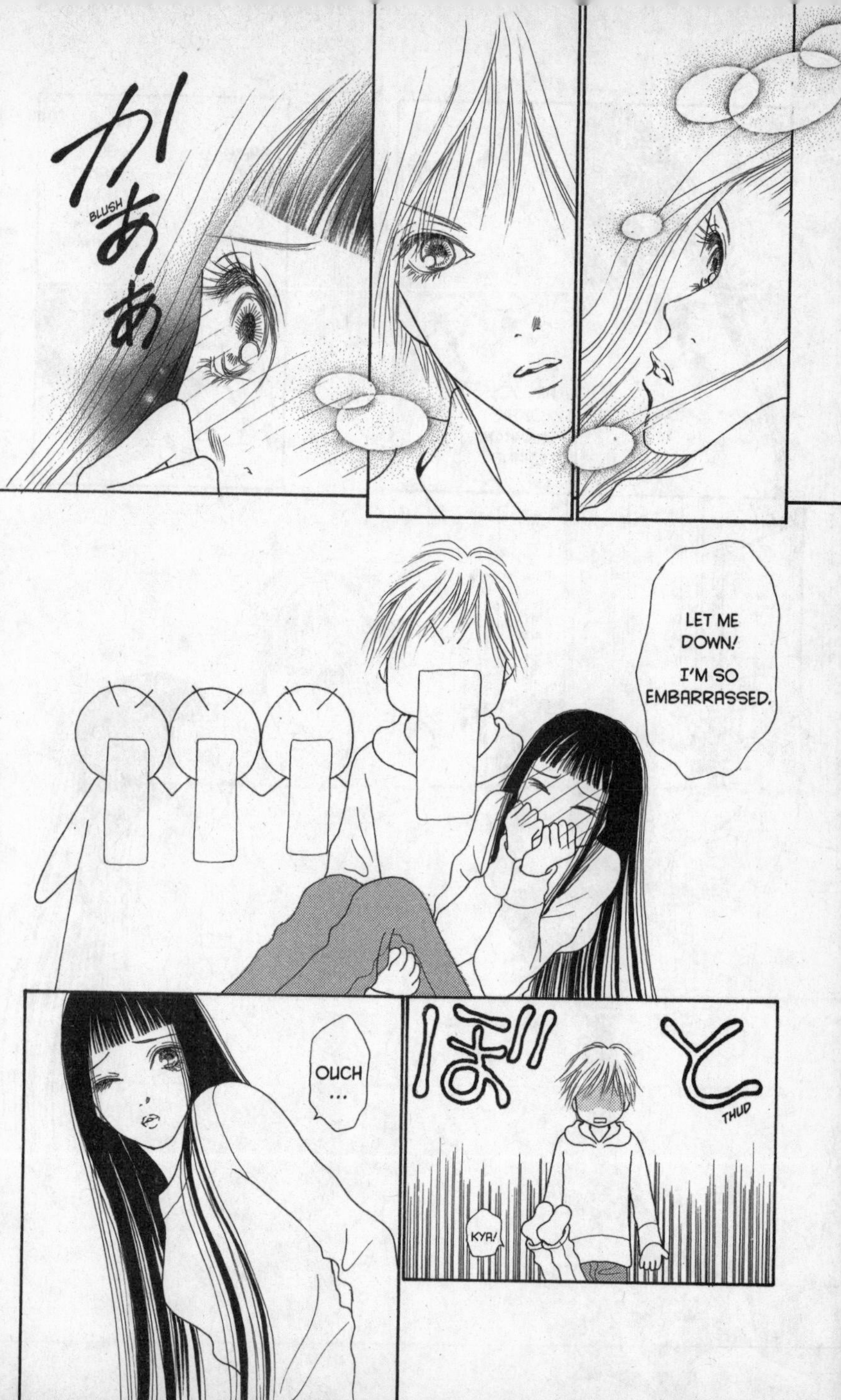
かぁぁ
BLUSH
LET ME DOWN! I'M SO EMBARRASSED.
ぼと
THUD
KYA!
OUCH ...

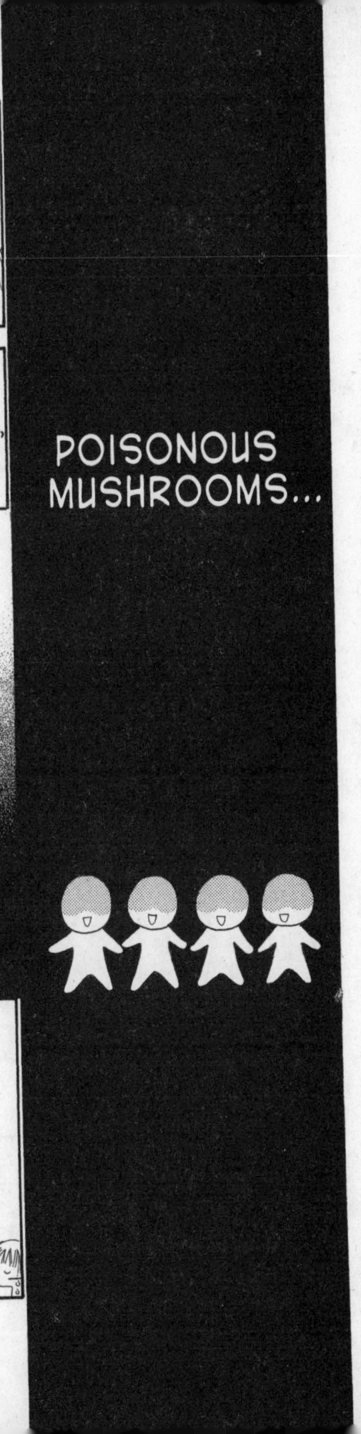
POISONOUS MUSHROOMS...

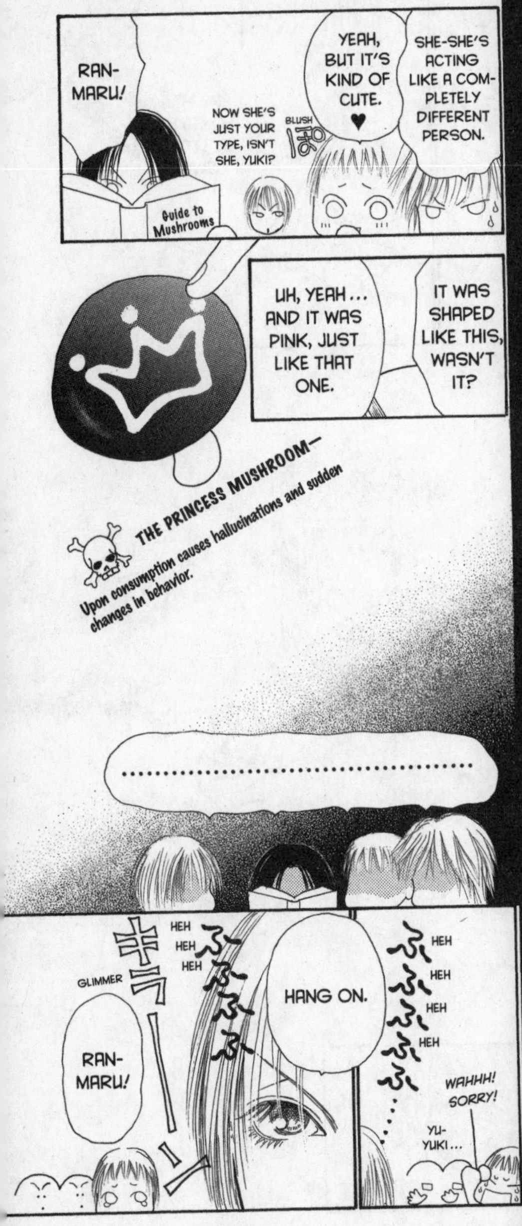
SHE-SHE'S ACTING LIKE A COM-PLETELY DIFFERENT PERSON.
YEAH, BUT IT'S KIND OF CUTE. ♥
BLUSH
NOW SHE'S JUST YOUR TYPE, ISN'T SHE, YUKI?
RAN-MARU!
Guide to Mushrooms
IT WAS SHAPED LIKE THIS, WASN'T IT?
UH, YEAH... AND IT WAS PINK, JUST LIKE THAT ONE.
THE PRINCESS MUSHROOM—
Upon consumption causes hallucinations and sudden changes in behavior.
....
HEH HEH HEH HEH
WAHHH! SORRY!
YU-YUKI...
HANG ON.
HEH HEH HEH
GLIMMER
RAN-MARU!

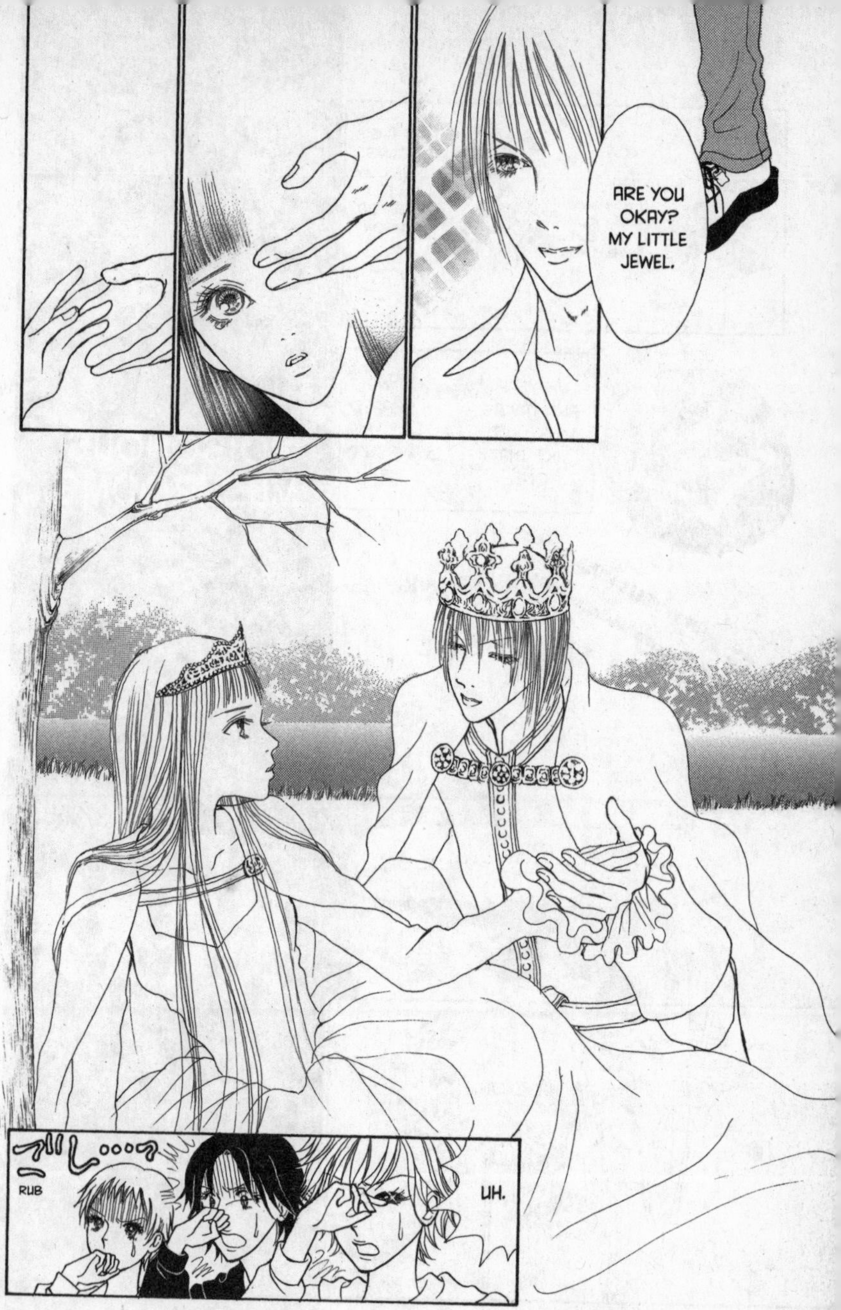
ARE YOU OKAY? MY LITTLE JEWEL.
UH.
RUB

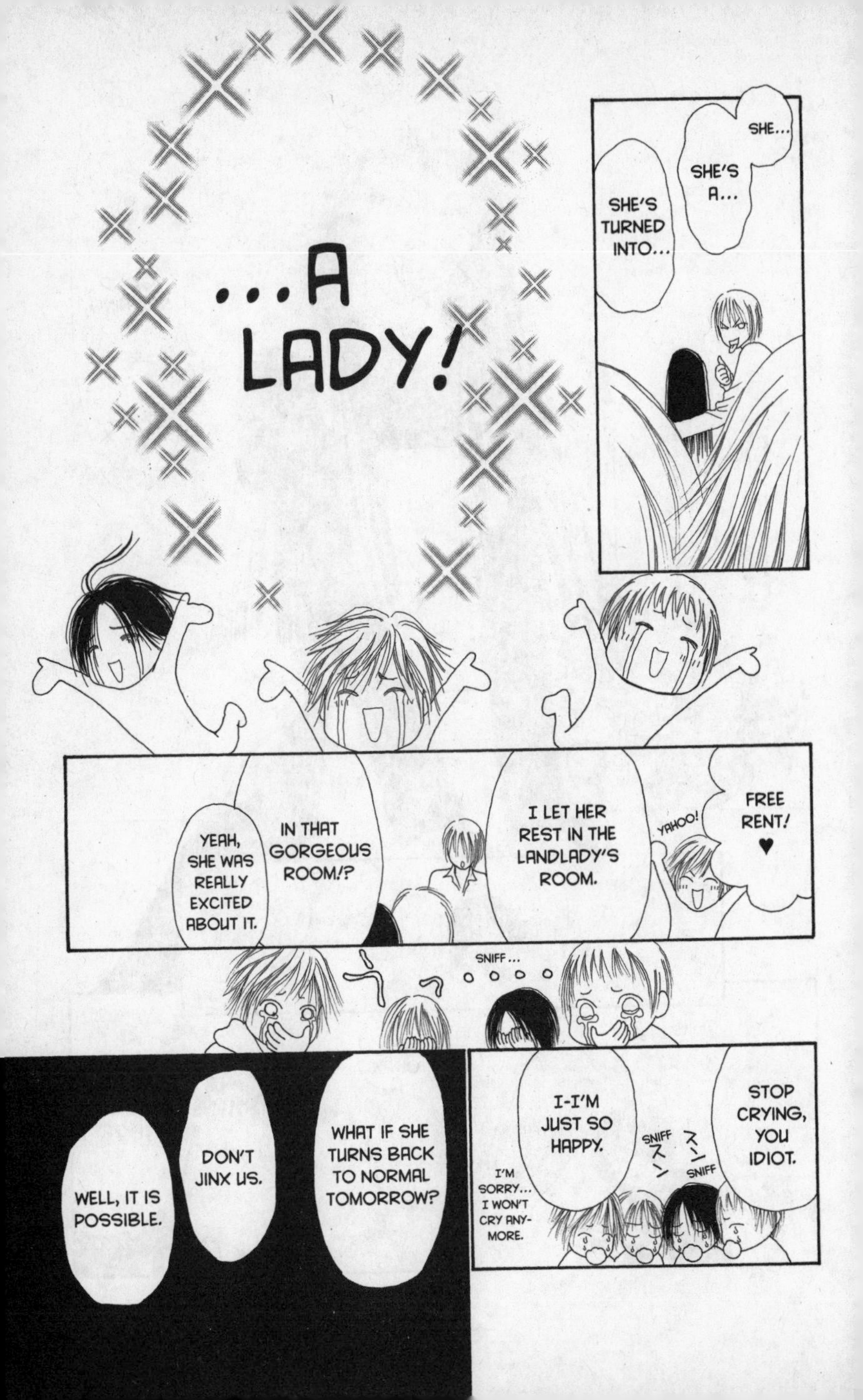
SHE...
SHE'S A...
SHE'S TURNED INTO...
...A LADY!
FREE RENT! ♥
YAHOO!
I LET HER REST IN THE LANDLADY'S ROOM.
IN THAT GORGEOUS ROOM!?
YEAH, SHE WAS REALLY EXCITED ABOUT IT.
SNIFF...
STOP CRYING, YOU IDIOT.
スン SNIFF
SNIFF スン
I-I'M JUST SO HAPPY.
I'M SORRY... I WON'T CRY ANYMORE.
WHAT IF SHE TURNS BACK TO NORMAL TOMORROW?
DON'T JINX US.
WELL, IT IS POSSIBLE.

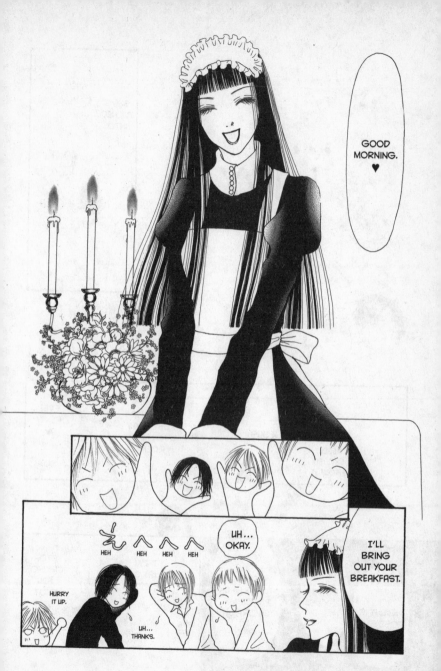

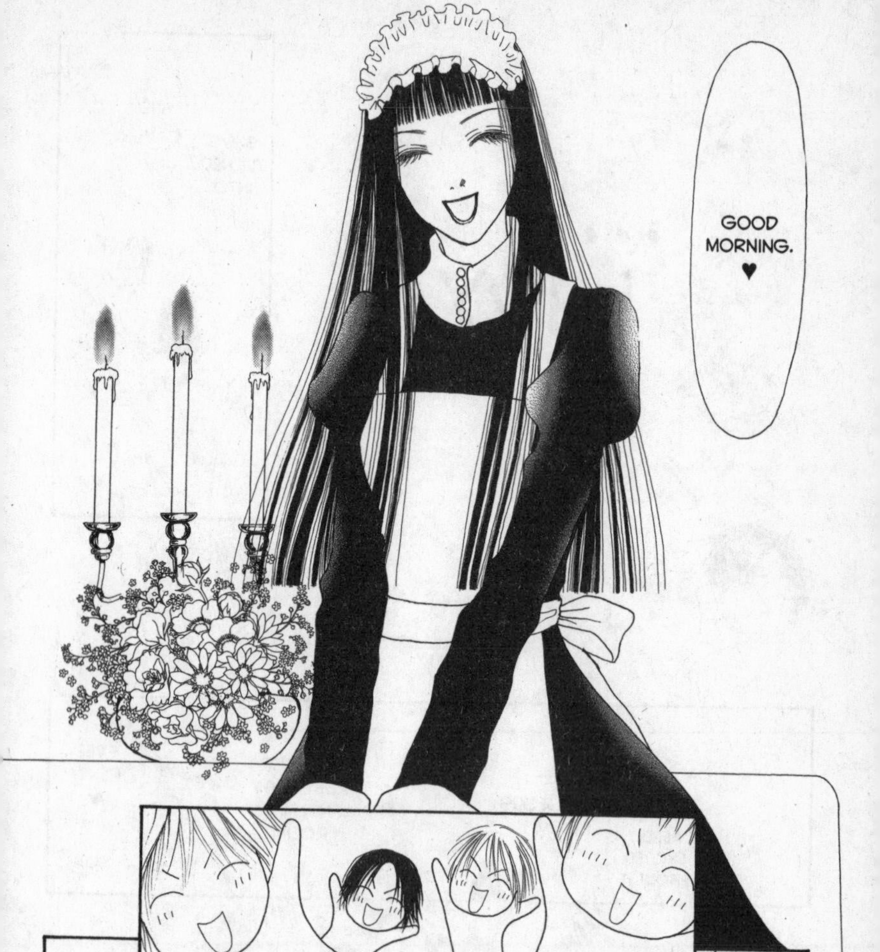
GOOD MORNING. ♥
I'LL BRING OUT YOUR BREAKFAST.
UH... OKAY.
えへへへ
HEH HEH HEH HEH
UH... THANKS.
HURRY IT UP.

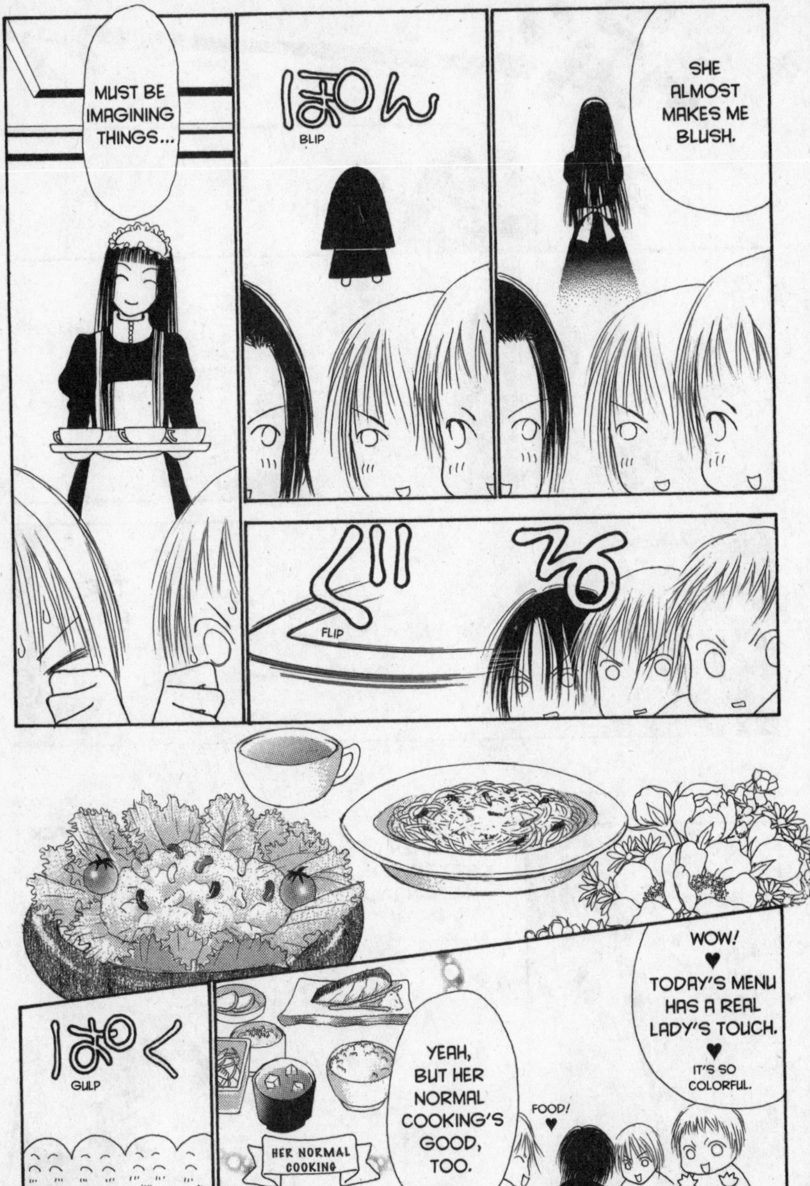

SHE ALMOST MAKES ME BLUSH.
BLIP
FLIP
MUST BE IMAGINING THINGS...
WOW! ♥ TODAY'S MENU HAS A REAL LADY'S TOUCH. ♥
IT'S SO COLORFUL.
FOOD! ♥
YEAH, BUT HER NORMAL COOKING'S GOOD, TOO.
HER NORMAL COOKING
GULP

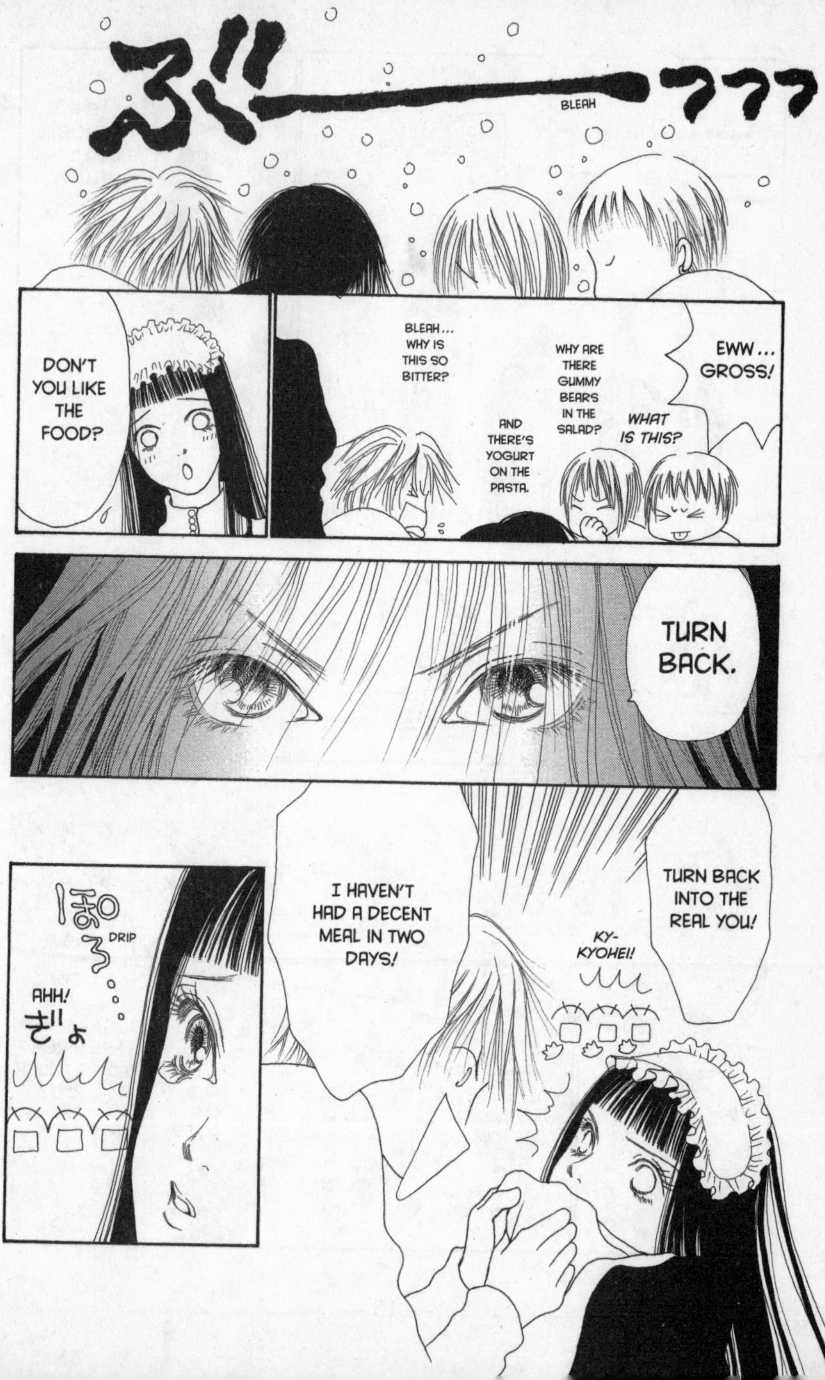
ぶ‼ーっっっ
BLEAH
EWW... GROSS!
WHAT IS THIS?
WHY ARE THERE GUMMY BEARS IN THE SALAD?
AND THERE'S YOGURT ON THE PASTA.
BLEAH... WHY IS THIS SO BITTER?
DON'T YOU LIKE THE FOOD?
TURN BACK.
TURN BACK INTO THE REAL YOU!
I HAVEN'T HAD A DECENT MEAL IN TWO DAYS!
KY-KYOHEI!
ぽろ
DRIP
AHH!
ぎょ

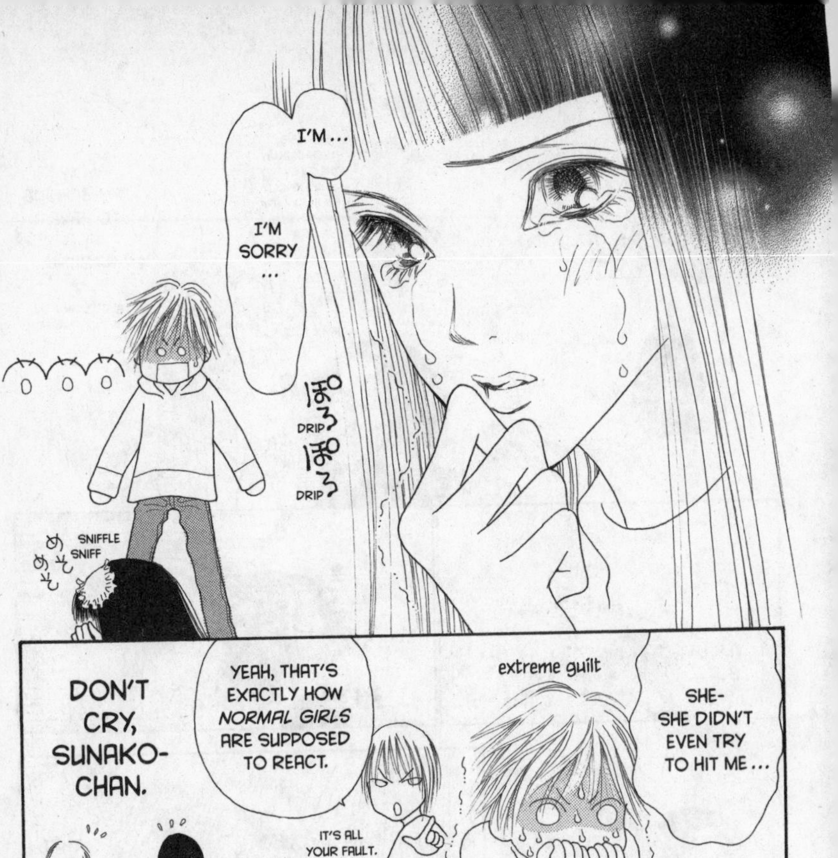
I'M...
I'M SORRY ...
DRIP
DRIP
SNIFFLE
SNIFF
SHE- SHE DIDN'T EVEN TRY TO HIT ME...
extreme guilt
YEAH, THAT'S EXACTLY HOW *NORMAL GIRLS* ARE SUPPOSED TO REACT.
IT'S ALL YOUR FAULT.
DON'T CRY, SUNAKO-CHAN.
SNIFF
I'LL MAKE SOME-THING ELSE.
NO, THAT'S OKAY. THIS IS FINE.
YEAH, WE'LL EAT THIS.
CHOMP CHOMP
YUM, YUM... GOOD.
OKAY, I'LL GO DO THE LAUNDRY.
BLUSH

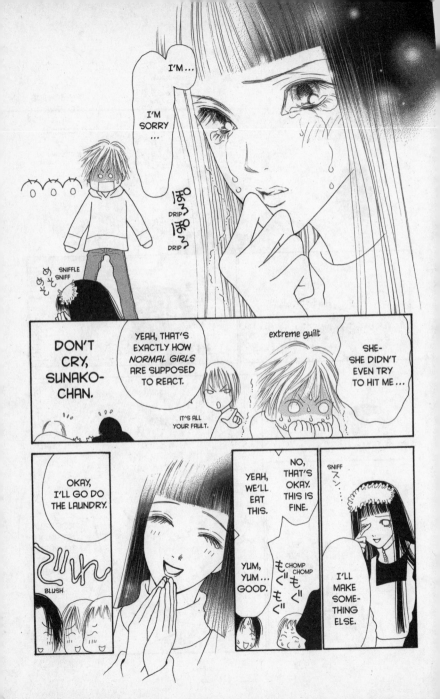

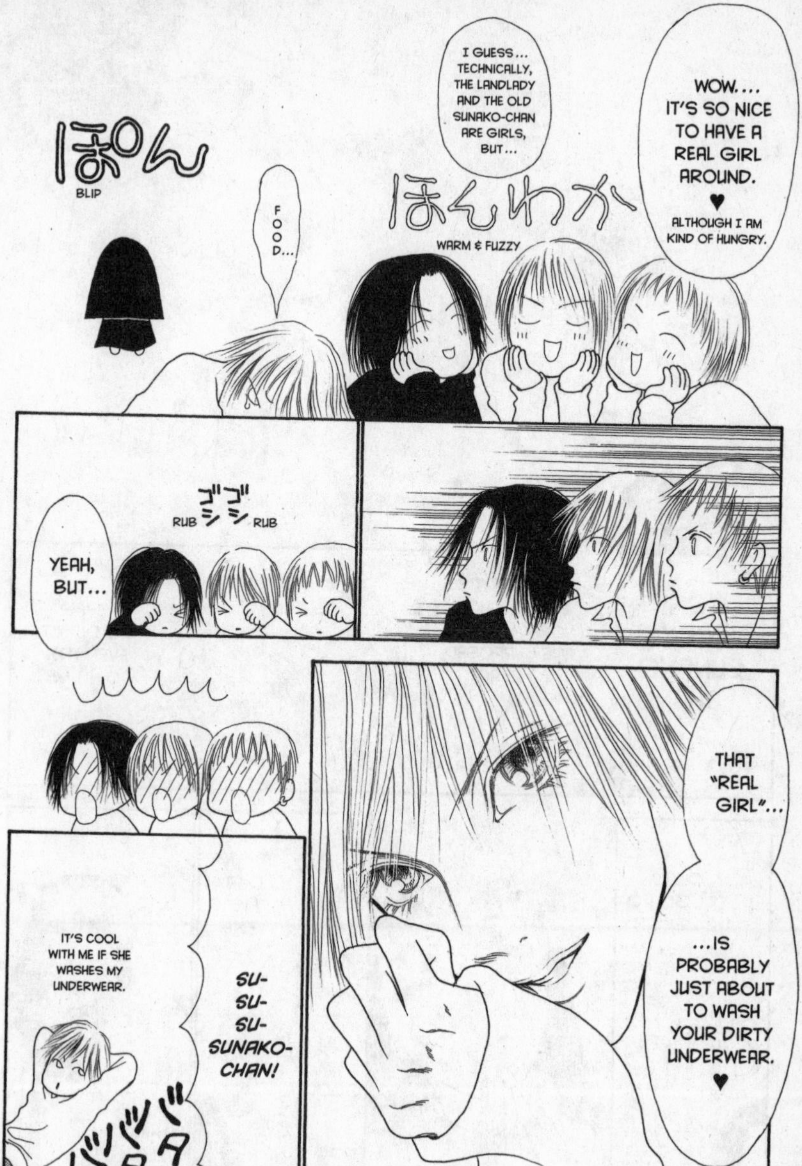
WOW.... IT'S SO NICE TO HAVE A REAL GIRL AROUND. ♥
ALTHOUGH I AM KIND OF HUNGRY.
I GUESS... TECHNICALLY, THE LANDLADY AND THE OLD SUNAKO-CHAN ARE GIRLS, BUT...
ほんわか
WARM & FUZZY
FOOD...
ぽん
BLIP
ゴシゴシ
RUB RUB
YEAH, BUT...
THAT "REAL GIRL"...
...IS PROBABLY JUST ABOUT TO WASH YOUR DIRTY UNDERWEAR. ♥
SU-SU-SU-SUNAKO-CHAN!
IT'S COOL WITH ME IF SHE WASHES MY UNDERWEAR.
バッバッバ
TAPPA TAPPA TAPPA

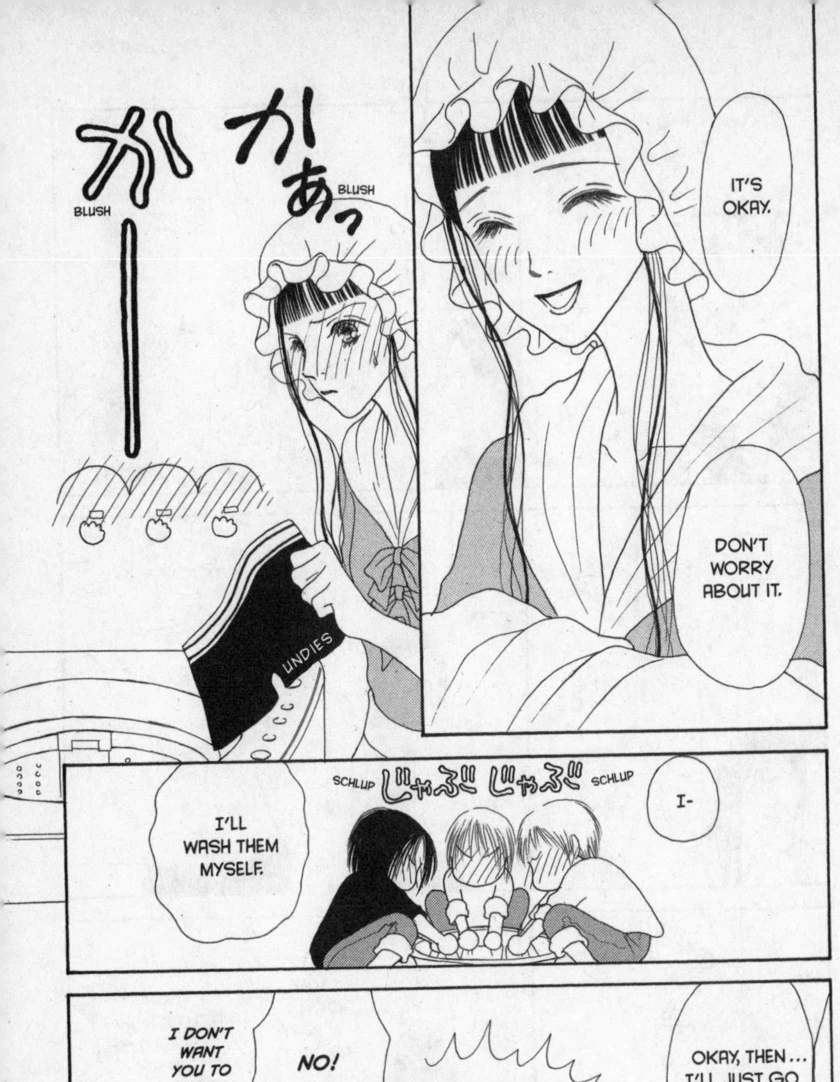
IT'S OKAY.
DON'T WORRY ABOUT IT.
かあっ
BLUSH
かー
BLUSH
UNDIES
I-
じゃぶ じゃぶ
SCHLUP SCHLUP
I'LL WASH THEM MYSELF.
OKAY, THEN... I'LL JUST GO CLEAN YOUR ROOM.
NO! I'LL DO THAT TOO!
I DON'T WANT YOU TO FIND MY SPECIAL MAGAZINES!
WE ARE GUYS, AFTER ALL.

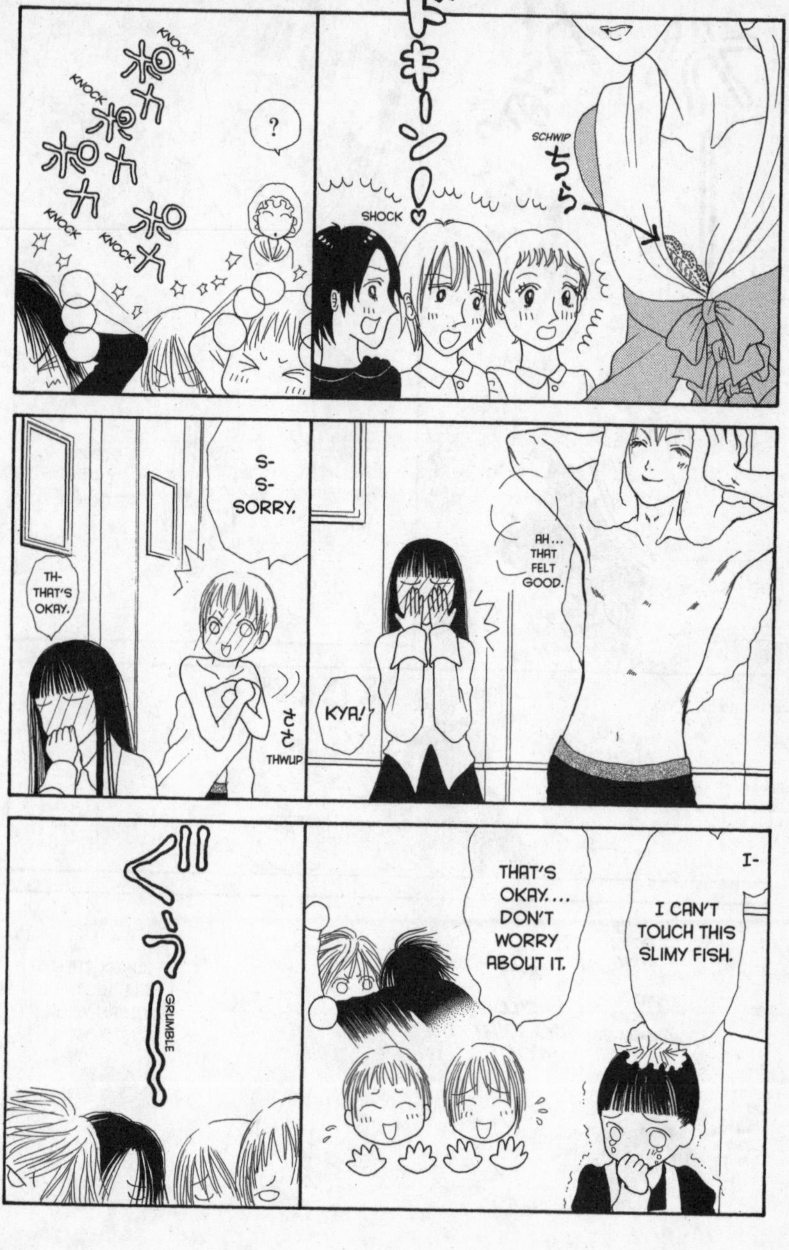
ドキーン!
SHOCK
ちら
SCHWIP
?
KNOCK
KNOCK
KNOCK
KNOCK
AH... THAT FELT GOOD.
KYA!
S-S-SORRY.
TH-THAT'S OKAY.
THWUP
I-
I CAN'T TOUCH THIS SLIMY FISH.
THAT'S OKAY.... DON'T WORRY ABOUT IT.
ぐ~う
GRUMBLE

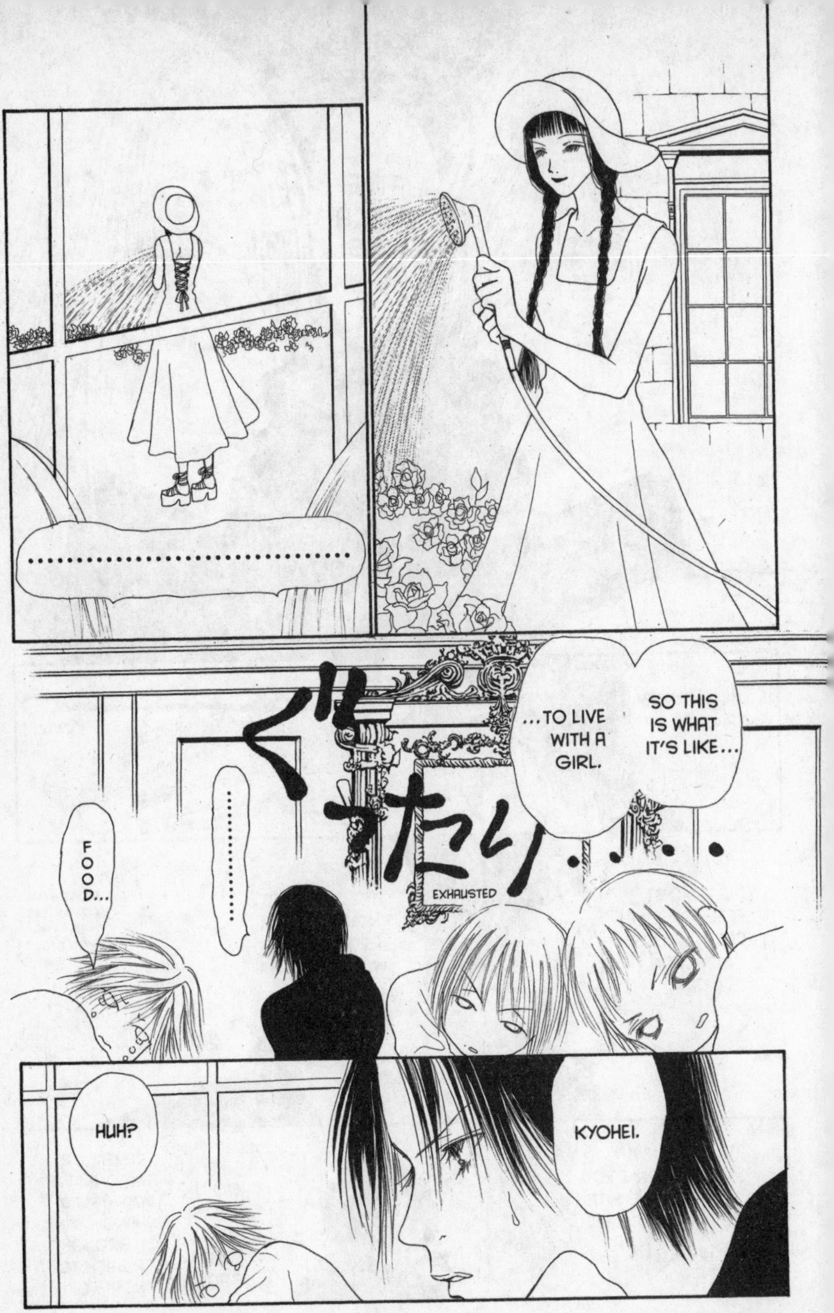

....
SO THIS IS WHAT IT'S LIKE...
...TO LIVE WITH A GIRL.
ぐったり...
EXHAUSTED
....
FOOD...
KYOHEI.
HUH?

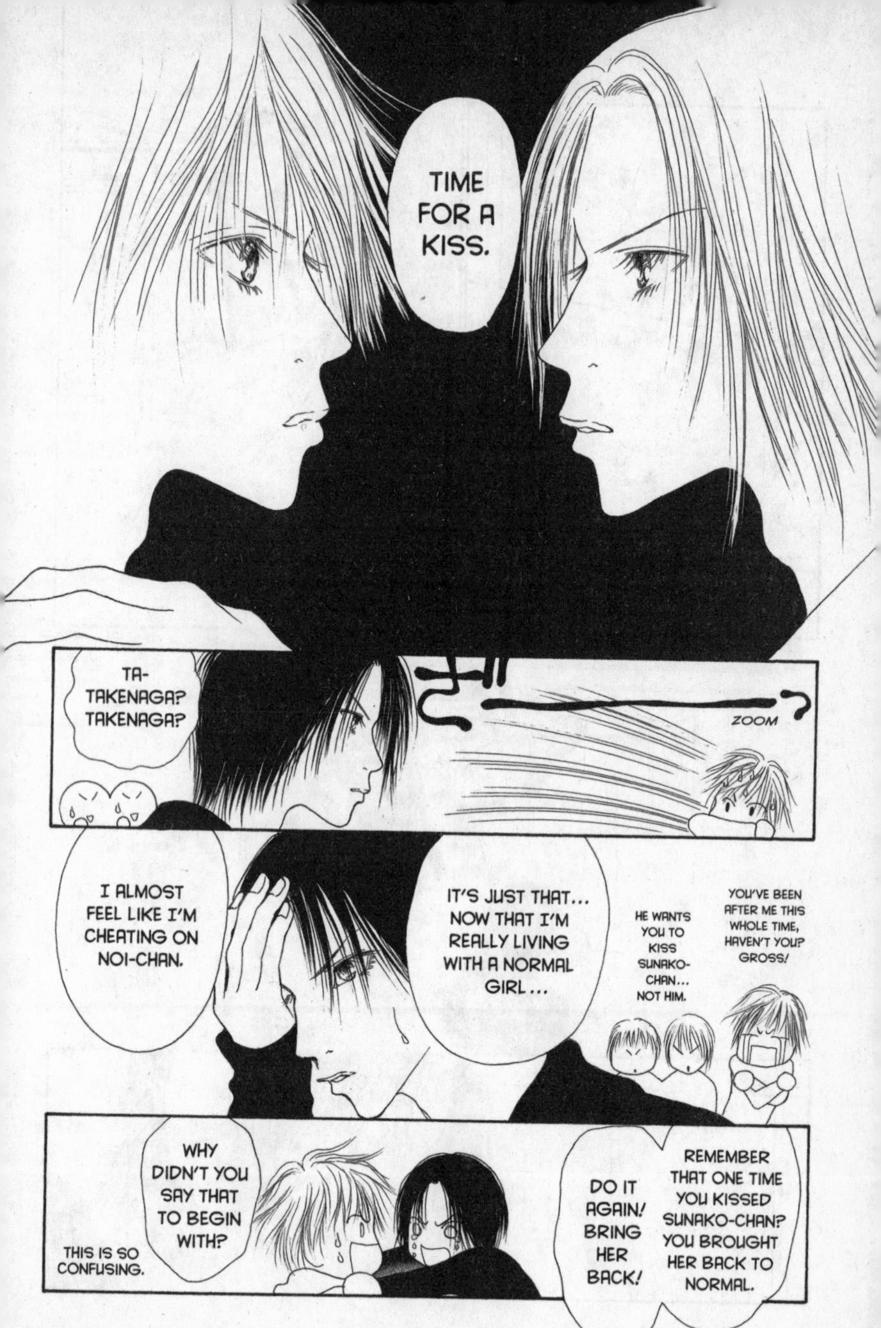
TIME FOR A KISS.
ZOOM
TA- TAKENAGA? TAKENAGA?
YOU'VE BEEN AFTER ME THIS WHOLE TIME, HAVEN'T YOU? GROSS!
HE WANTS YOU TO KISS SUNAKO-CHAN... NOT HIM.
IT'S JUST THAT... NOW THAT I'M REALLY LIVING WITH A NORMAL GIRL...
I ALMOST FEEL LIKE I'M CHEATING ON NOI-CHAN.
REMEMBER THAT ONE TIME YOU KISSED SUNAKO-CHAN? YOU BROUGHT HER BACK TO NORMAL.
DO IT AGAIN! BRING HER BACK!
WHY DIDN'T YOU SAY THAT TO BEGIN WITH?
THIS IS SO CONFUSING.

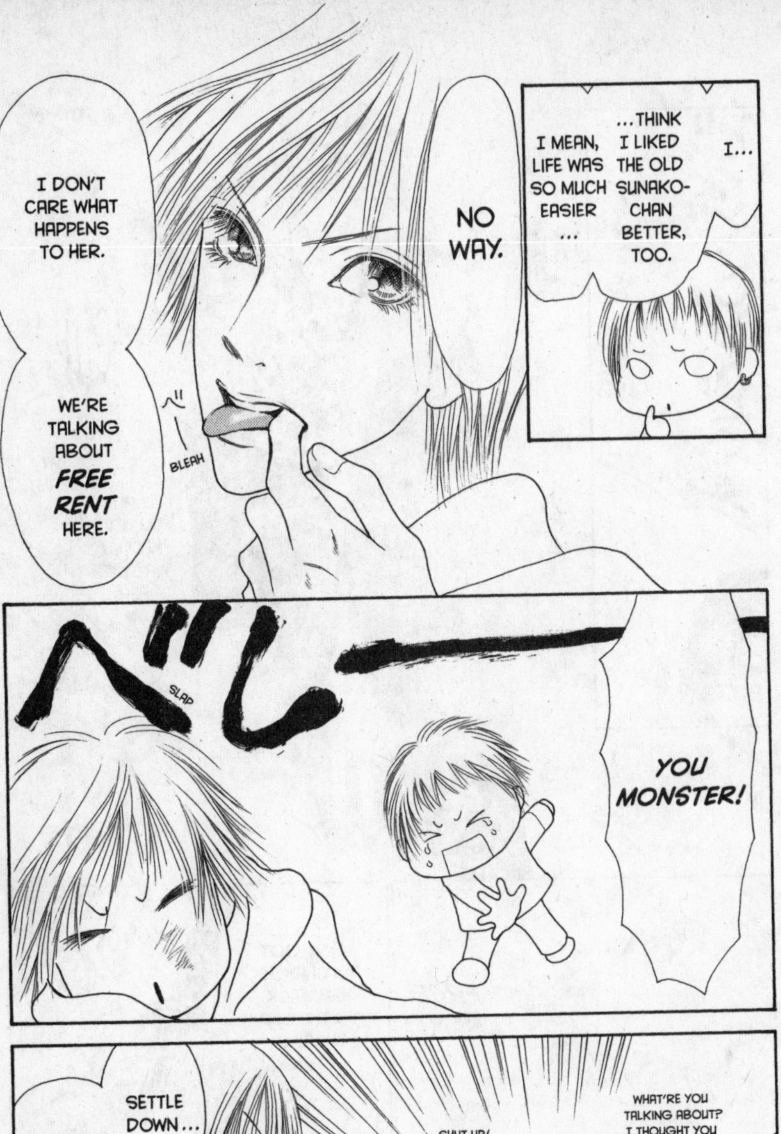
I...
...THINK I LIKED THE OLD SUNAKO-CHAN BETTER, TOO.
I MEAN, LIFE WAS SO MUCH EASIER ...
NO WAY.
I DON'T CARE WHAT HAPPENS TO HER.
WE'RE TALKING ABOUT *FREE RENT* HERE.
BLEAH
YOU MONSTER!
SLAP
WHAT'RE YOU TALKING ABOUT? I THOUGHT YOU WANTED HER TO CHANGE BACK!
SHUT UP! THINK ABOUT THE RENT!
SETTLE DOWN...
LET'S JUST GIVE IT SOME TIME, AND SEE WHAT HAPPENS.

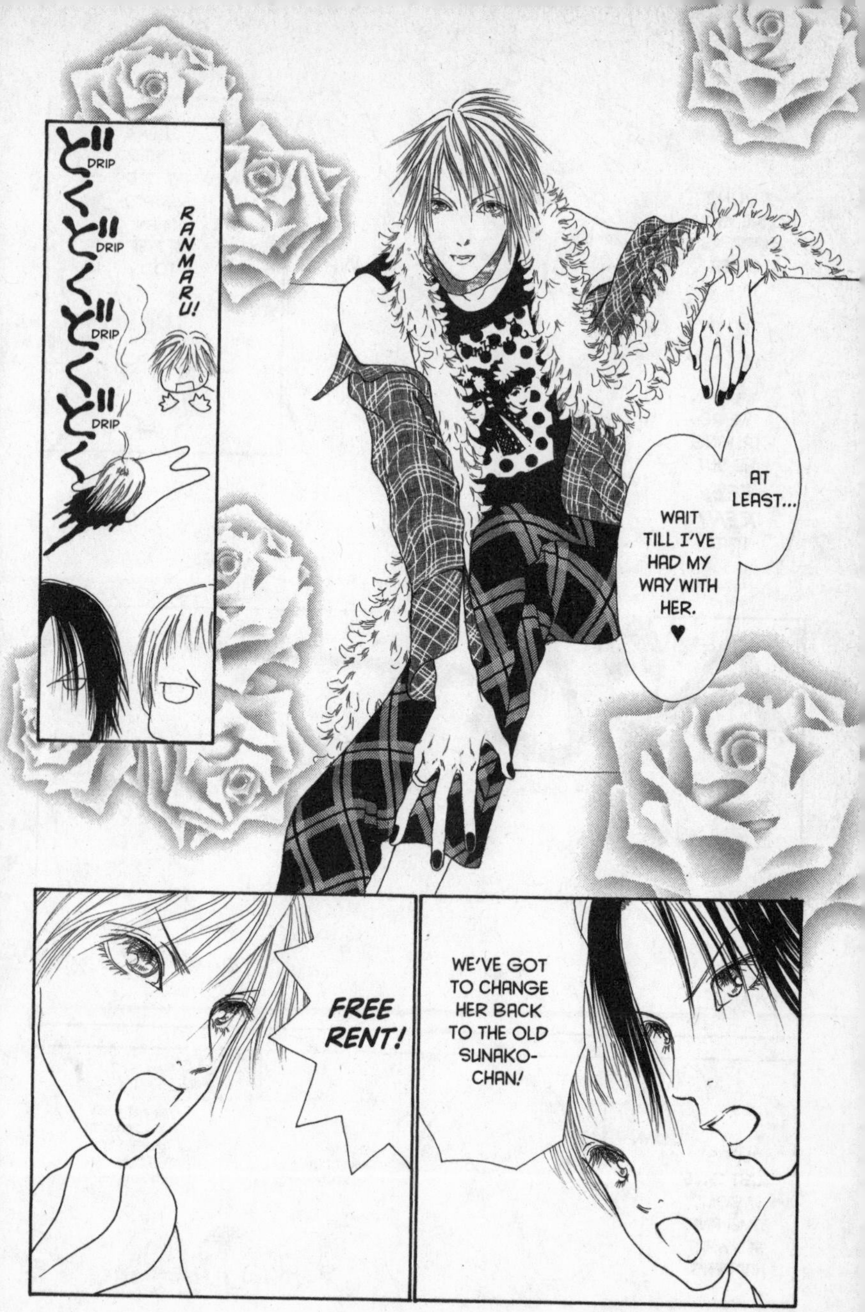
AT LEAST...
WAIT TILL I'VE HAD MY WAY WITH HER. ♥
どくどくどくどく
DRIP
DRIP
DRIP
DRIP
RANMARU!
WE'VE GOT TO CHANGE HER BACK TO THE OLD SUNAKO-CHAN!
FREE RENT!

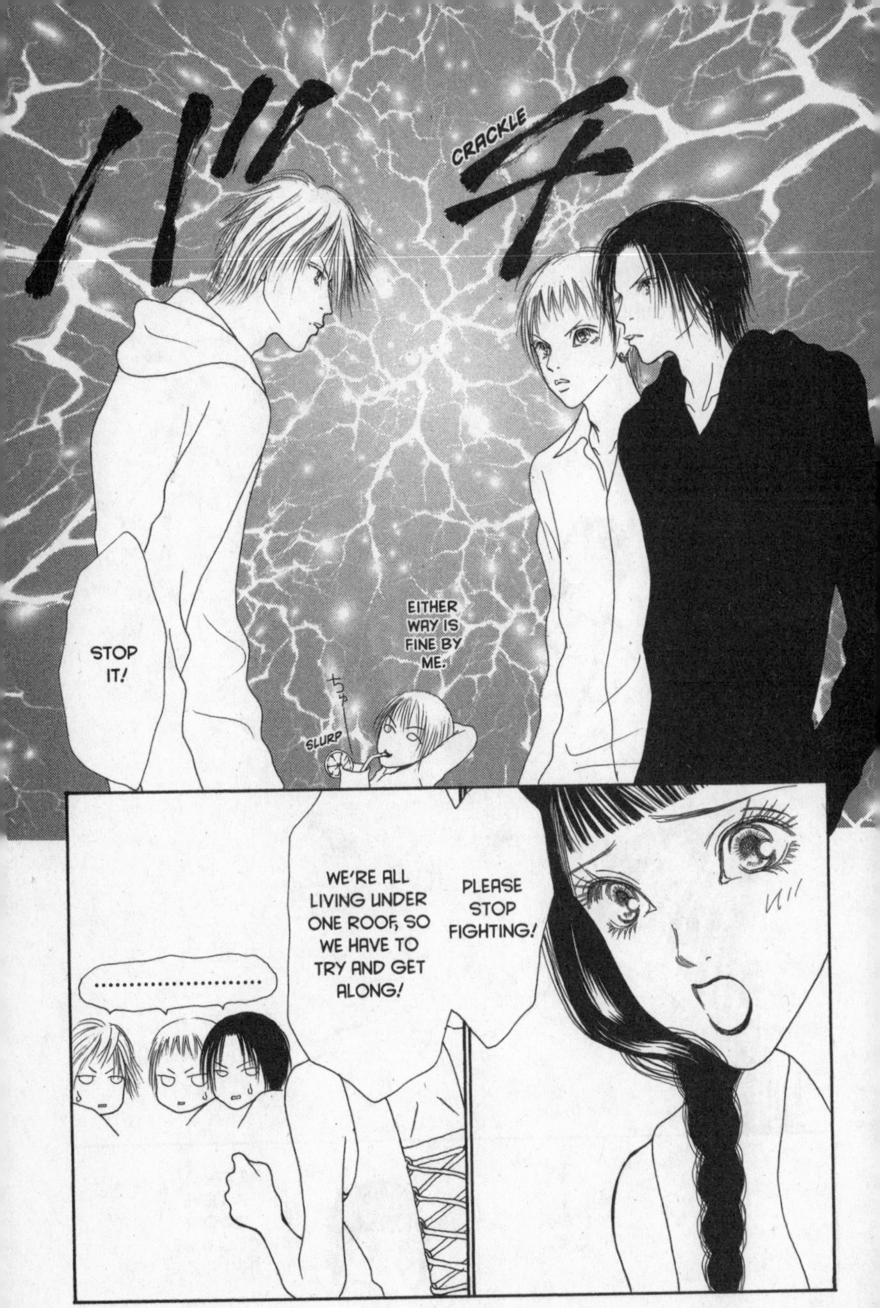
CRACKLE
EITHER WAY IS FINE BY ME.
ちゅ
SLURP
STOP IT!
PLEASE STOP FIGHTING!
WE'RE ALL LIVING UNDER ONE ROOF, SO WE HAVE TO TRY AND GET ALONG!
....

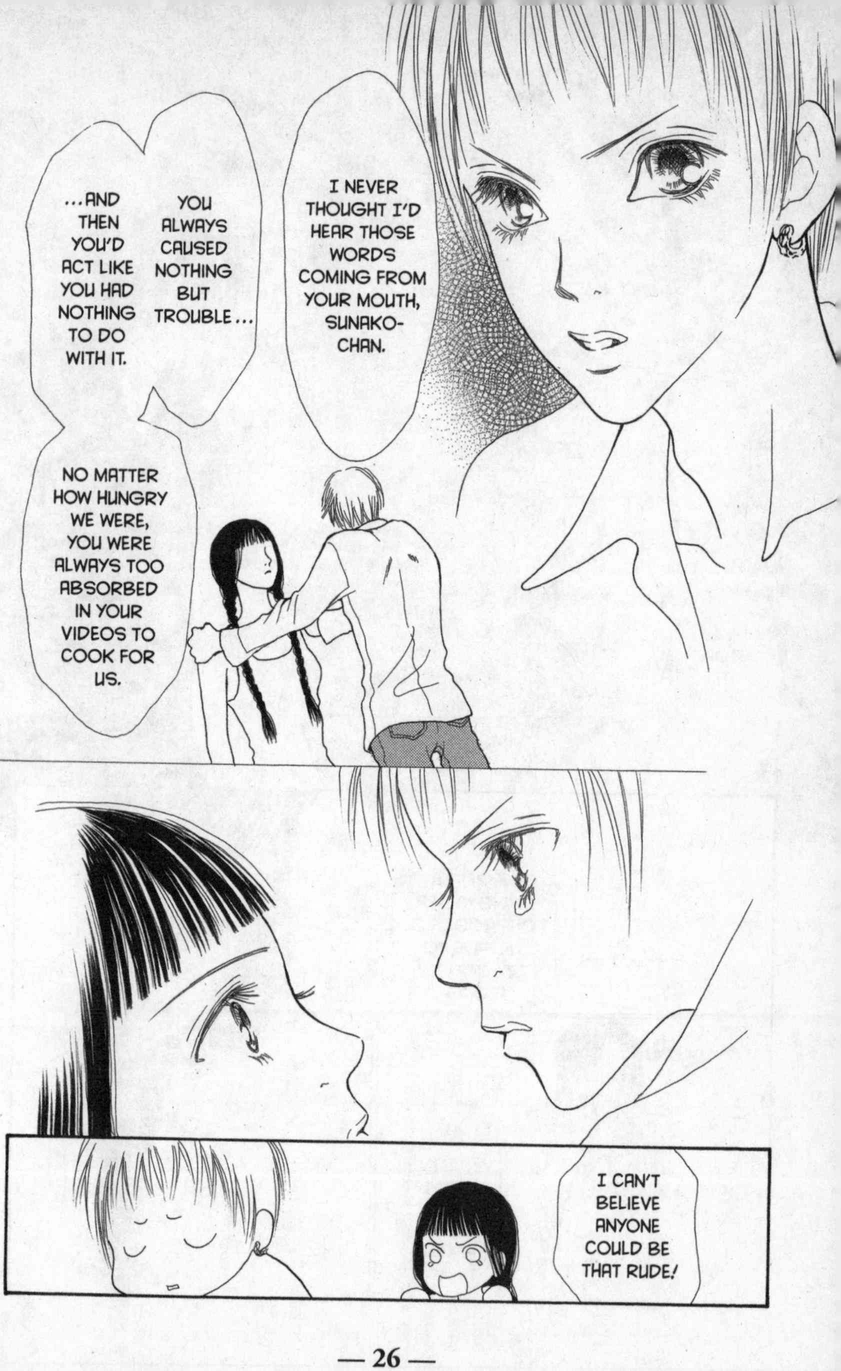
I NEVER THOUGHT I'D HEAR THOSE WORDS COMING FROM YOUR MOUTH, SUNAKO-CHAN.
YOU ALWAYS CAUSED NOTHING BUT TROUBLE...
...AND THEN YOU'D ACT LIKE YOU HAD NOTHING TO DO WITH IT.
NO MATTER HOW HUNGRY WE WERE, YOU WERE ALWAYS TOO ABSORBED IN YOUR VIDEOS TO COOK FOR US.
I CAN'T BELIEVE ANYONE COULD BE THAT RUDE!

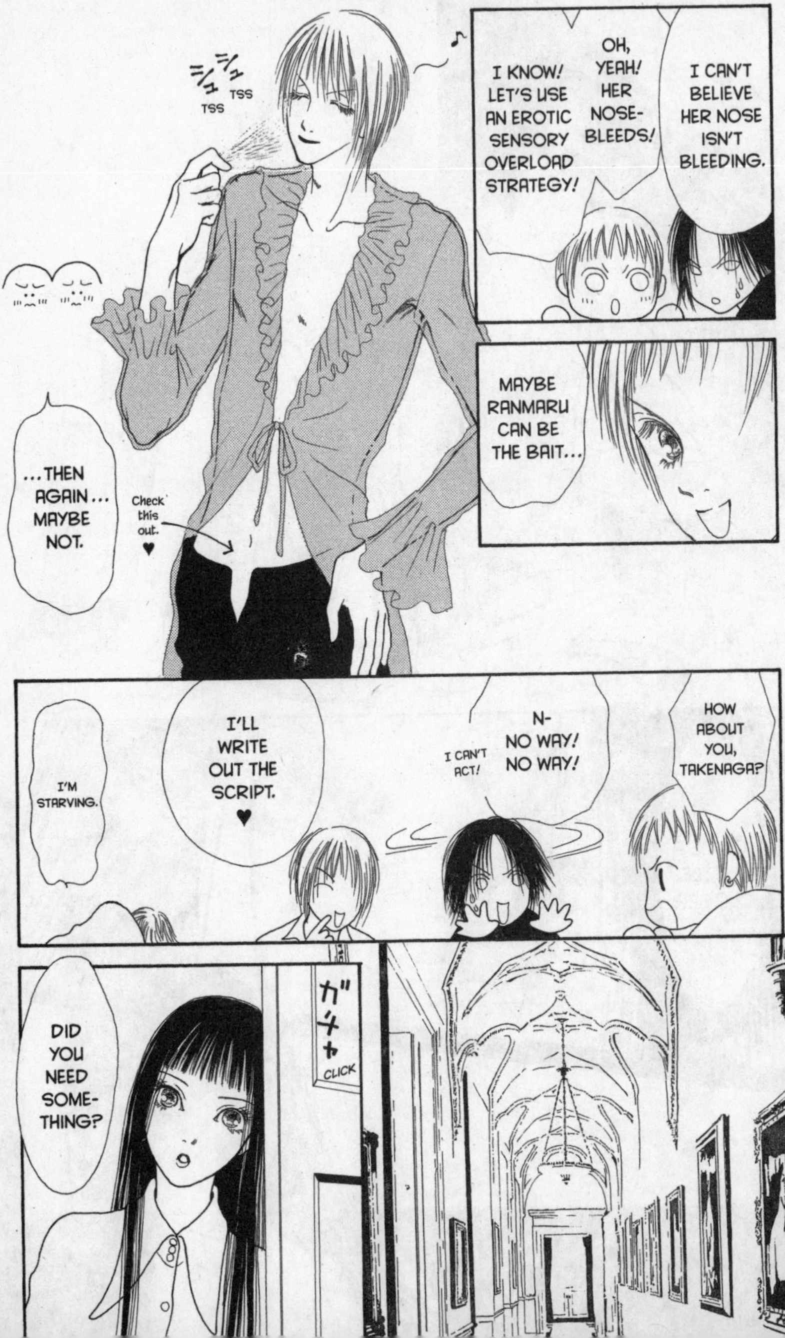

I CAN'T BELIEVE HER NOSE ISN'T BLEEDING.
OH, YEAH! HER NOSE-BLEEDS!
I KNOW! LET'S USE AN EROTIC SENSORY OVERLOAD STRATEGY!
MAYBE RANMARU CAN BE THE BAIT...
♪
シュ シュ
TSS TSS
Check this out. ♥
...THEN AGAIN... MAYBE NOT.
HOW ABOUT YOU, TAKENAGA?
N- NO WAY! NO WAY!
I CAN'T ACT!
I'LL WRITE OUT THE SCRIPT. ♥
I'M STARVING.
ガチャ
CLICK
DID YOU NEED SOME-THING?

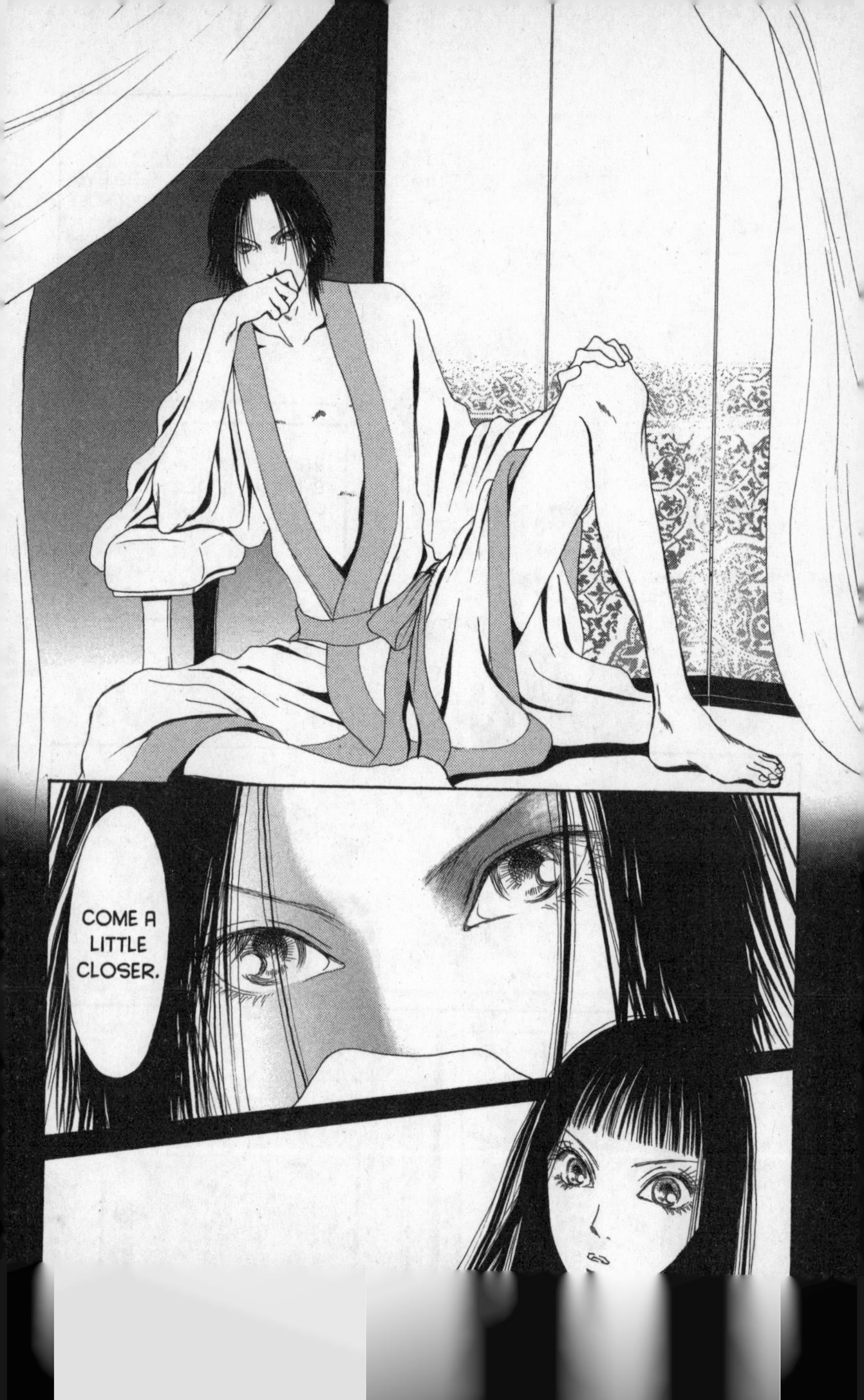
COME A LITTLE CLOSER.

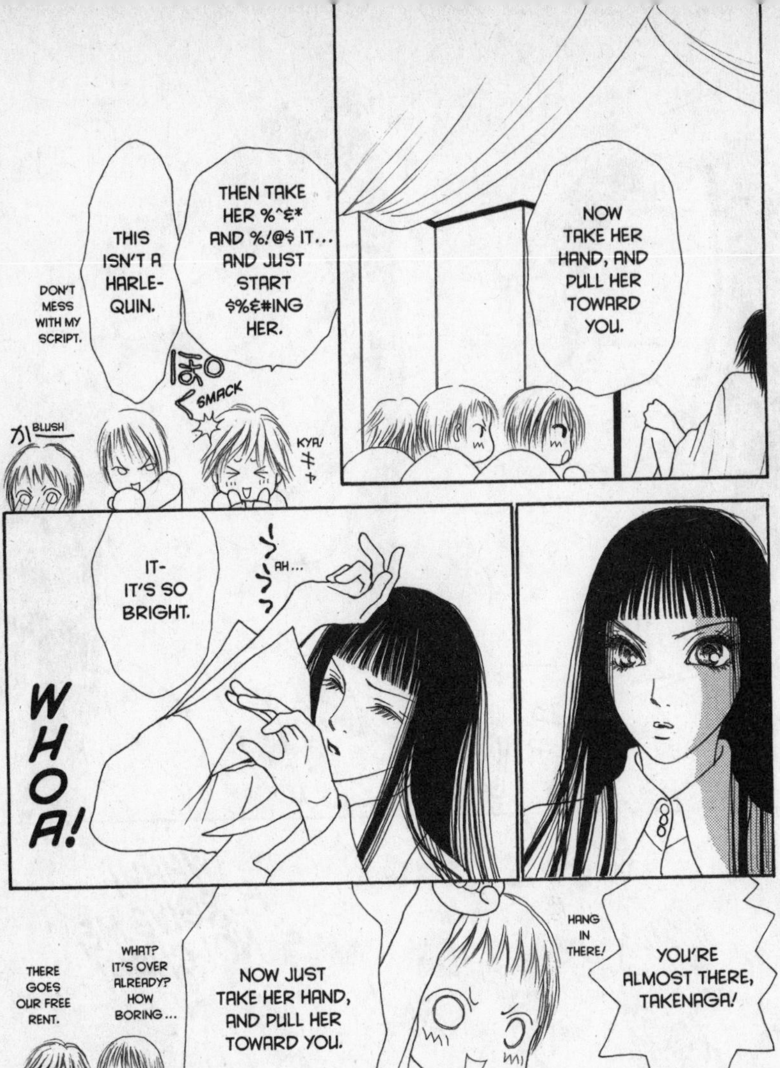
NOW TAKE HER HAND, AND PULL HER TOWARD YOU.
THEN TAKE HER %^&* AND %!@$ IT... AND JUST START $%&#ING HER.
THIS ISN'T A HARLEQUIN.
DON'T MESS WITH MY SCRIPT.
SMACK
KYA!
BLUSH
AH...
IT- IT'S SO BRIGHT.
WHOA!
YOU'RE ALMOST THERE, TAKENAGA!
HANG IN THERE!
NOW JUST TAKE HER HAND, AND PULL HER TOWARD YOU.
WHAT? IT'S OVER ALREADY? HOW BORING...
THERE GOES OUR FREE RENT.
YANK

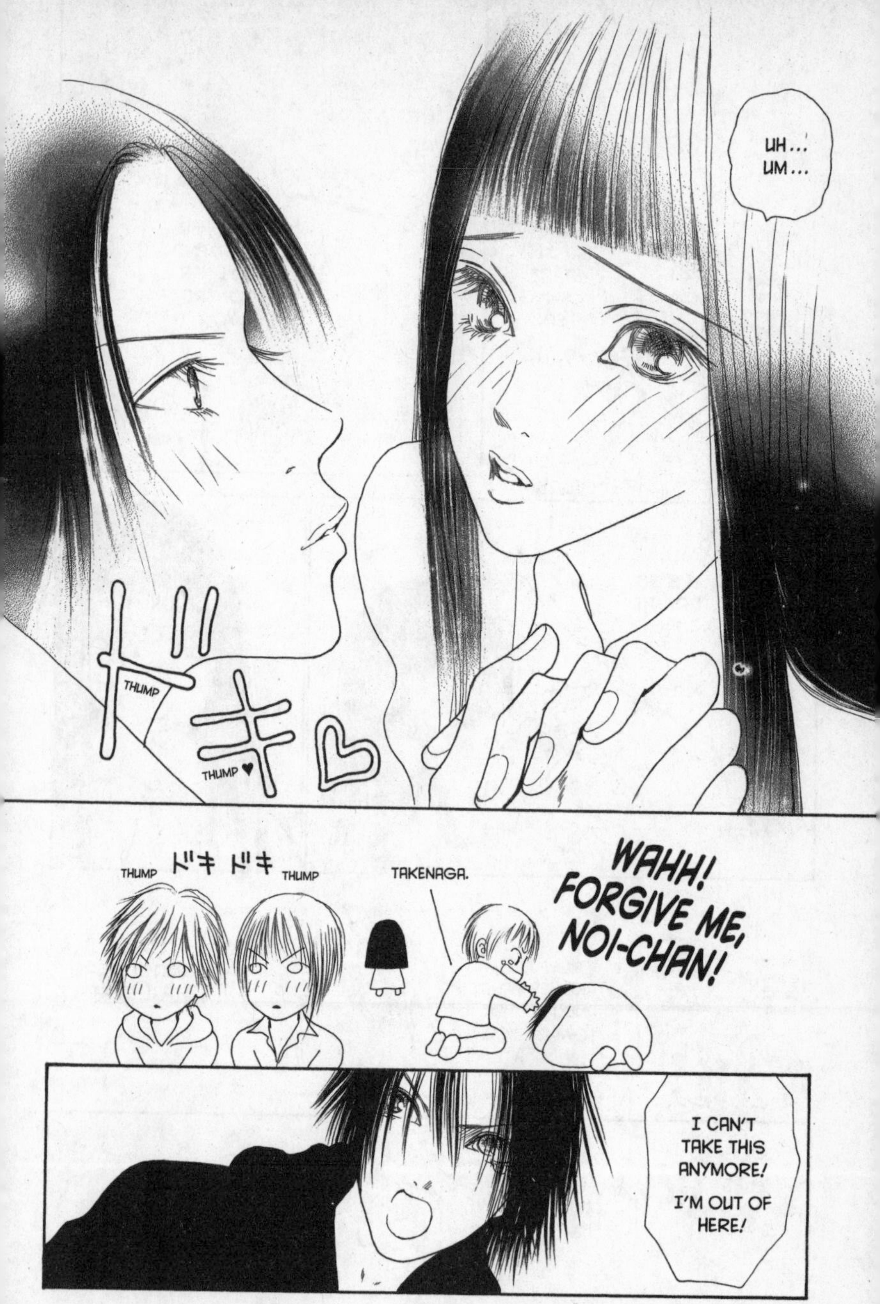
UH...
UM...
ドキ
THUMP
THUMP ♥
WAHH! FORGIVE ME, NOI-CHAN!
TAKENAGA.
ドキ ドキ
THUMP
THUMP
I CAN'T TAKE THIS ANYMORE!
I'M OUT OF HERE!

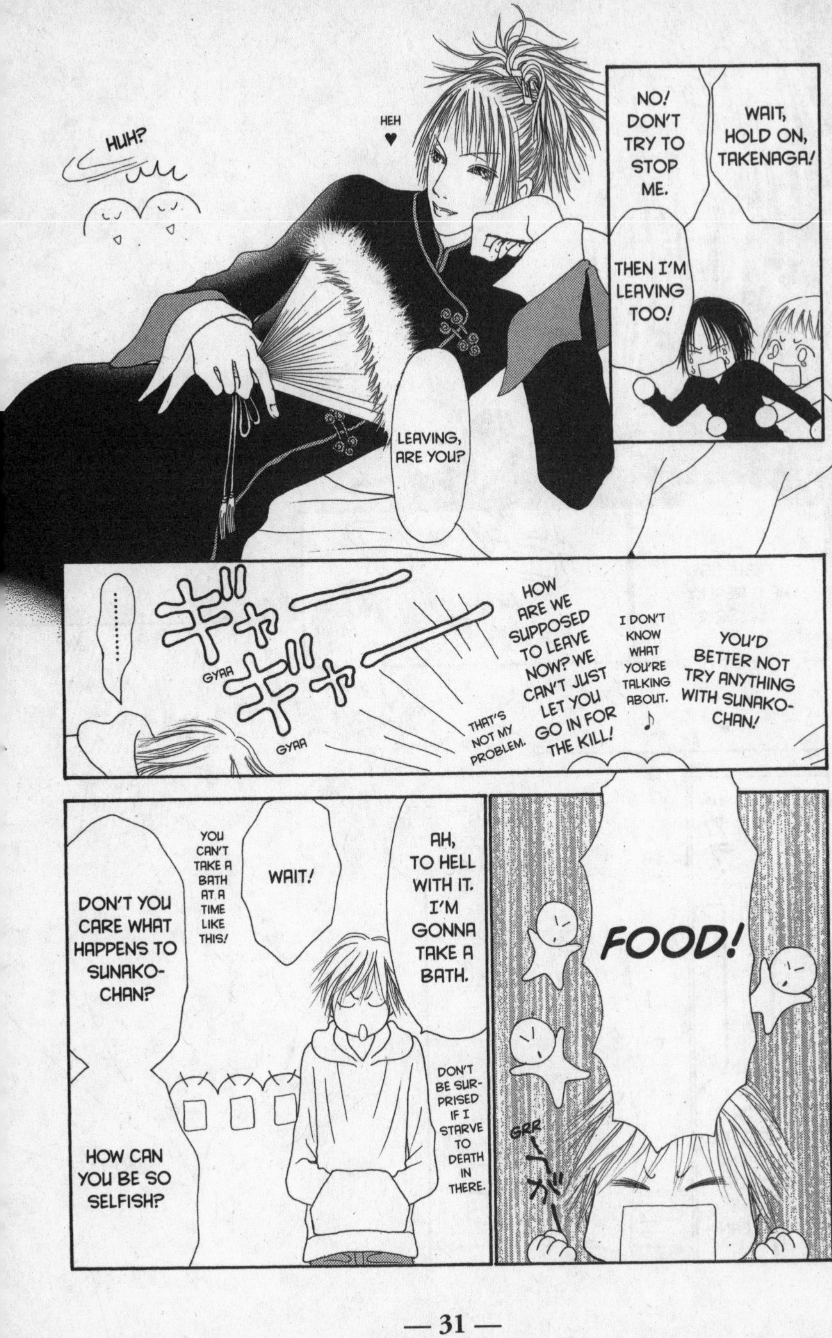
WAIT, HOLD ON, TAKENAGA!
NO! DON'T TRY TO STOP ME.
THEN I'M LEAVING TOO!
HEH ♥
LEAVING, ARE YOU?
HUH?
YOU'D BETTER NOT TRY ANYTHING WITH SUNAKO-CHAN!
I DON'T KNOW WHAT YOU'RE TALKING ABOUT. ♪
HOW ARE WE SUPPOSED TO LEAVE NOW? WE CAN'T JUST LET YOU GO IN FOR THE KILL!
THAT'S NOT MY PROBLEM.
ギャーー GYAA
ギャーー GYAA
......
FOOD!
GRR
ガー
AH, TO HELL WITH IT. I'M GONNA TAKE A BATH.
DON'T BE SURPRISED IF I STARVE TO DEATH IN THERE.
WAIT!
YOU CAN'T TAKE A BATH AT A TIME LIKE THIS!
DON'T YOU CARE WHAT HAPPENS TO SUNAKO-CHAN?
HOW CAN YOU BE SO SELFISH?

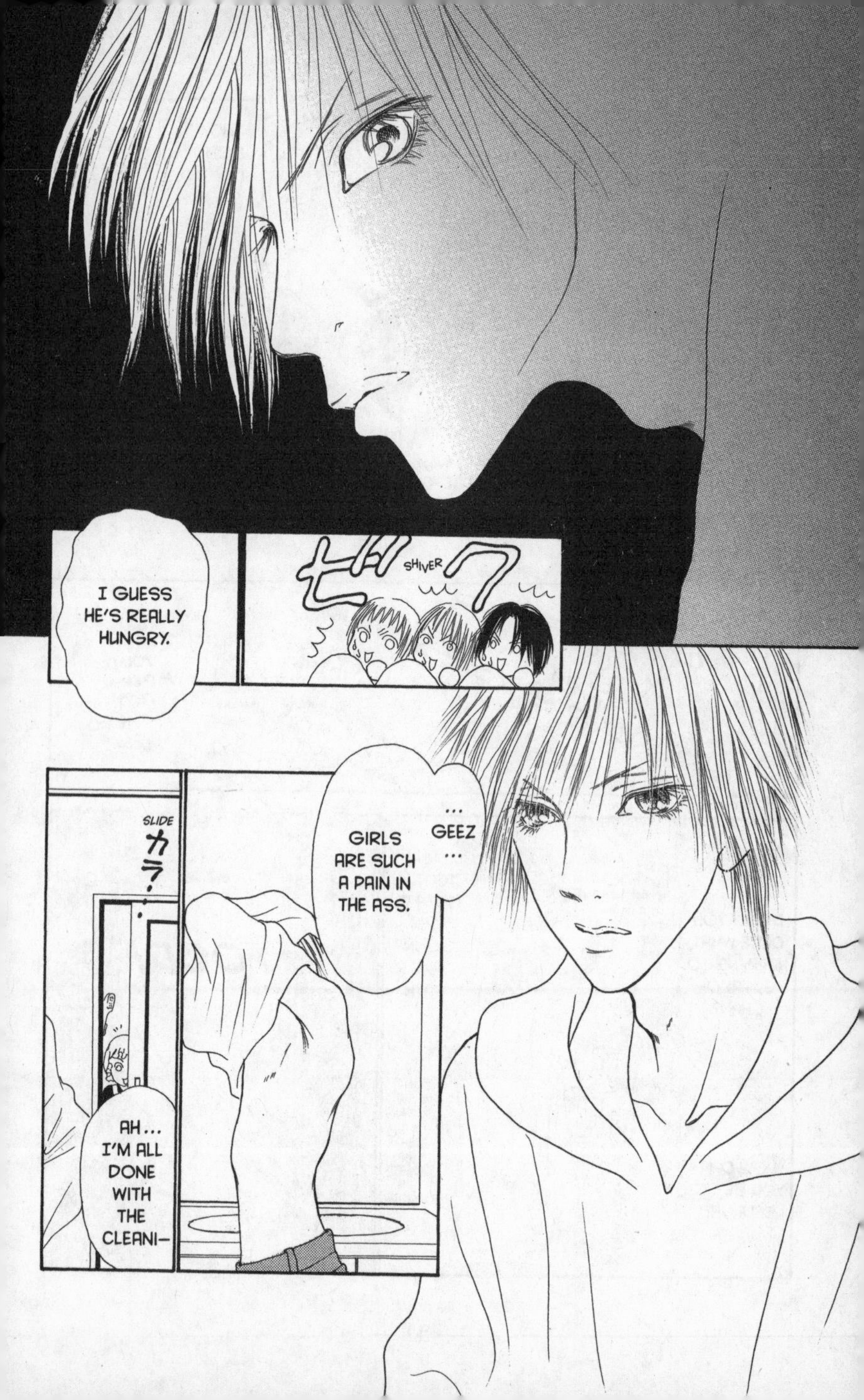
SHIVER
I GUESS HE'S REALLY HUNGRY.
... GEEZ ...
GIRLS ARE SUCH A PAIN IN THE ASS.
SLIDE
カラ
AH... I'M ALL DONE WITH THE CLEANI-

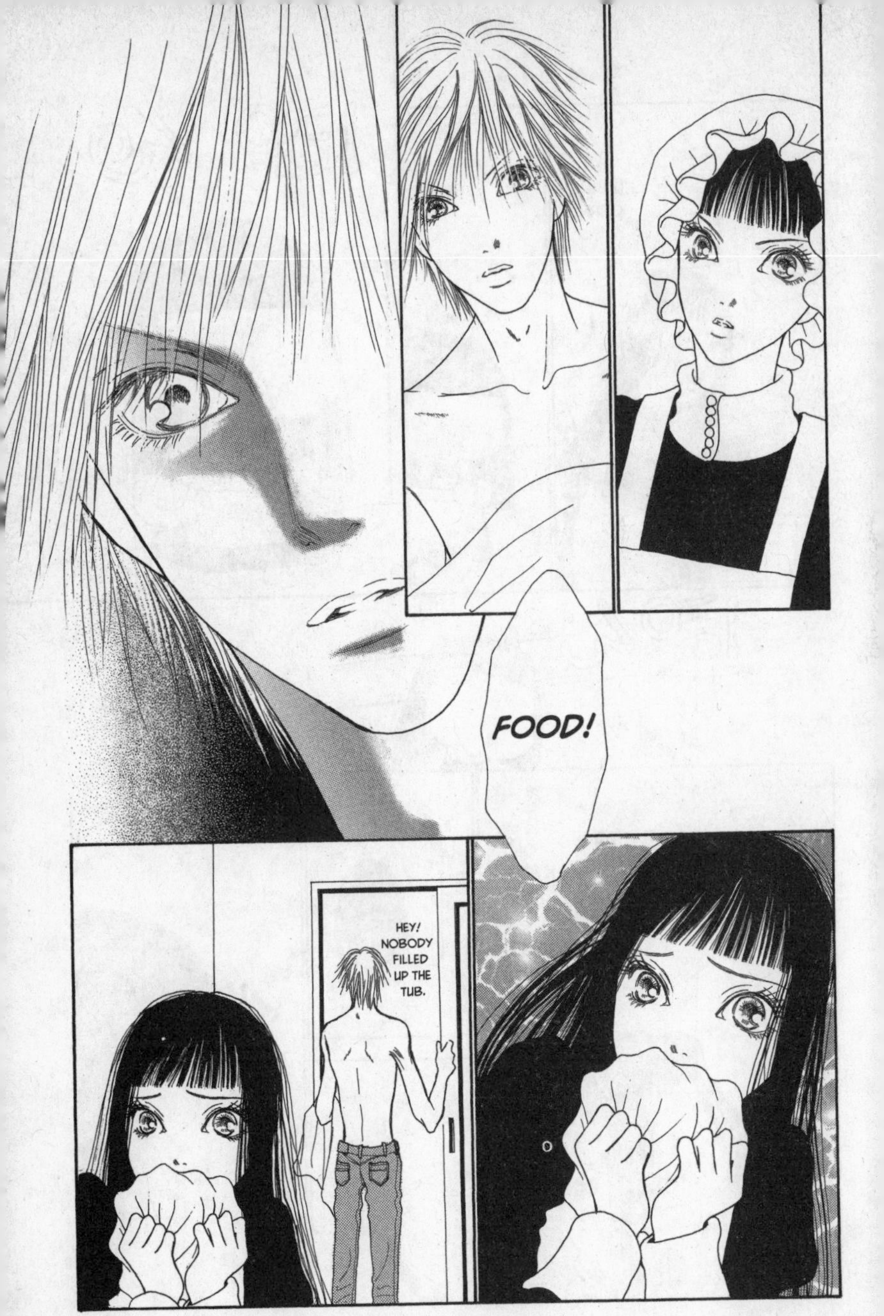
FOOD!
HEY! NOBODY FILLED UP THE TUB.

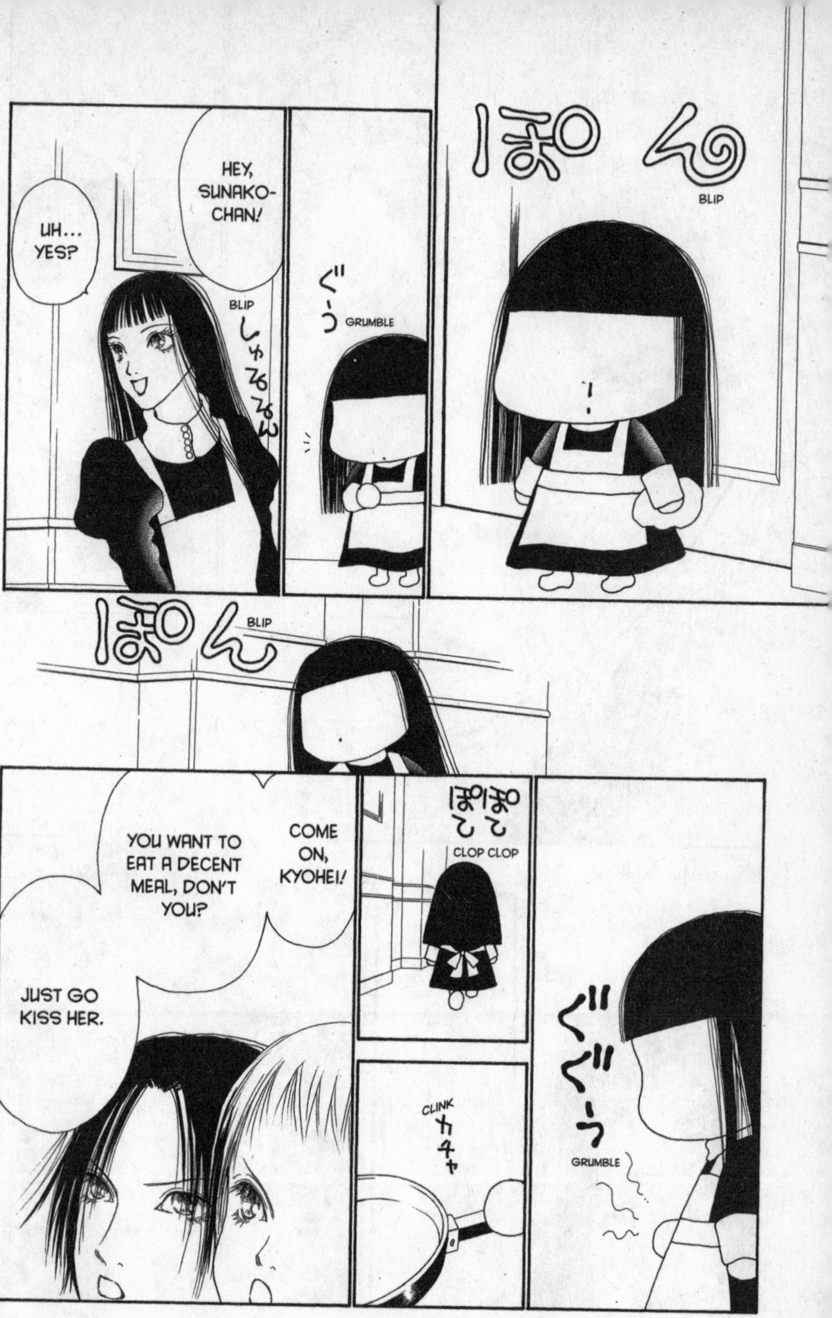
ぽん
BLIP
ぐう
GRUMBLE
HEY, SUNAKO-CHAN!
UH... YES?
BLIP
しゅるるん
ぽん
BLIP
ぐぐう
GRUMBLE
ぽてぽて
CLOP CLOP
CLINK
カチャ
COME ON, KYOHEI!
YOU WANT TO EAT A DECENT MEAL, DON'T YOU?
JUST GO KISS HER.

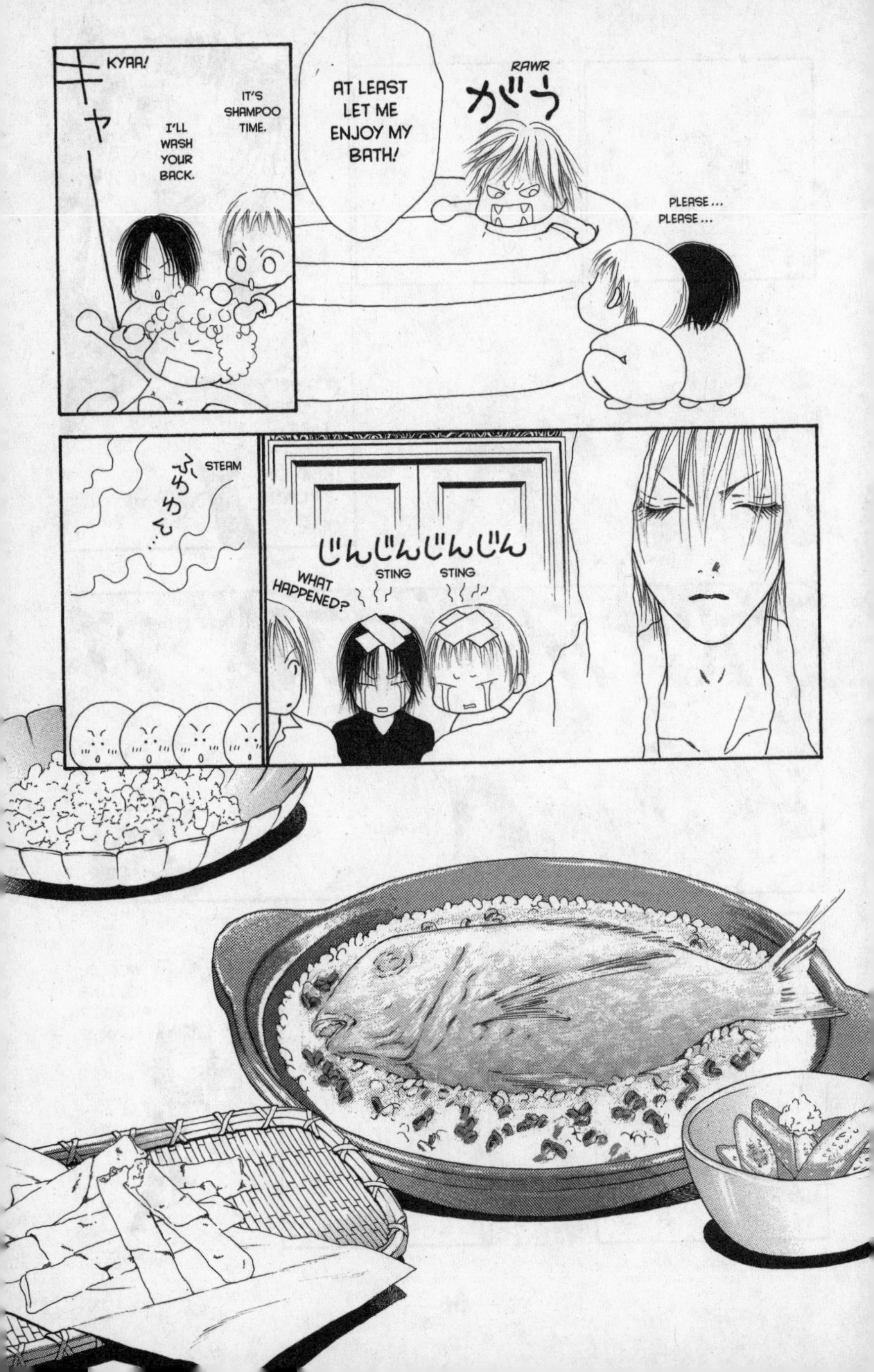
がう
RAWR
AT LEAST LET ME ENJOY MY BATH!
PLEASE... PLEASE...
キャー
KYAA!
IT'S SHAMPOO TIME.
I'LL WASH YOUR BACK.
じんじんじんじん
STING STING
WHAT HAPPENED?
ふわわ〜…
STEAM

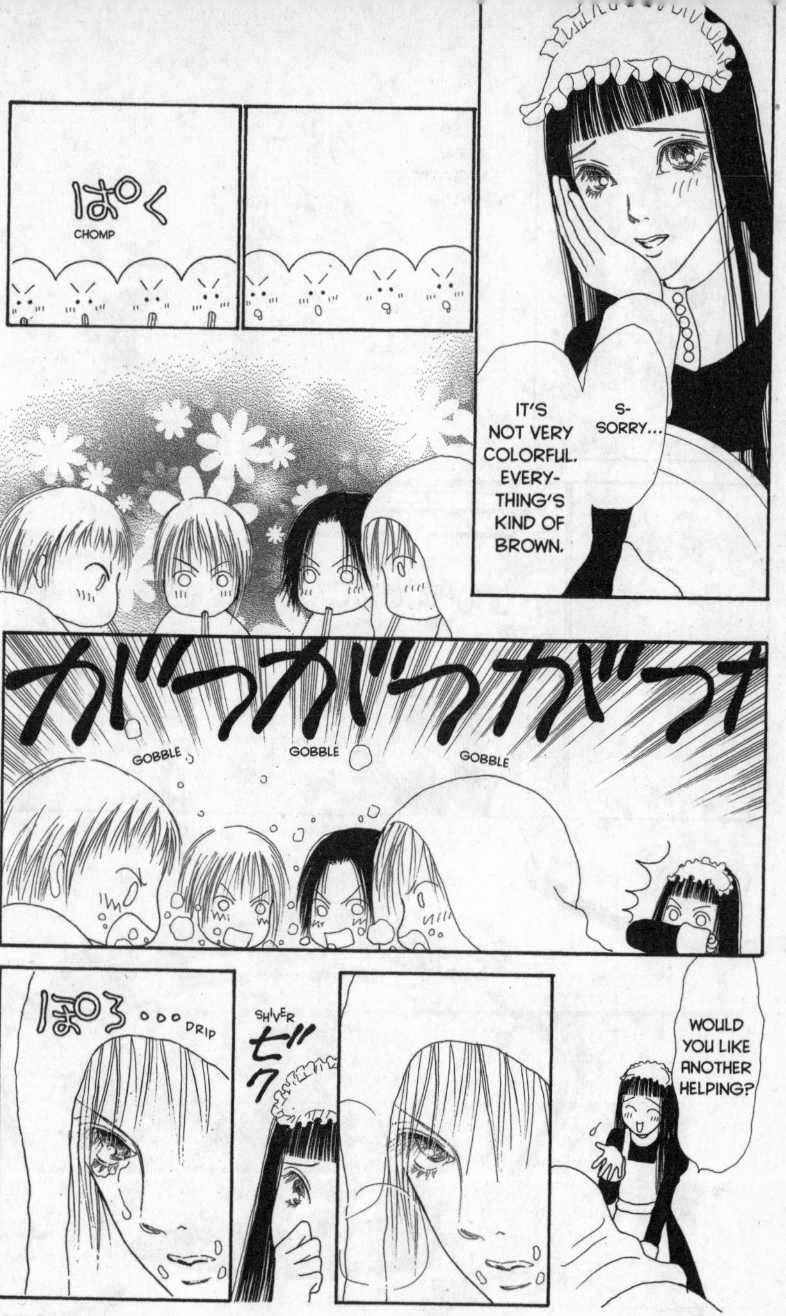
S-SORRY...
IT'S NOT VERY COLORFUL. EVERYTHING'S KIND OF BROWN.
ぱく
CHOMP
がつがつがつ
GOBBLE
GOBBLE
GOBBLE
WOULD YOU LIKE ANOTHER HELPING?
ビク
SHIVER
ぽろ
DRIP

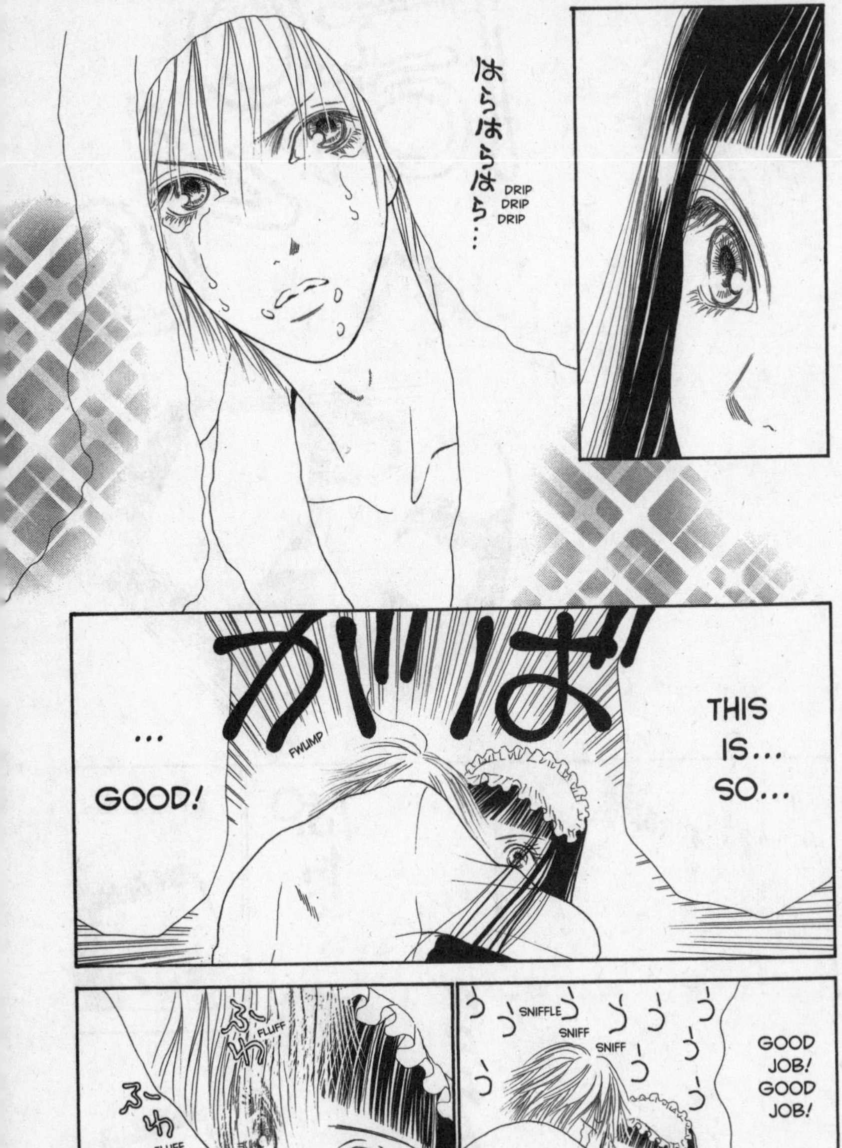
はらはらはら…
DRIP
DRIP
DRIP
THIS IS... SO...
がばっ
FWUMP
... GOOD!
GOOD JOB! GOOD JOB!
うっうっ
SNIFFLE
SNIFF
SNIFF
ふわ
FLUFF
ふわ
FLUFF

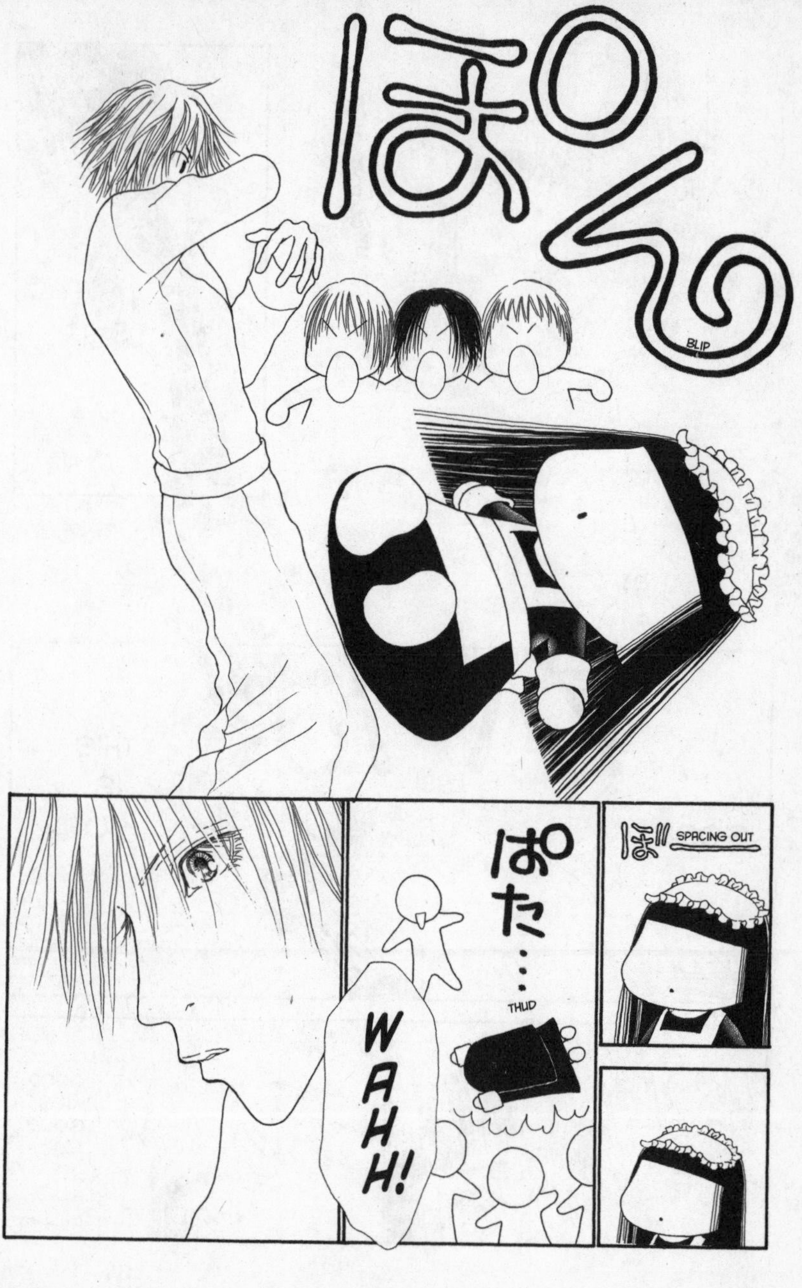
ぽん
BLIP
ぼ〃
SPACING OUT
ぱた…
THUD
WAHH!

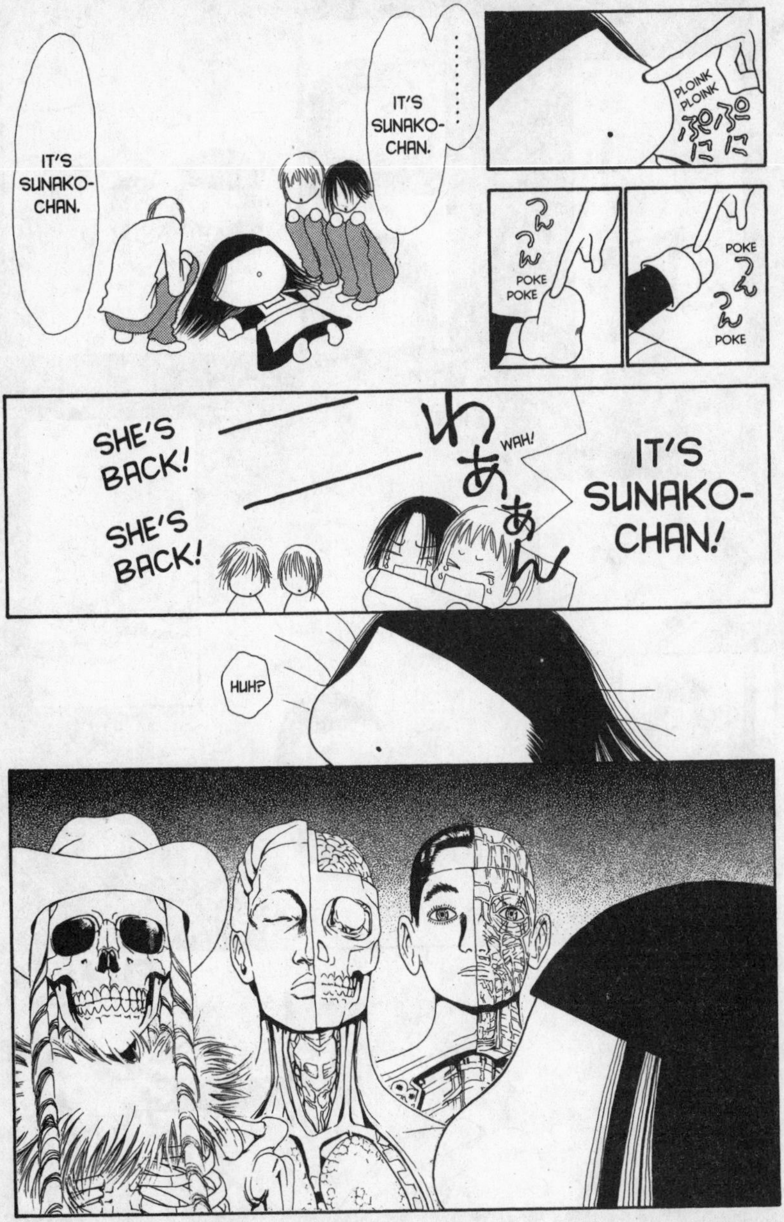

PLOINK PLOINK
ぷにぷに
POKE
つんつん
POKE
つんつん
POKE POKE
......
IT'S SUNAKO-CHAN.
IT'S SUNAKO-CHAN.
IT'S SUNAKO-CHAN!
わああん
WAH!
SHE'S BACK!
SHE'S BACK!
HUH?

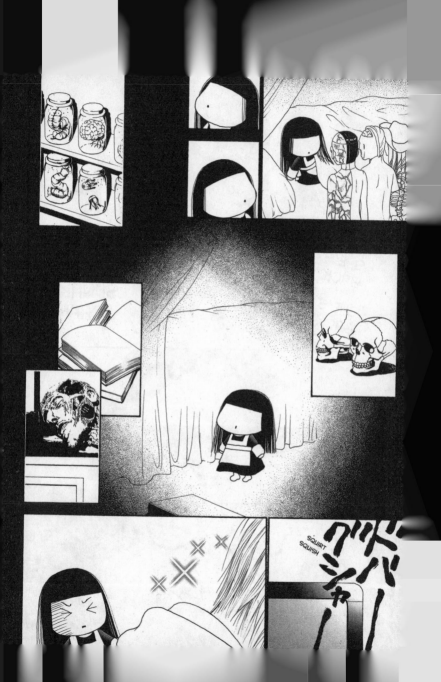

SQUIRT
SQUISH

ワッド
バシャ
シャ

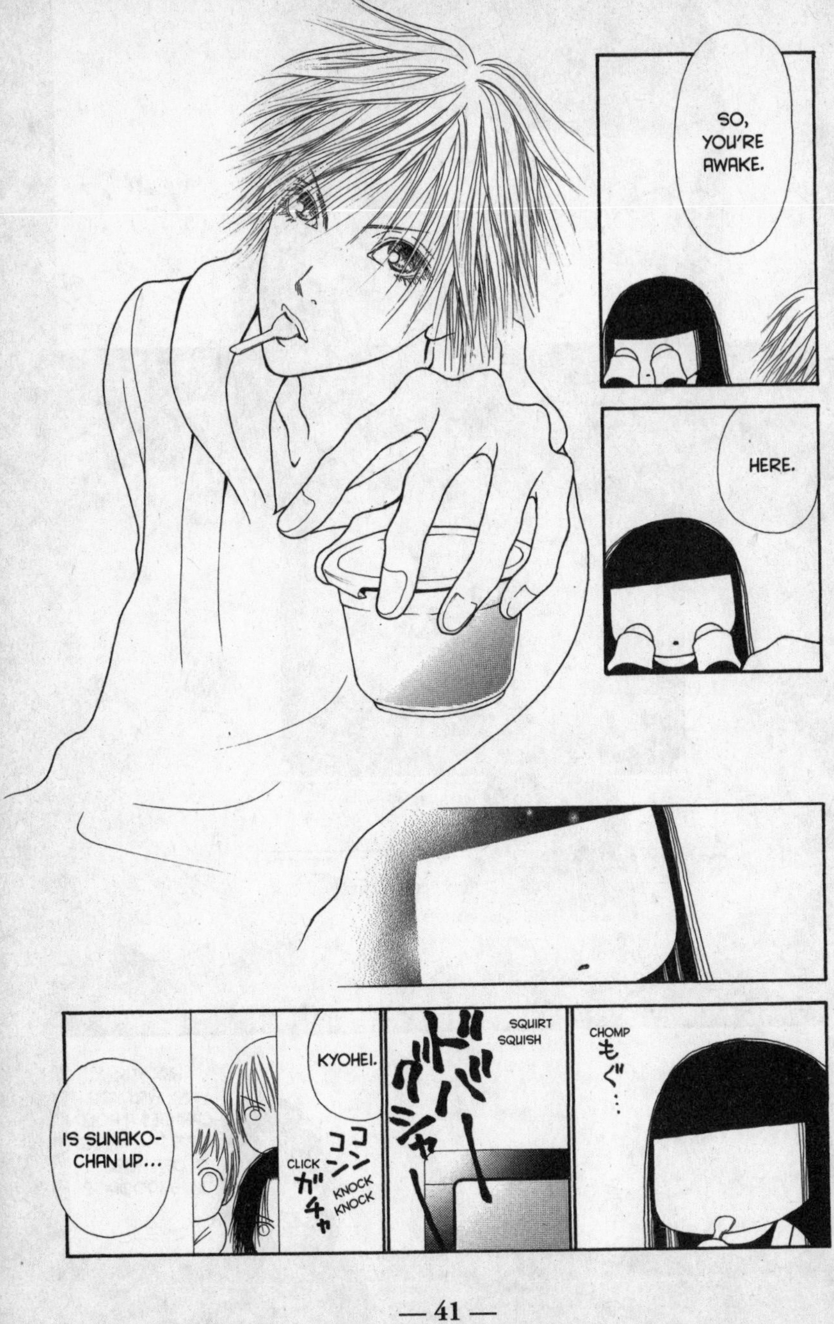
SO, YOU'RE AWAKE.
HERE.
CHOMP
もぐ…
SQUIRT
SQUISH
ドバー
シャー
KYOHEI.
CLICK
KNOCK KNOCK
コンコン
ガチャ
IS SUNAKO-CHAN UP...

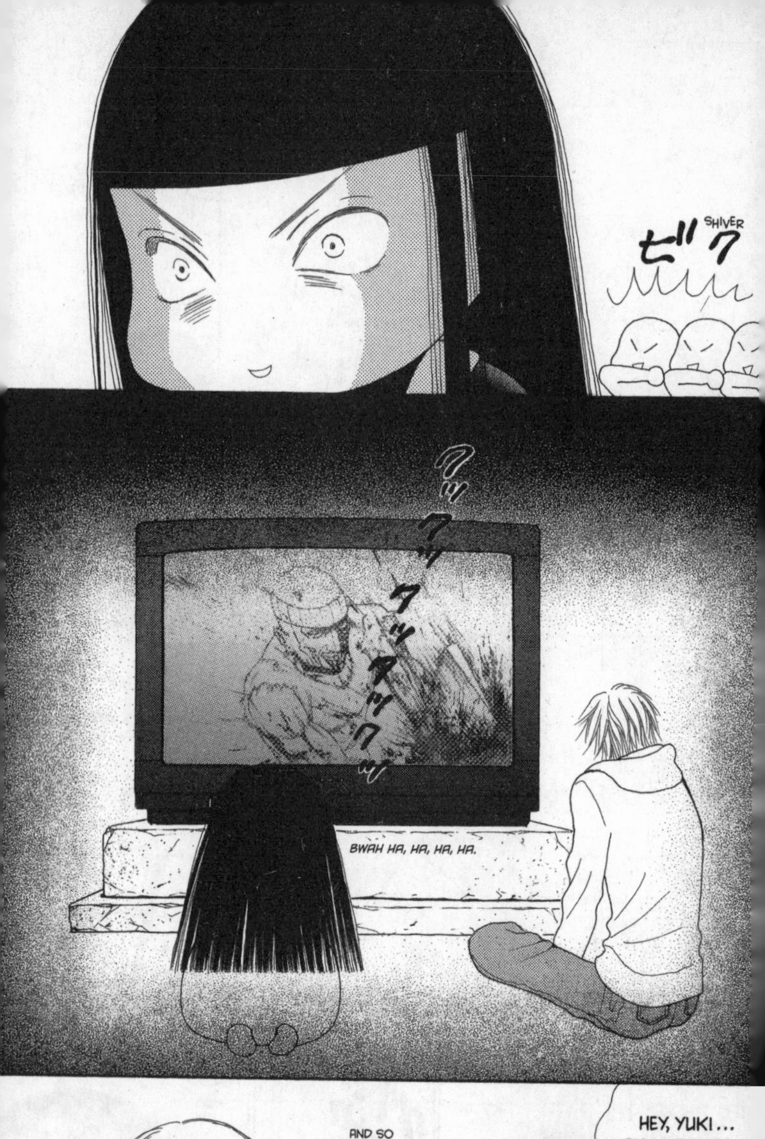
SHIVER
ビク
BWAH HA, HA, HA, HA.
HEY, YUKI... ANY WAY YOU CAN GET A HOLD OF SOME MORE OF THOSE MUSHROOMS?
AND SO IT BEGINS AGAIN.

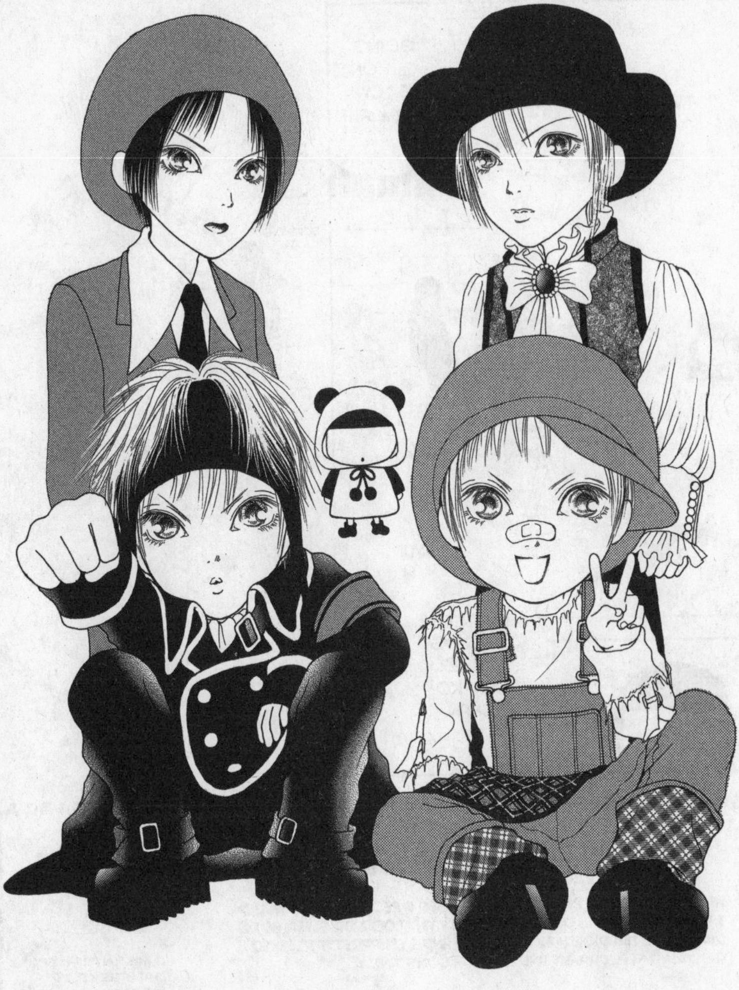

Chapter 28
Little Lost Boy

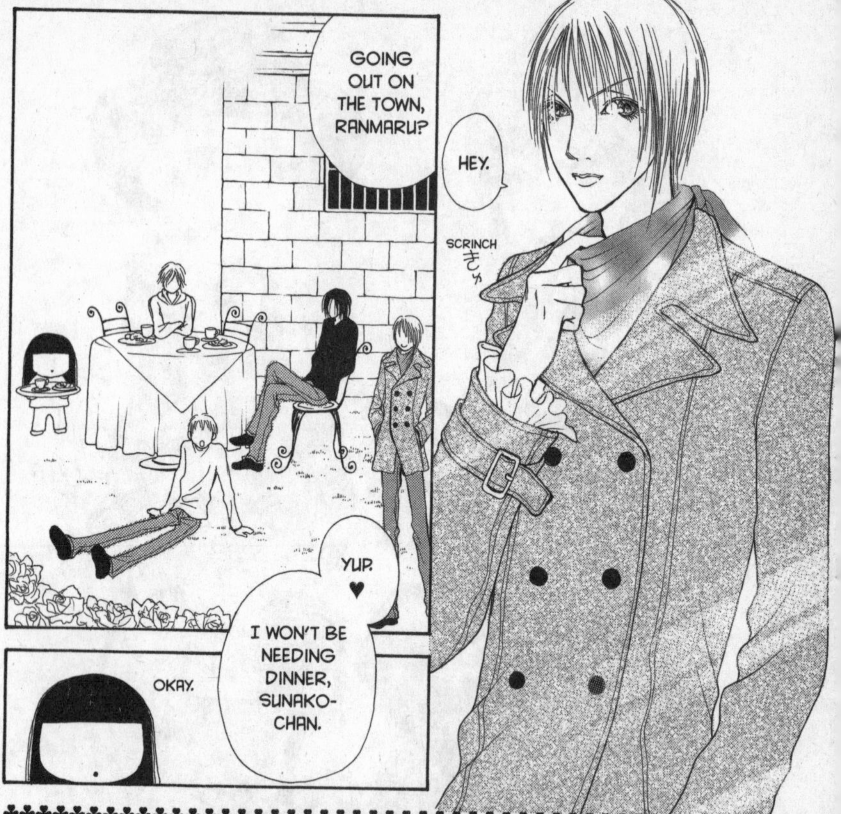
HEY.
SCRINCH
GOING OUT ON THE TOWN, RANMARU?
YUP. ♥
I WON'T BE NEEDING DINNER, SUNAKO-CHAN.
OKAY.

BEHIND THE SCENES

WHILE WRITING THIS CHAPTER, I WITNESSED A PECULIAR PHENOMENON. I WENT THREE WHOLE DAYS WITH HARDLY ANY FOOD OR SLEEP, BUT I DIDN'T FEEL TIRED OR HUNGRY AT ALL. AND I FELT PRETTY RELAXED. (USUALLY I FEEL CRANKY AND I LAUGH CONSTANTLY.)

I WAS JUST STARTING TO WONDER WHY, WHEN FOR SOME REASON A BUNCH OF WINGED ANTS SUDDENLY APPEARED OUT OF NOWHERE. AND AS SOON AS I FINISHED MY STORYBOARDS, THEY VANISHED. WHERE'D THEY GO?

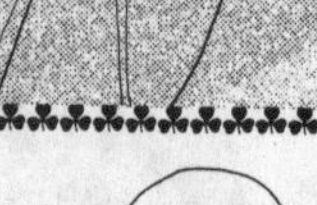

IT WAS FUN DRAWING THAT LITTLE KID. I'D LIKE TO DRAW HIM AGAIN SOMEDAY.

IT TOOK ME FIVE HOURS TO DRAW RANMARU IN COSPLAY.

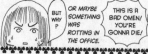

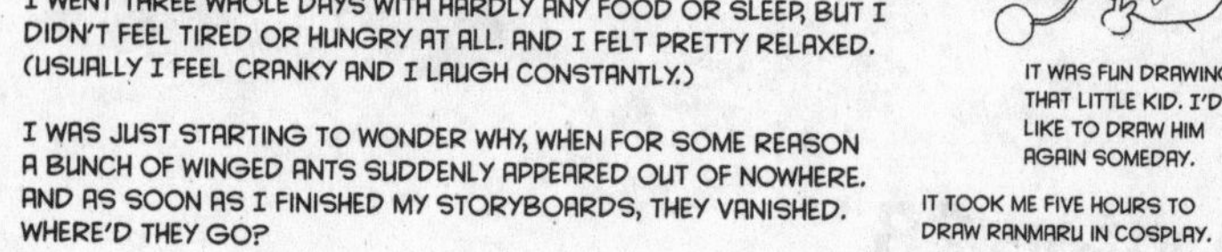
I WONDER IF THOSE ANTS CAME OUT OF MY BRAIN...
BUT WHY?
OR MAYBE SOMETHING WAS ROTTING IN THE OFFICE.
THIS IS A BAD OMEN! YOU'RE GONNA DIE!
THEY'RE OVER HERE TOO!
KYAA! THEY'RE EVERYWHERE!

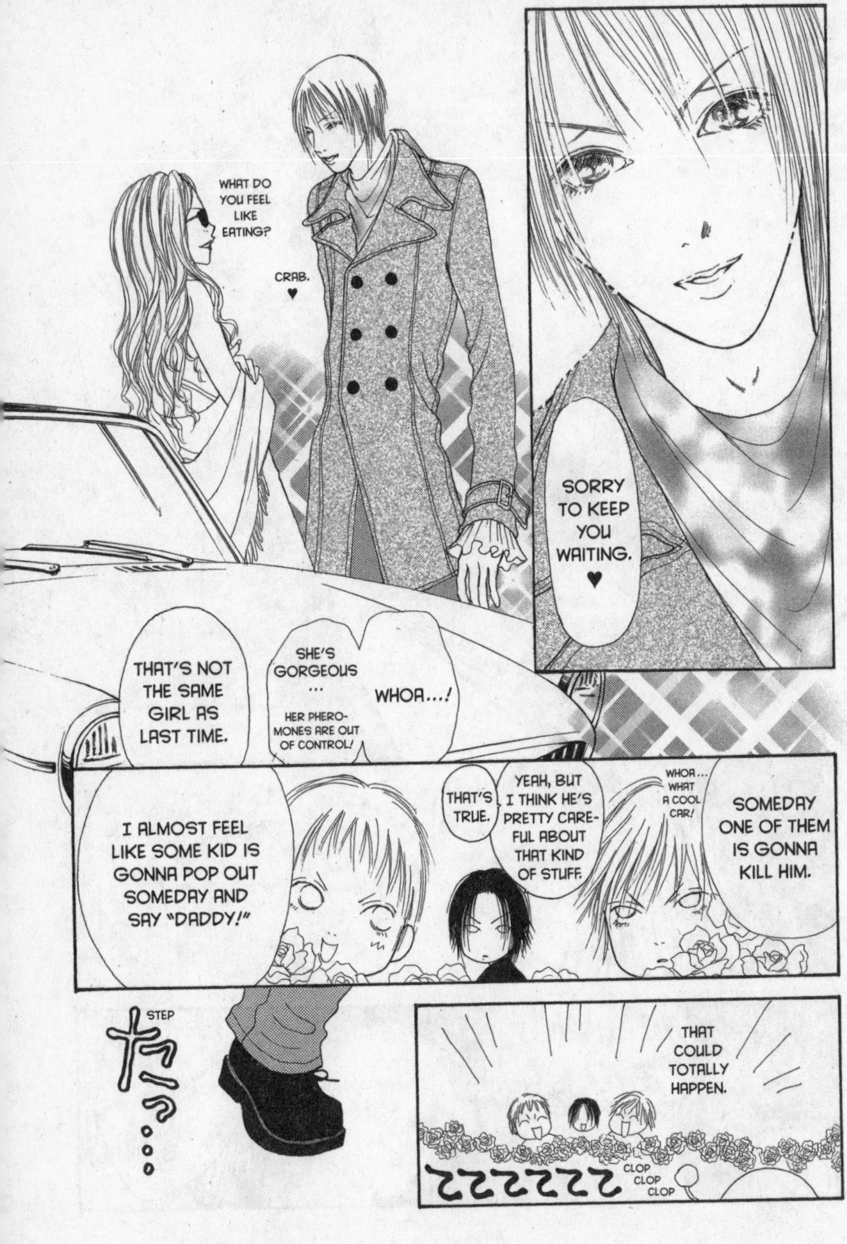
SORRY TO KEEP YOU WAITING. ♥
WHAT DO YOU FEEL LIKE EATING?
CRAB. ♥
WHOA...!
SHE'S GORGEOUS...
HER PHEROMONES ARE OUT OF CONTROL!
THAT'S NOT THE SAME GIRL AS LAST TIME.
SOMEDAY ONE OF THEM IS GONNA KILL HIM.
WHOA... WHAT A COOL CAR!
YEAH, BUT I THINK HE'S PRETTY CAREFUL ABOUT THAT KIND OF STUFF.
THAT'S TRUE.
I ALMOST FEEL LIKE SOME KID IS GONNA POP OUT SOMEDAY AND SAY "DADDY!"
THAT COULD TOTALLY HAPPEN.
CLOP CLOP CLOP
STEP

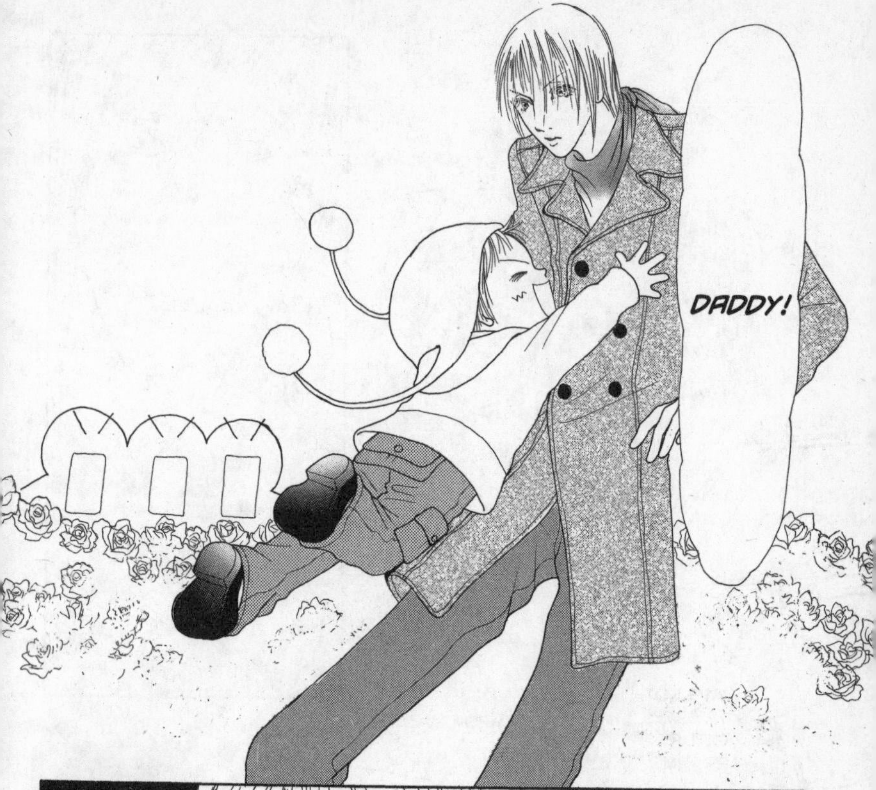
DADDY!

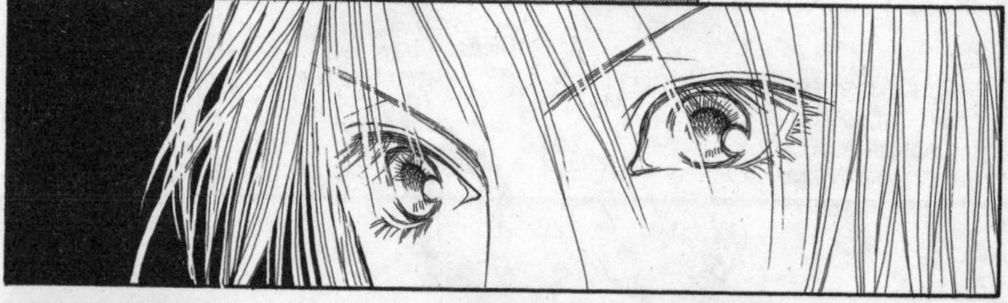

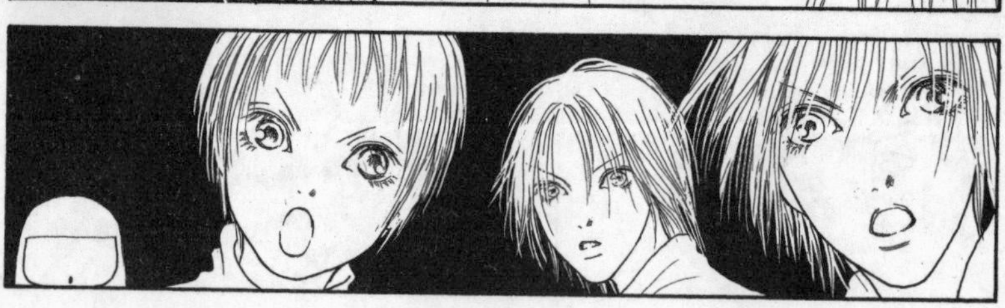

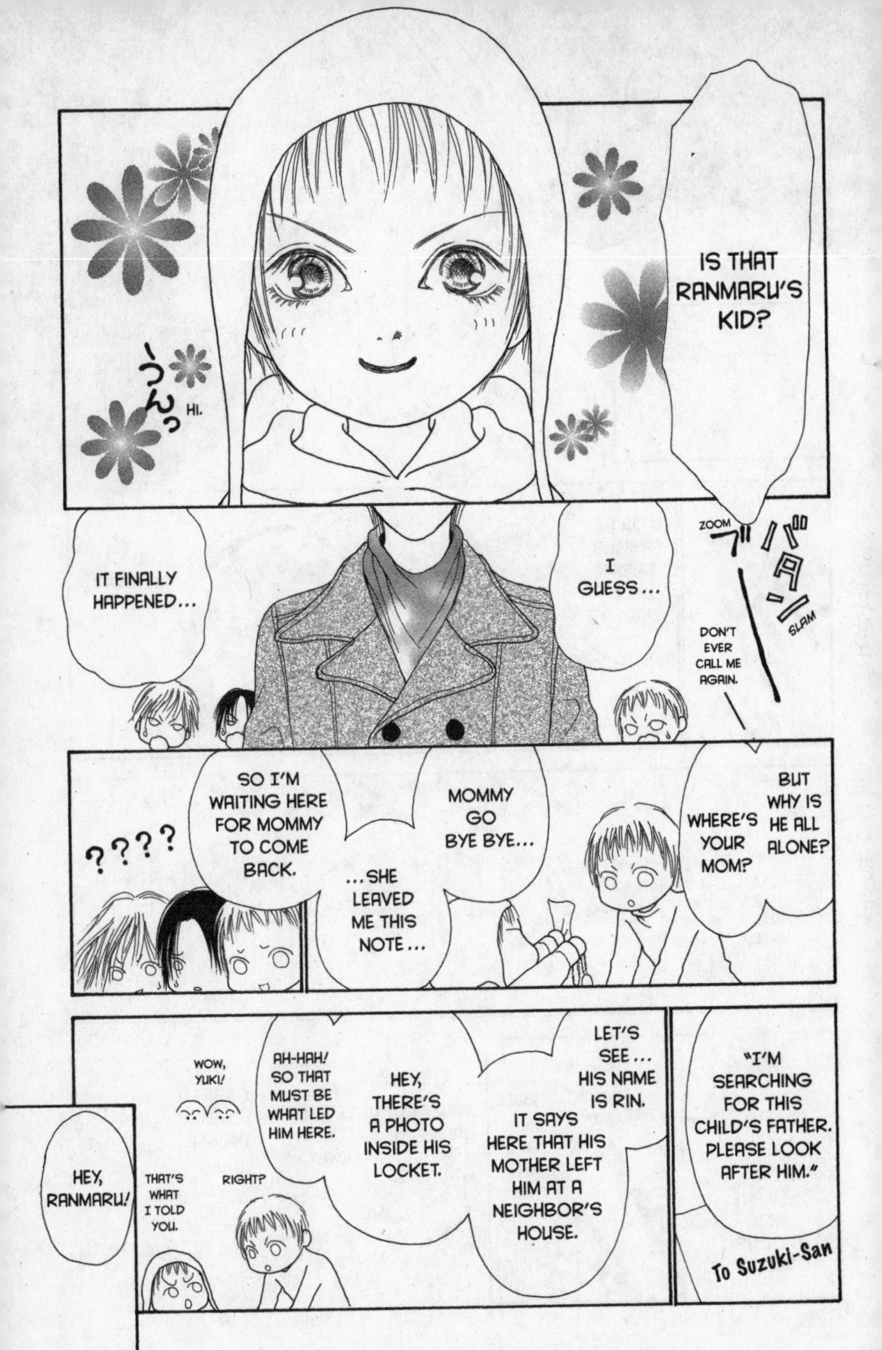
IS THAT RANMARU'S KID?
うんっ
HI.
ZOOM
SLAM
DON'T EVER CALL ME AGAIN.
I GUESS...
IT FINALLY HAPPENED...
BUT WHY IS HE ALL ALONE?
WHERE'S YOUR MOM?
MOMMY GO BYE BYE...
...SHE LEFT ME THIS NOTE...
SO I'M WAITING HERE FOR MOMMY TO COME BACK.
????
"I'M SEARCHING FOR THIS CHILD'S FATHER. PLEASE LOOK AFTER HIM."
To Suzuki-San
LET'S SEE... HIS NAME IS RIN.
IT SAYS HERE THAT HIS MOTHER LEFT HIM AT A NEIGHBOR'S HOUSE.
HEY, THERE'S A PHOTO INSIDE HIS LOCKET.
AH-HAH! SO THAT MUST BE WHAT LED HIM HERE.
WOW, YUKI!
RIGHT?
THAT'S WHAT I TOLD YOU.
HEY, RANMARU!

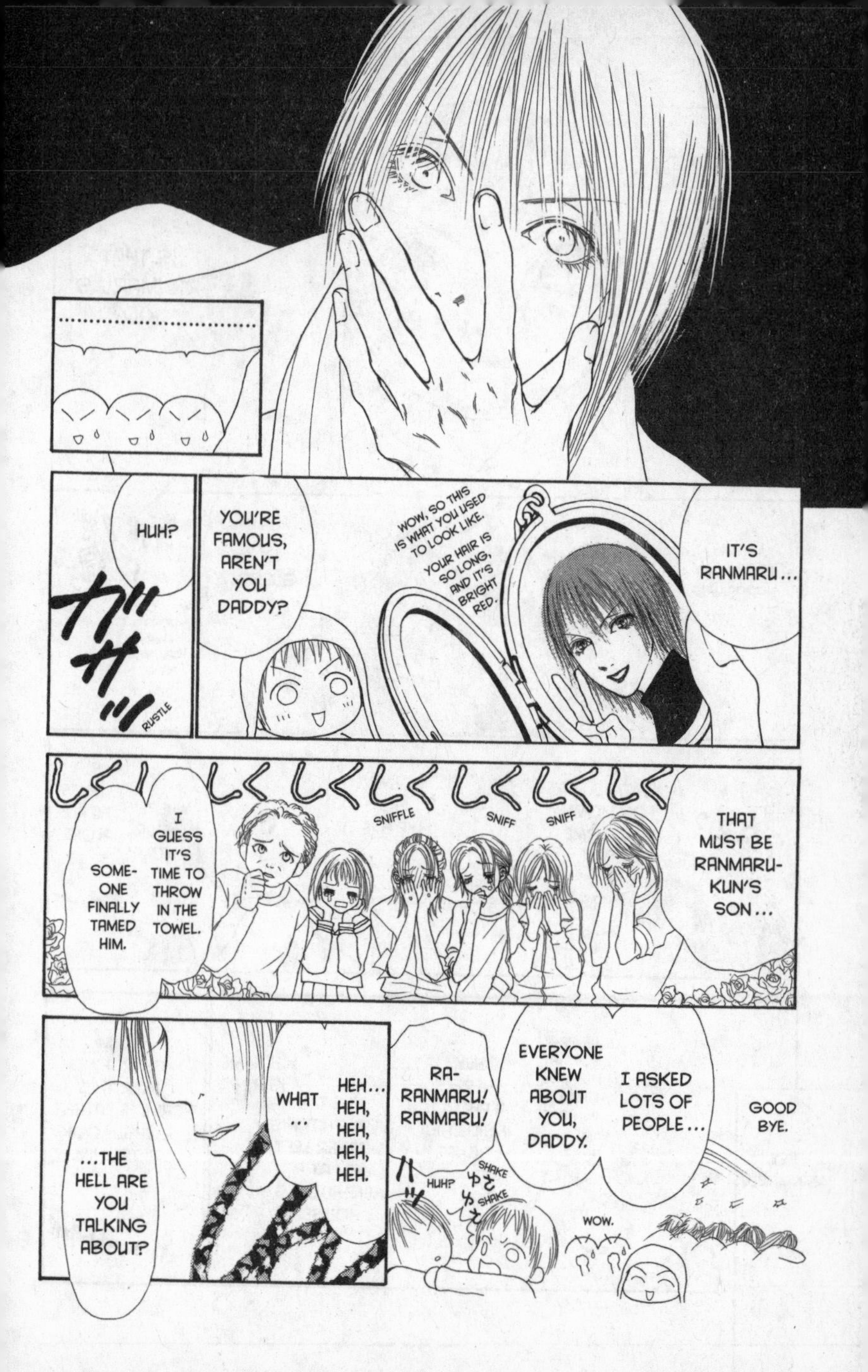
……………
IT'S RANMARU…
WOW, SO THIS IS WHAT YOU USED TO LOOK LIKE.
YOUR HAIR IS SO LONG, AND IT'S BRIGHT RED.
YOU'RE FAMOUS, AREN'T YOU DADDY?
HUH?
ガサッ
RUSTLE
THAT MUST BE RANMARU-KUN'S SON…
しくしくしくしくしくしくしく
SNIFF
SNIFF
SNIFFLE
I GUESS IT'S TIME TO THROW IN THE TOWEL.
SOME-ONE FINALLY TAMED HIM.
GOOD BYE.
I ASKED LOTS OF PEOPLE…
EVERYONE KNEW ABOUT YOU, DADDY.
WOW.
RA-RANMARU! RANMARU!
ゆさゆさ
SHAKE
SHAKE
HUH?
ハッ
HEH… HEH, HEH, HEH, HEH.
WHAT …
…THE HELL ARE YOU TALKING ABOUT?

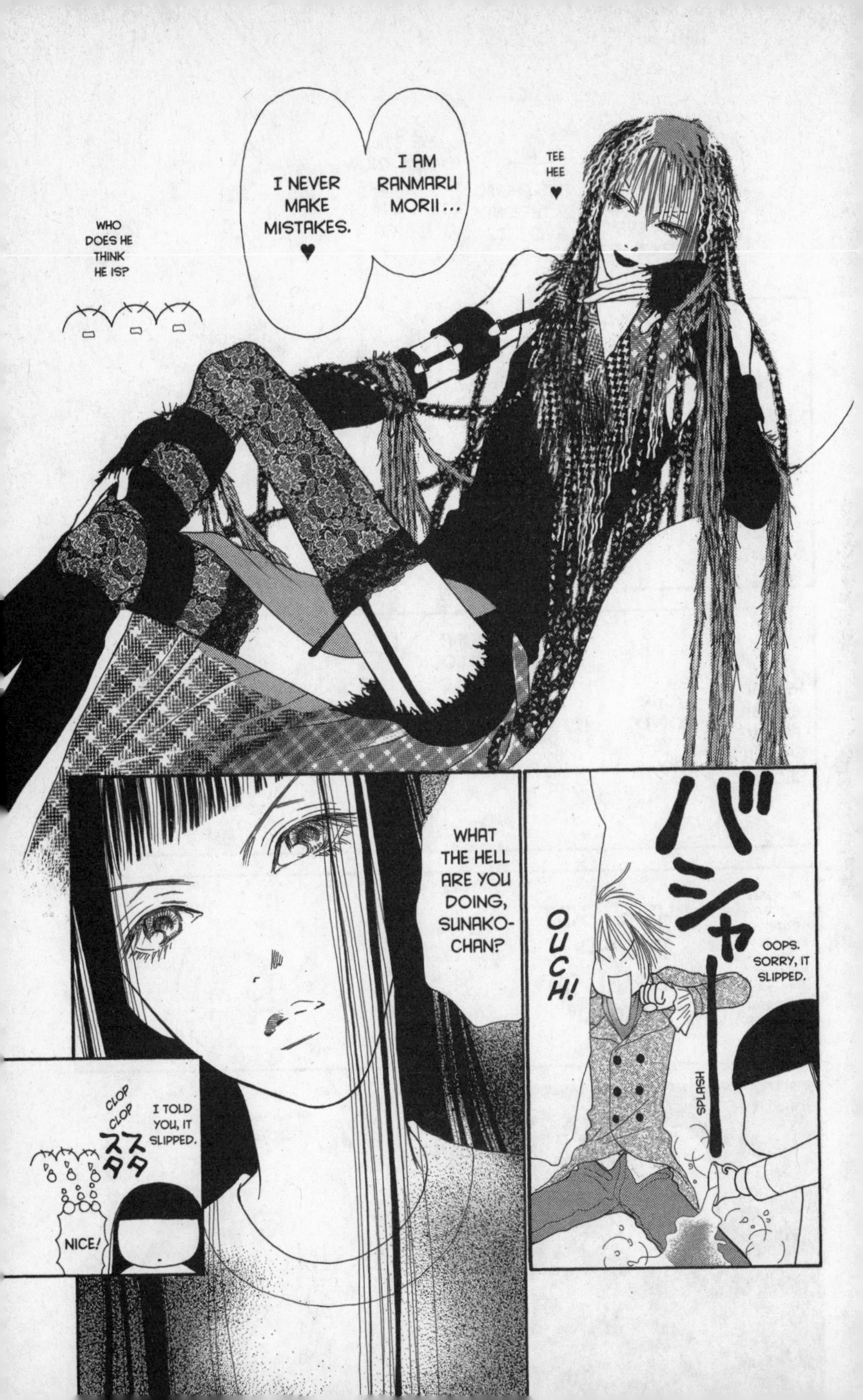
TEE HEE ♥
I AM RANMARU MORII...
I NEVER MAKE MISTAKES. ♥
WHO DOES HE THINK HE IS?
バシャー
OOPS. SORRY, IT SLIPPED.
OUCH!
SPLASH
WHAT THE HELL ARE YOU DOING, SUNAKO-CHAN?
I TOLD YOU, IT SLIPPED.
スタスタ
CLOP CLOP
NICE!

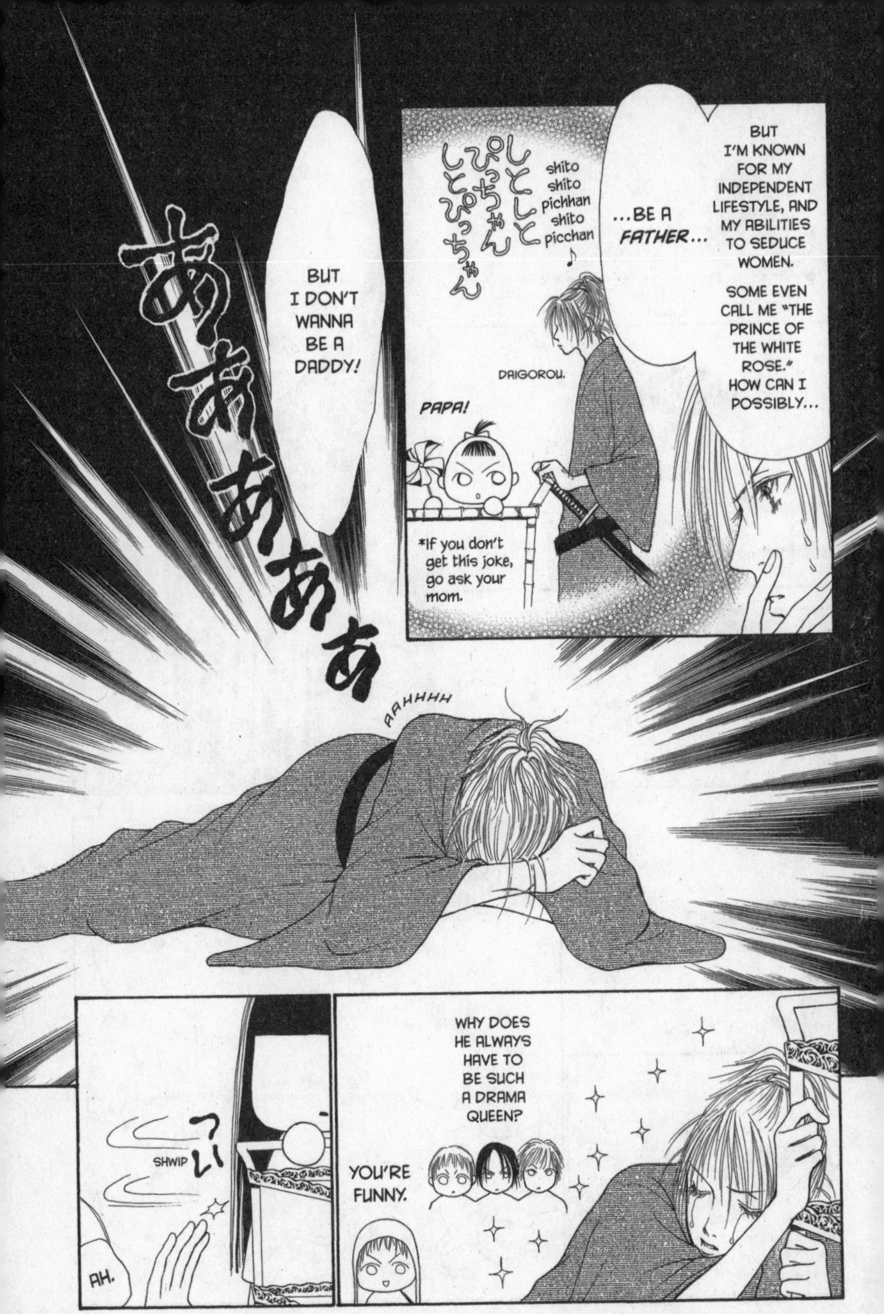
BUT I'M KNOWN FOR MY INDEPENDENT LIFESTYLE, AND MY ABILITIES TO SEDUCE WOMEN.
SOME EVEN CALL ME "THE PRINCE OF THE WHITE ROSE." HOW CAN I POSSIBLY...
...BE A *FATHER*...
しとしとぴっちゃんしとぴっちゃん
shito shito pichhan shito picchan ♪
DAIGOROU.
PAPA!
*If you don't get this joke, go ask your mom.
BUT I DON'T WANNA BE A DADDY!
ああああああ
AAHHHH
WHY DOES HE ALWAYS HAVE TO BE SUCH A DRAMA QUEEN?
YOU'RE FUNNY.
つい
SHWIP
AH.

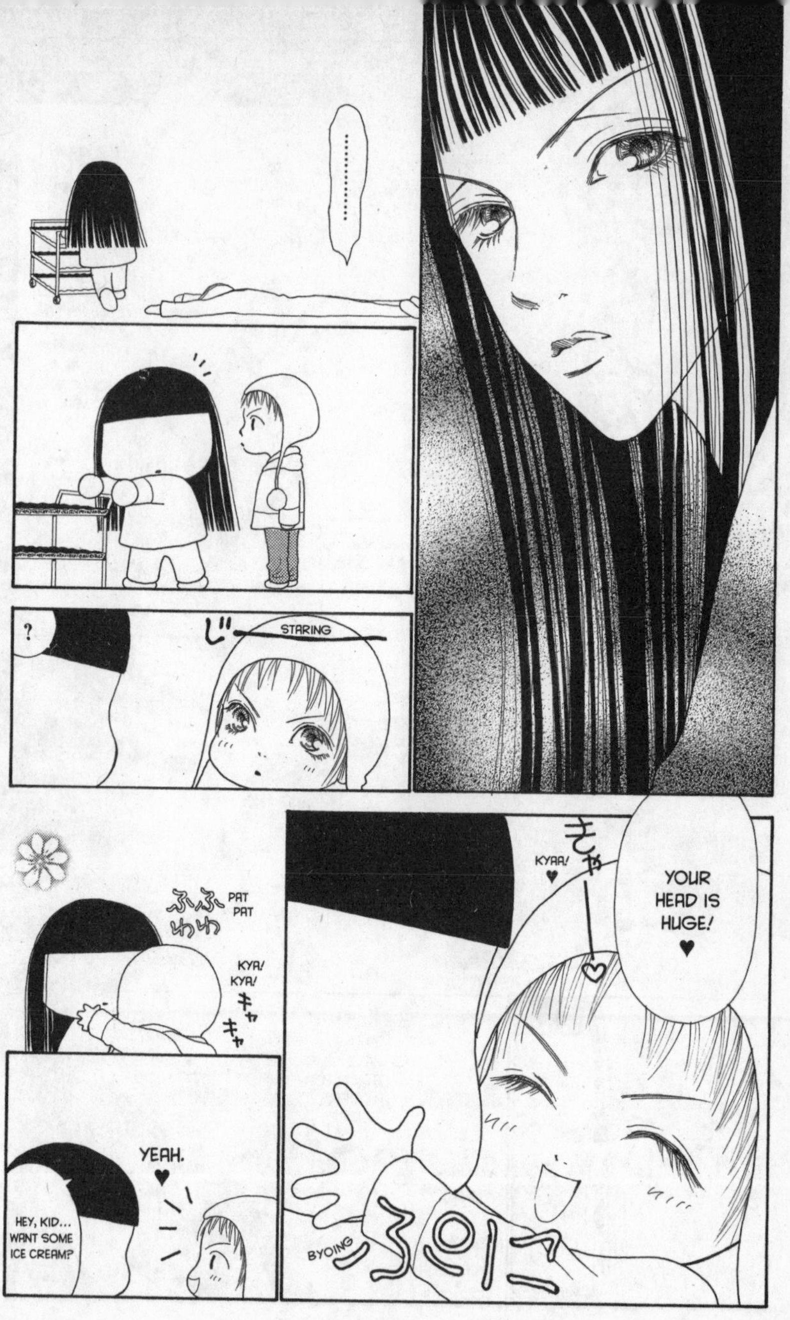
......
?
じ— STARING
きゃー KYAA! ♥
YOUR HEAD IS HUGE! ♥
BYOING
PAT PAT
KYA! KYA! キャ キャ
YEAH. ♥
HEY, KID... WANT SOME ICE CREAM?

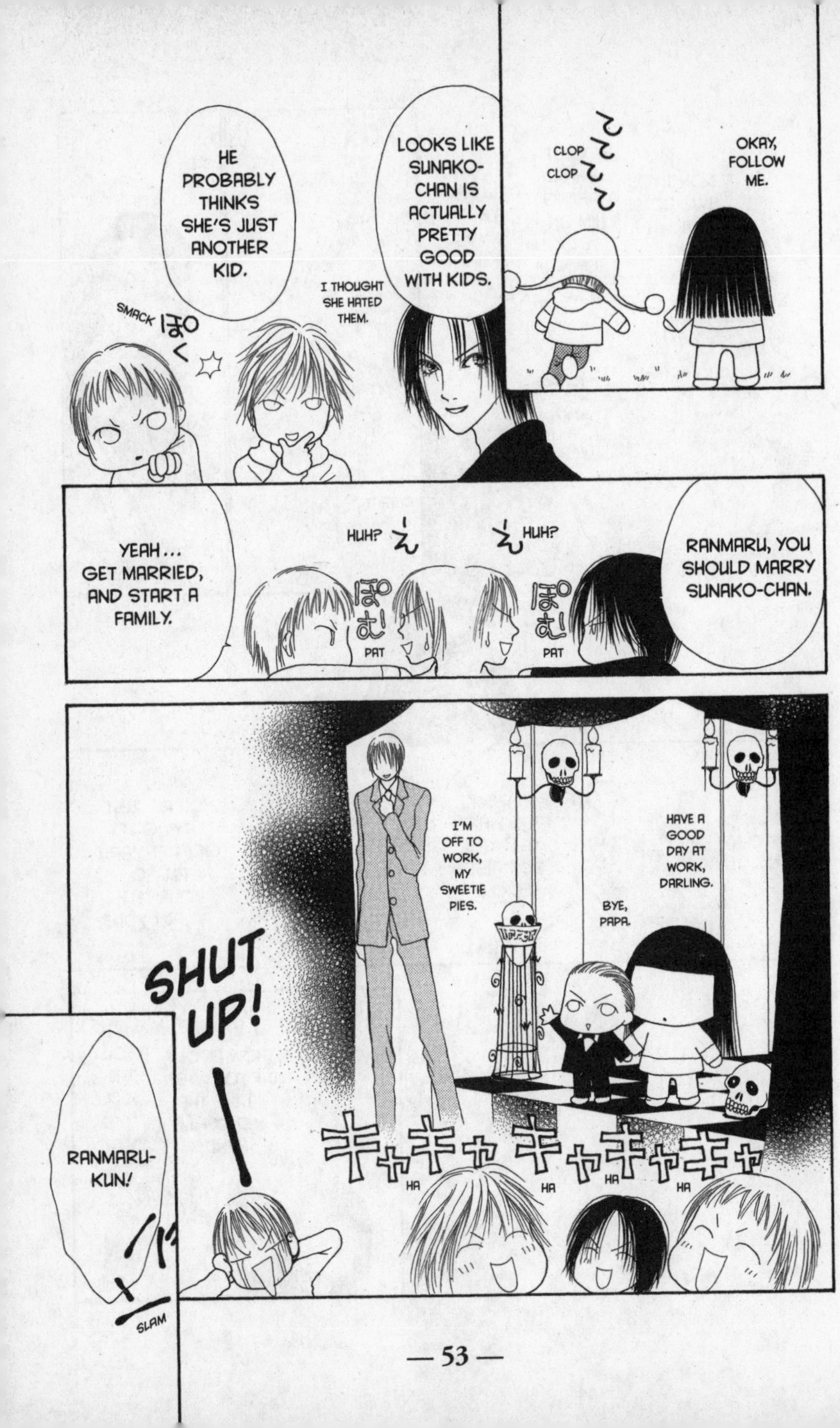
OKAY, FOLLOW ME.
CLOP CLOP
LOOKS LIKE SUNAKO-CHAN IS ACTUALLY PRETTY GOOD WITH KIDS.
I THOUGHT SHE HATED THEM.
HE PROBABLY THINKS SHE'S JUST ANOTHER KID.
SMACK
RANMARU, YOU SHOULD MARRY SUNAKO-CHAN.
HUH?
PAT
HUH?
PAT
YEAH... GET MARRIED, AND START A FAMILY.
HAVE A GOOD DAY AT WORK, DARLING.
BYE, PAPA.
I'M OFF TO WORK, MY SWEETIE PIES.
HA HA HA HA
SHUT UP!
RANMARU-KUN!
SLAM

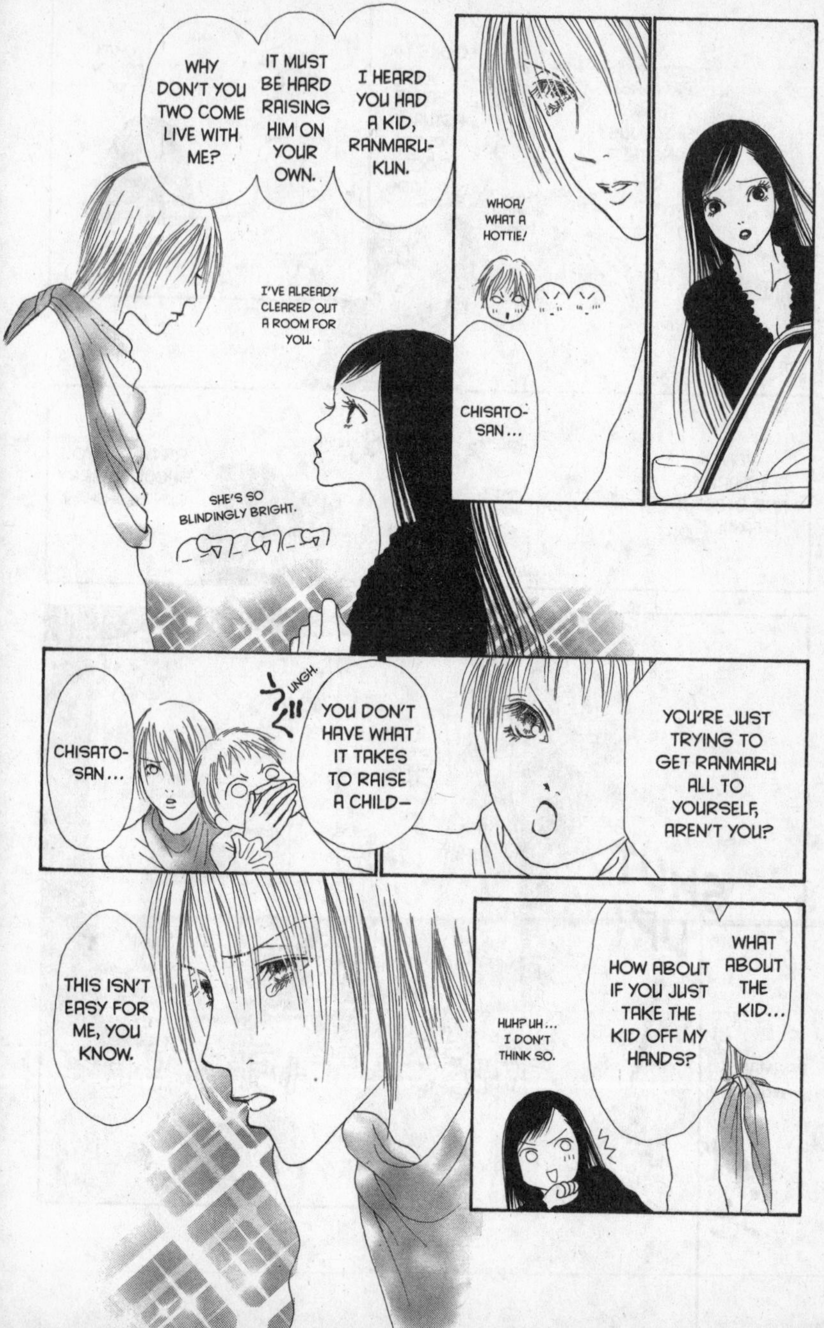
WHOA! WHAT A HOTTIE!
CHISATO-SAN...
I HEARD YOU HAD A KID, RANMARU-KUN.
IT MUST BE HARD RAISING HIM ON YOUR OWN.
WHY DON'T YOU TWO COME LIVE WITH ME?
I'VE ALREADY CLEARED OUT A ROOM FOR YOU.
SHE'S SO BLINDINGLY BRIGHT.
YOU'RE JUST TRYING TO GET RANMARU ALL TO YOURSELF, AREN'T YOU?
YOU DON'T HAVE WHAT IT TAKES TO RAISE A CHILD—
UNGH.
CHISATO-SAN...
WHAT ABOUT THE KID...
HOW ABOUT IF YOU JUST TAKE THE KID OFF MY HANDS?
HUH? UH... I DON'T THINK SO.
THIS ISN'T EASY FOR ME, YOU KNOW.

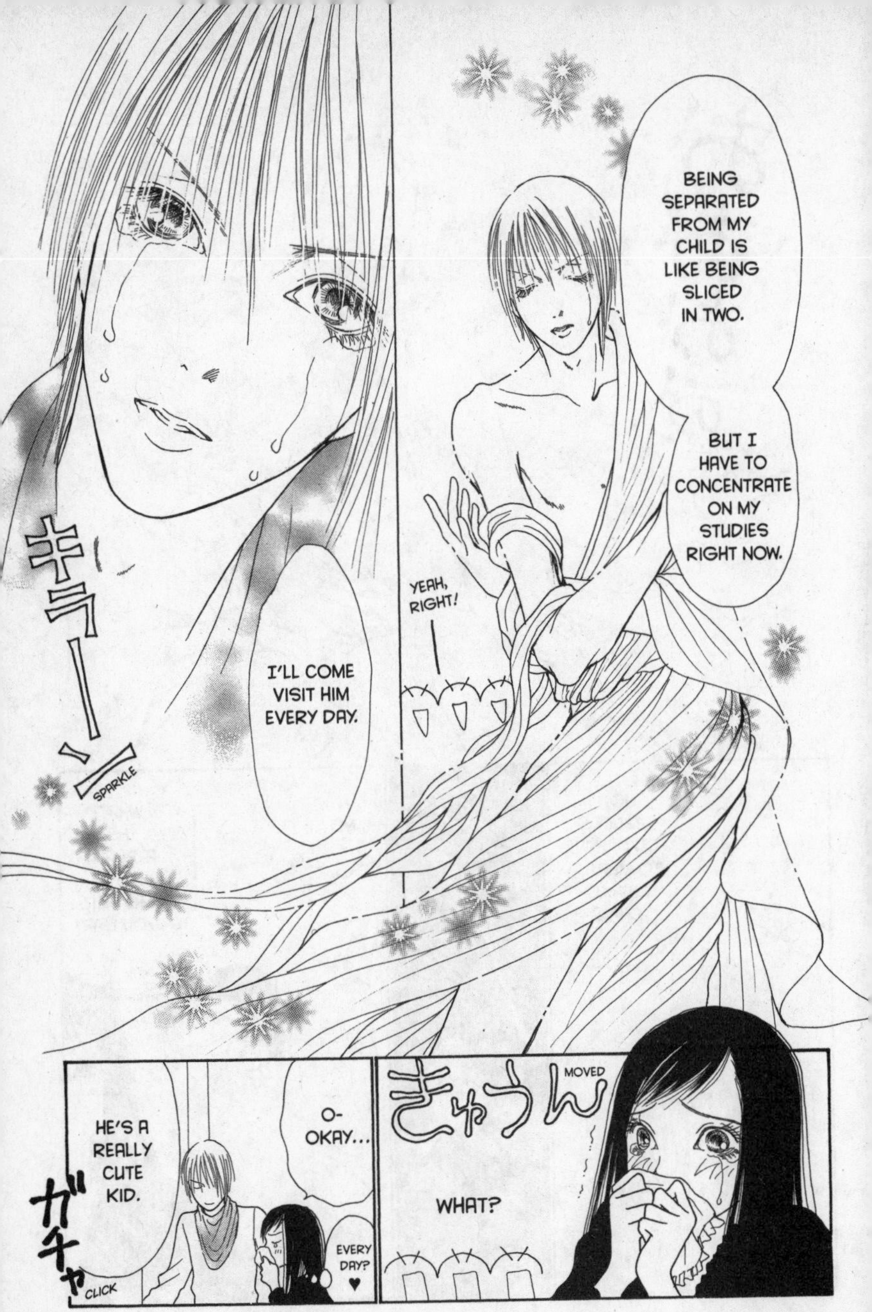
BEING SEPARATED FROM MY CHILD IS LIKE BEING SLICED IN TWO.
BUT I HAVE TO CONCENTRATE ON MY STUDIES RIGHT NOW.
YEAH, RIGHT!
I'LL COME VISIT HIM EVERY DAY.
キラーン
SPARKLE
きゅうん
MOVED
WHAT?
O-OKAY...
HE'S A REALLY CUTE KID.
EVERY DAY? ♥
ガチャ
CLICK

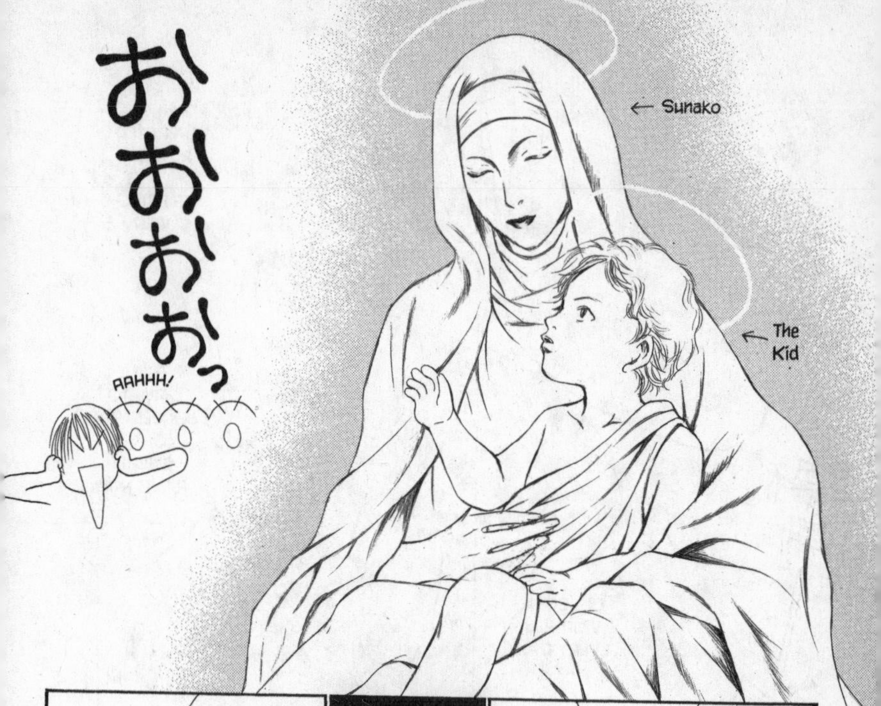
← Sunako
← The Kid
おおおおっ
AAHHH!

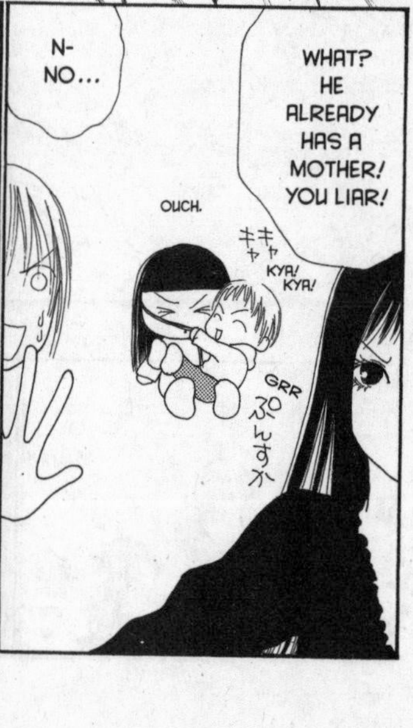
WHAT? HE ALREADY HAS A MOTHER! YOU LIAR!
N-NO...
OUCH.
キャキャ
KYA! KYA!
ぷんすか
GRR

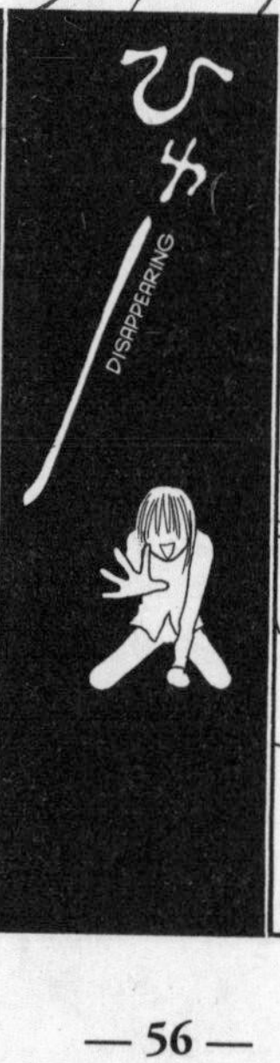
ひゅー
DISAPPEARING

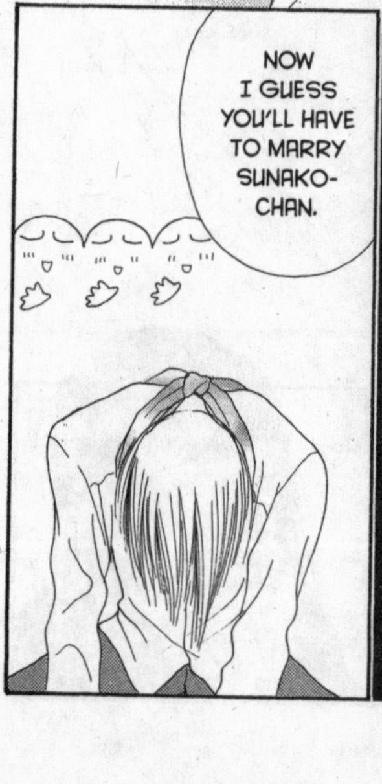
NOW I GUESS YOU'LL HAVE TO MARRY SUNAKO-CHAN.

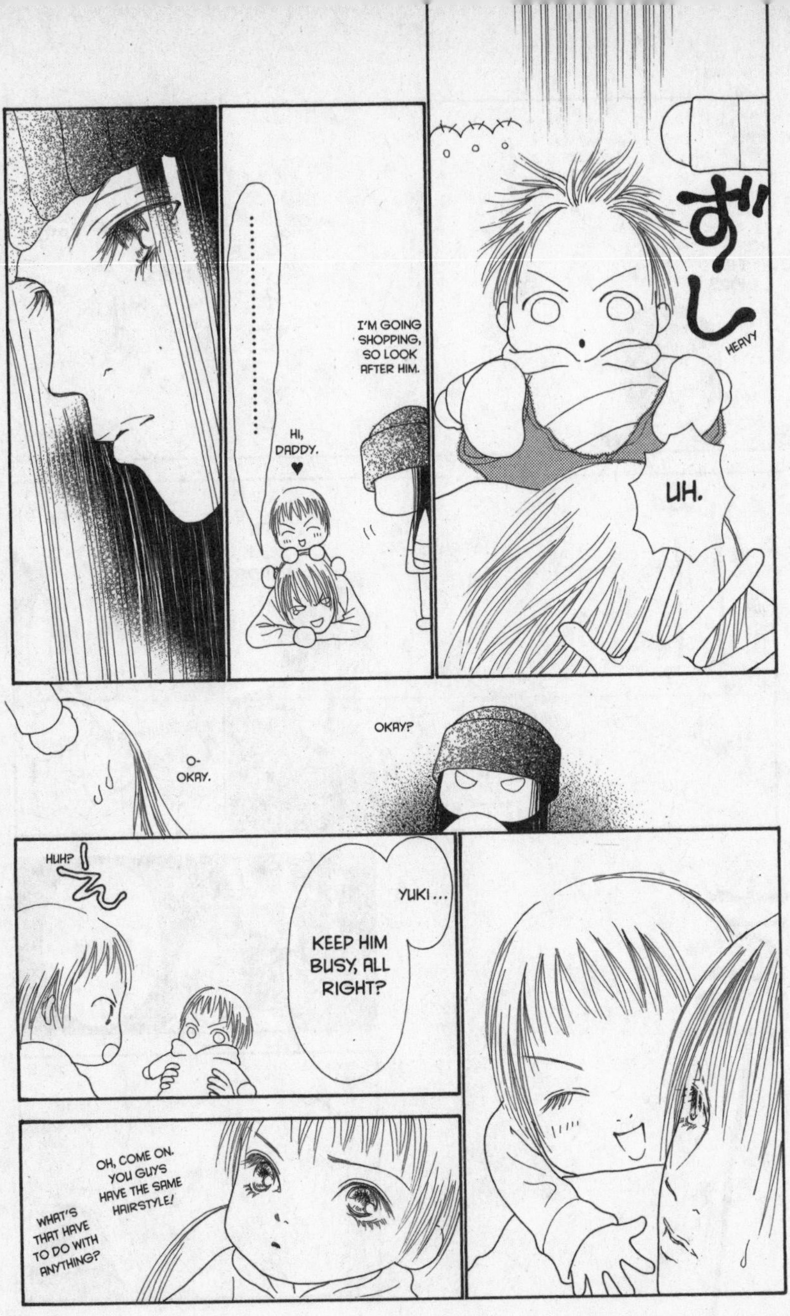
ずし
HEAVY
UH.
I'M GOING SHOPPING, SO LOOK AFTER HIM.
....
HI, DADDY. ♥
OKAY?
O- OKAY.
YUKI...
KEEP HIM BUSY, ALL RIGHT?
HUH? ん
OH, COME ON. YOU GUYS HAVE THE SAME HAIRSTYLE!
WHAT'S THAT HAVE TO DO WITH ANYTHING?

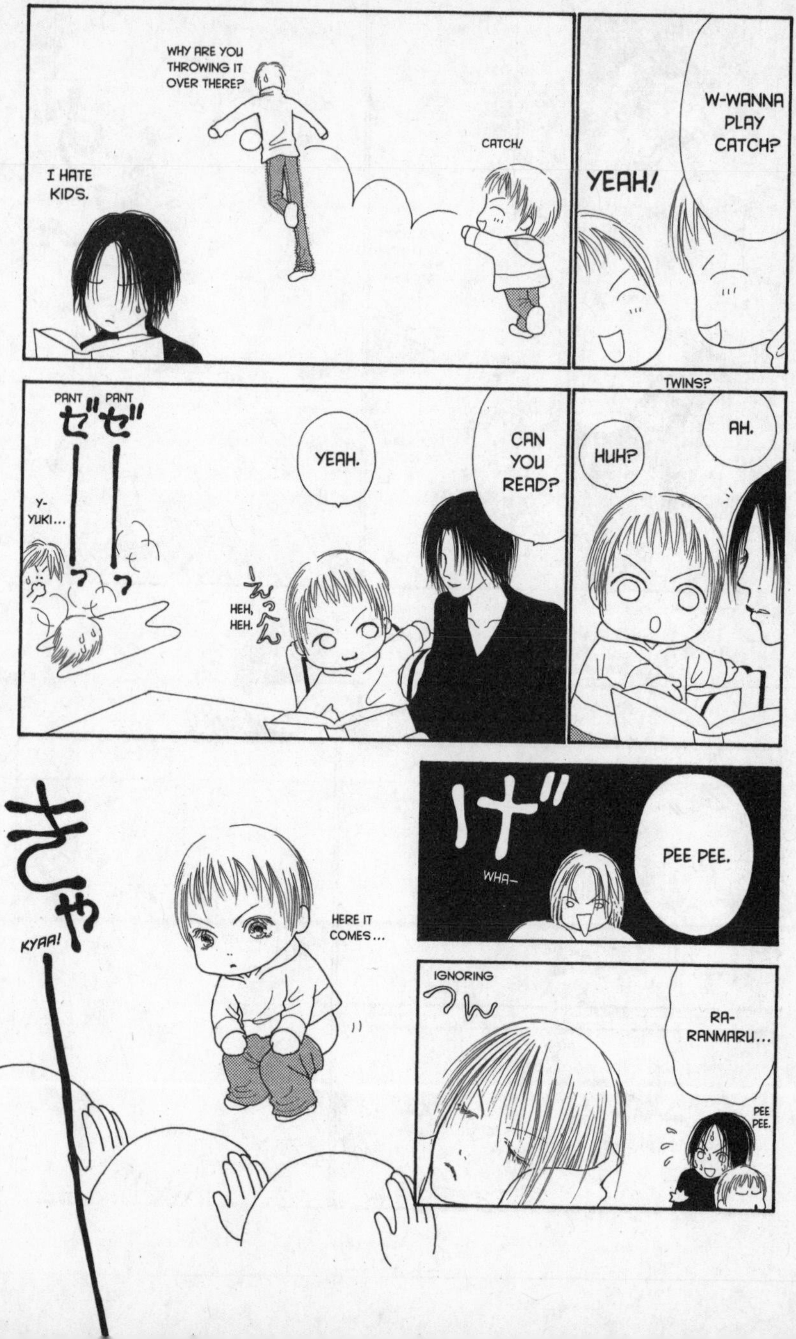
W-WANNA PLAY CATCH?
YEAH!
CATCH!
WHY ARE YOU THROWING IT OVER THERE?
I HATE KIDS.
TWINS?
AH.
HUH?
CAN YOU READ?
YEAH.
えっへん
HEH, HEH.
ぜーぜー
PANT PANT
Y-YUKI...
PEE PEE.
ゲ
WHA-
RA-RANMARU...
つん
IGNORING
PEE PEE.
HERE IT COMES...
きゃー
KYAA!

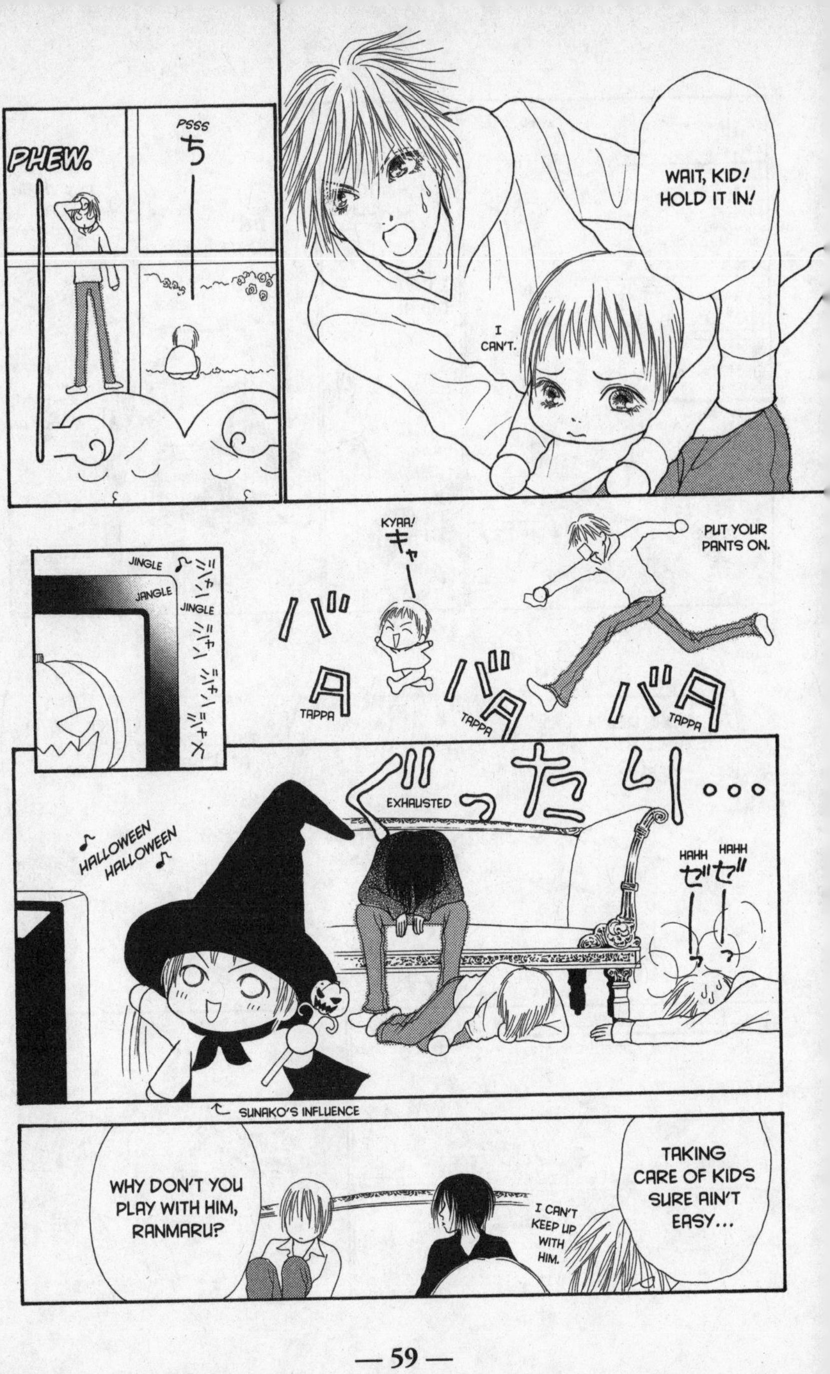
WAIT, KID! HOLD IT IN!
I CAN'T.
PSSS
ち
PHEW.
PUT YOUR PANTS ON.
KYAA!
キャー
バタ
TAPPA
バタ
TAPPA
バタ
TAPPA
JINGLE
JANGLE
JINGLE
HAHH
HAHH
ぜぜ
EXHAUSTED
HALLOWEEN HALLOWEEN
SUNAKO'S INFLUENCE
TAKING CARE OF KIDS SURE AIN'T EASY...
I CAN'T KEEP UP WITH HIM.
WHY DON'T YOU PLAY WITH HIM, RANMARU?

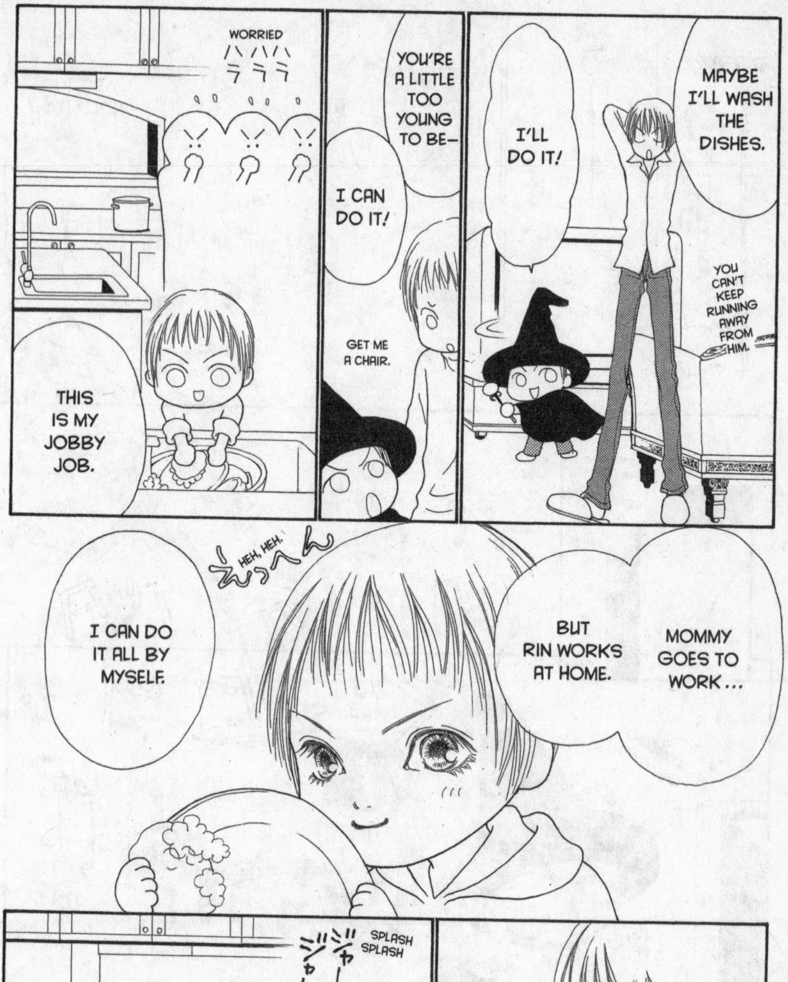
MAYBE I'LL WASH THE DISHES.
YOU CAN'T KEEP RUNNING AWAY FROM HIM.
I'LL DO IT!
YOU'RE A LITTLE TOO YOUNG TO BE—
I CAN DO IT!
GET ME A CHAIR.
WORRIED
ハラ ハラ ハラ
THIS IS MY JOBBY JOB.
MOMMY GOES TO WORK...
BUT RIN WORKS AT HOME.
HEH, HEH.
えっへん
I CAN DO IT ALL BY MYSELF.
RUB RUB
ゴシゴシ
SPLASH SPLASH
ジャー ジャー
CLINK CLINK
カチャ カチャ
....

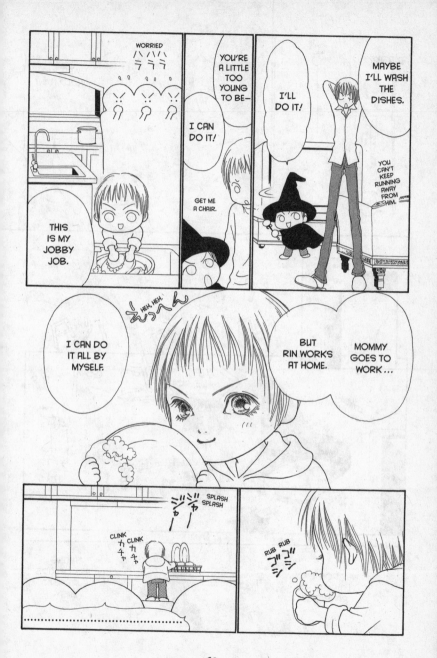

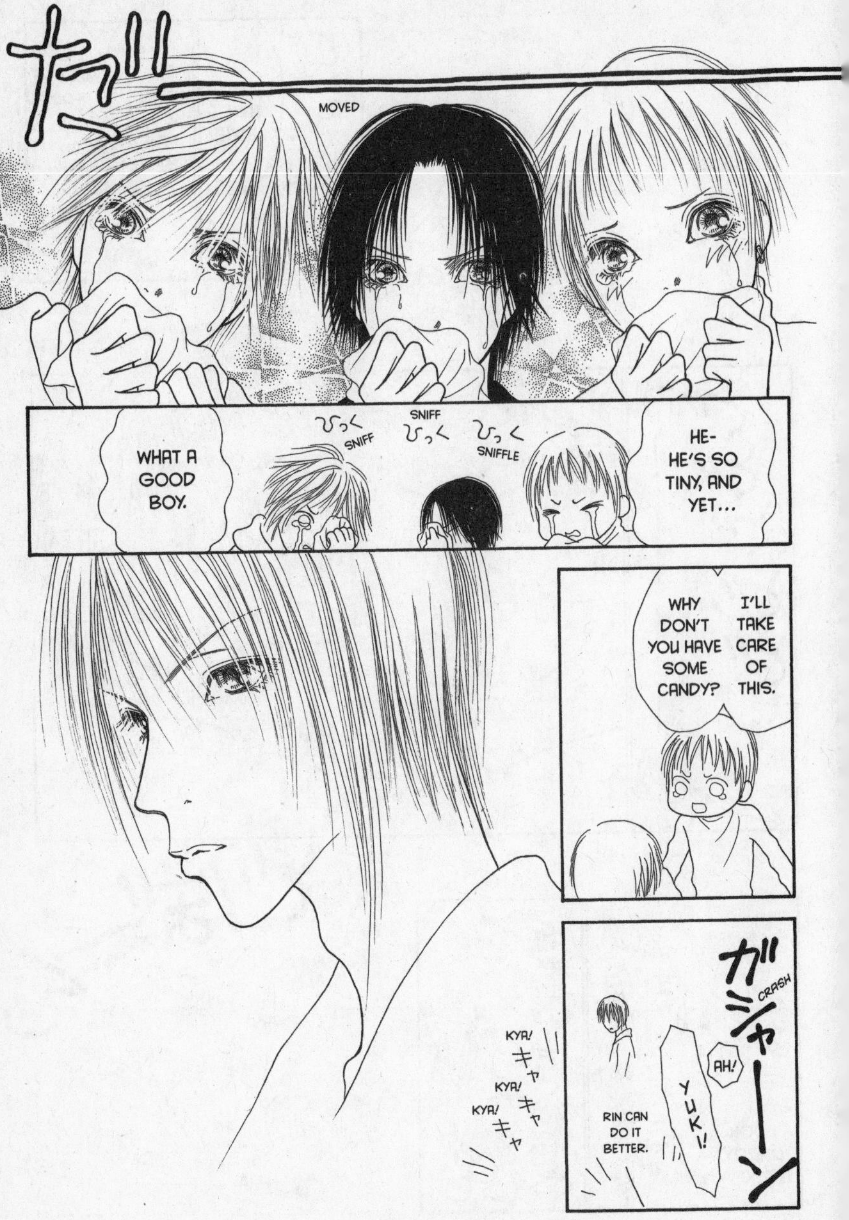
たっ
MOVED
HE- HE'S SO TINY, AND YET...
ひっく SNIFFLE
ひっく SNIFF
ひっく SNIFF
WHAT A GOOD BOY.
I'LL TAKE CARE OF THIS.
WHY DON'T YOU HAVE SOME CANDY?
ガシャーン CRASH
AH!
YUKI!
RIN CAN DO IT BETTER.
KYA! キャ
KYA! キャ
KYA! キャ

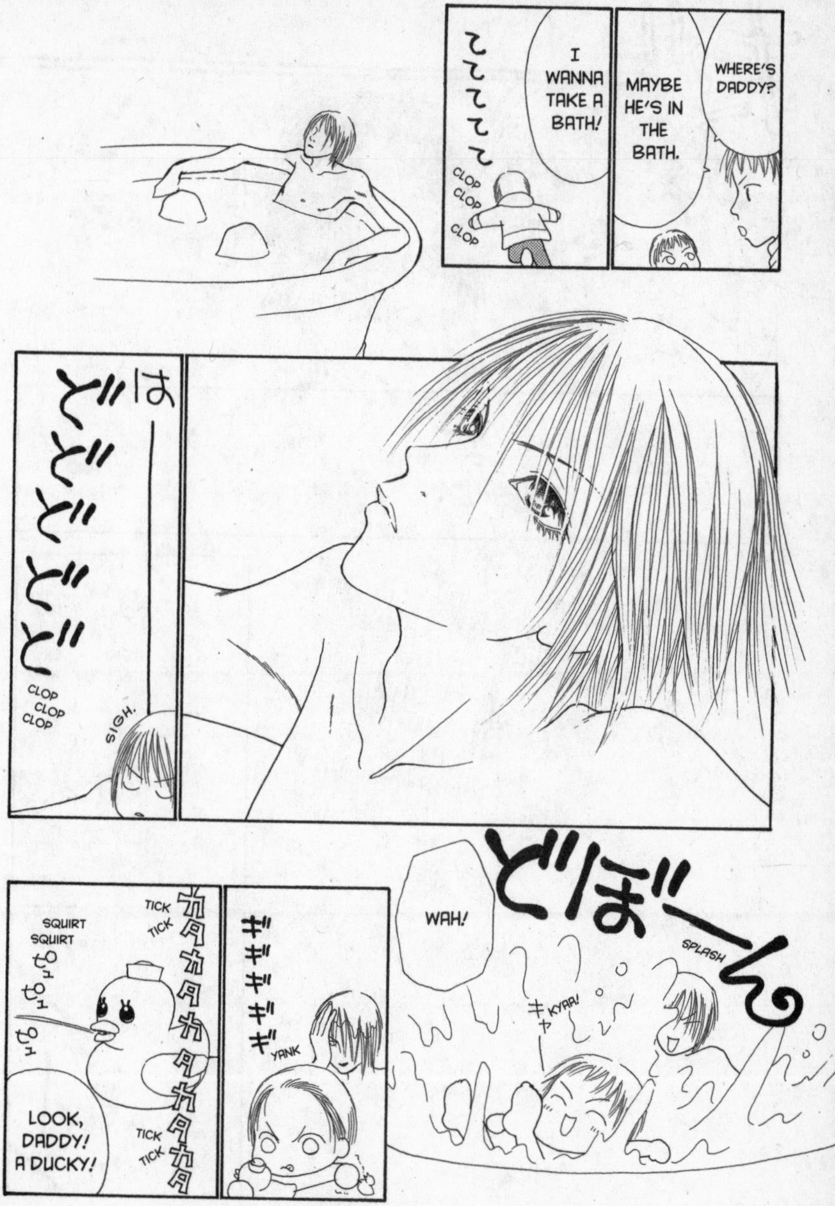
WHERE'S DADDY?
MAYBE HE'S IN THE BATH.
I WANNA TAKE A BATH!
てててて
CLOP CLOP CLOP
は—
どどどどど
CLOP CLOP CLOP
SIGH.
どぼーん
WAH!
SPLASH
キャー
KYAA!
ギギギギ
YANK
カタカタカタカタ
TICK TICK
SQUIRT SQUIRT
ぴゅぴゅぴゅ
LOOK, DADDY! A DUCKY!
TICK TICK

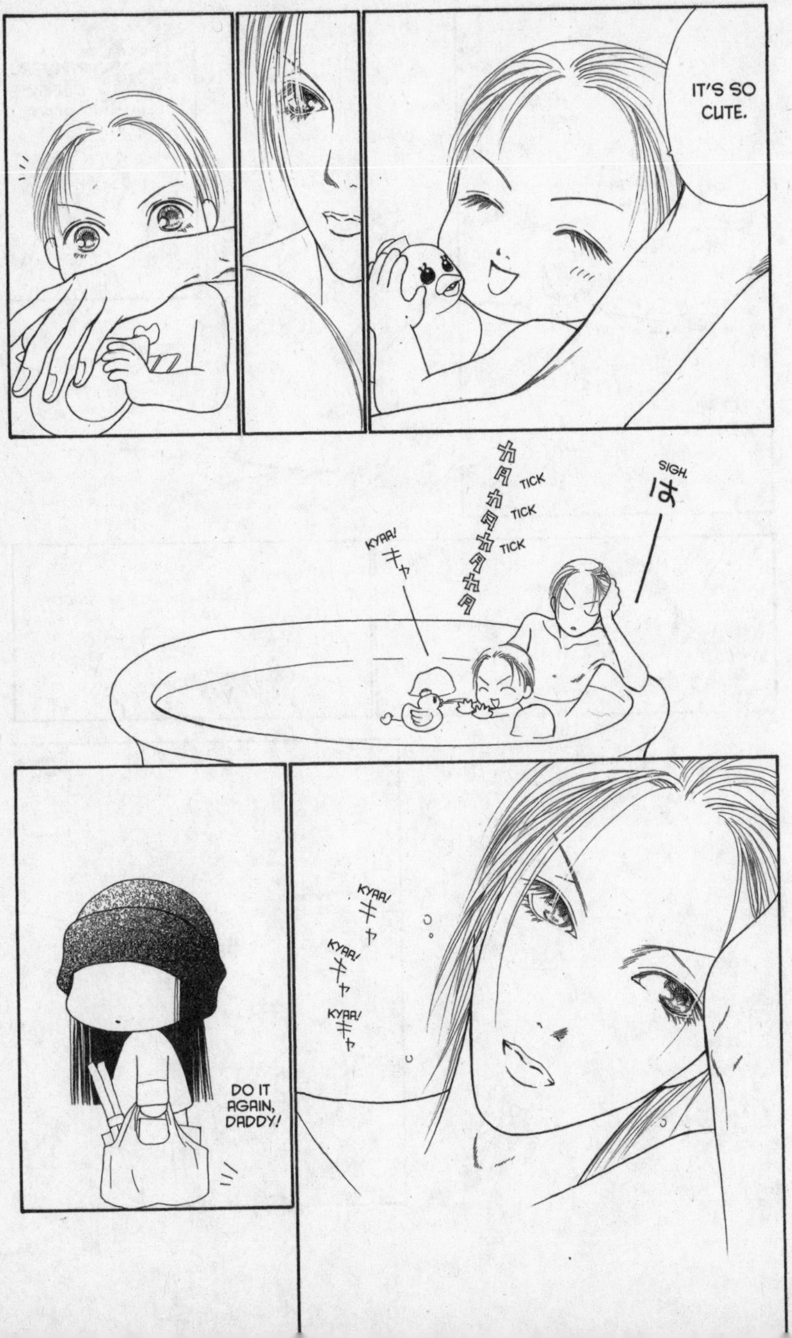
IT'S SO CUTE.
SIGH.
はー
カタカタカタカタ
TICK
TICK
TICK
KYAA!
キャー
KYAA!
キャ
KYAA!
キャ
KYAA!
キャ
DO IT AGAIN, DADDY!

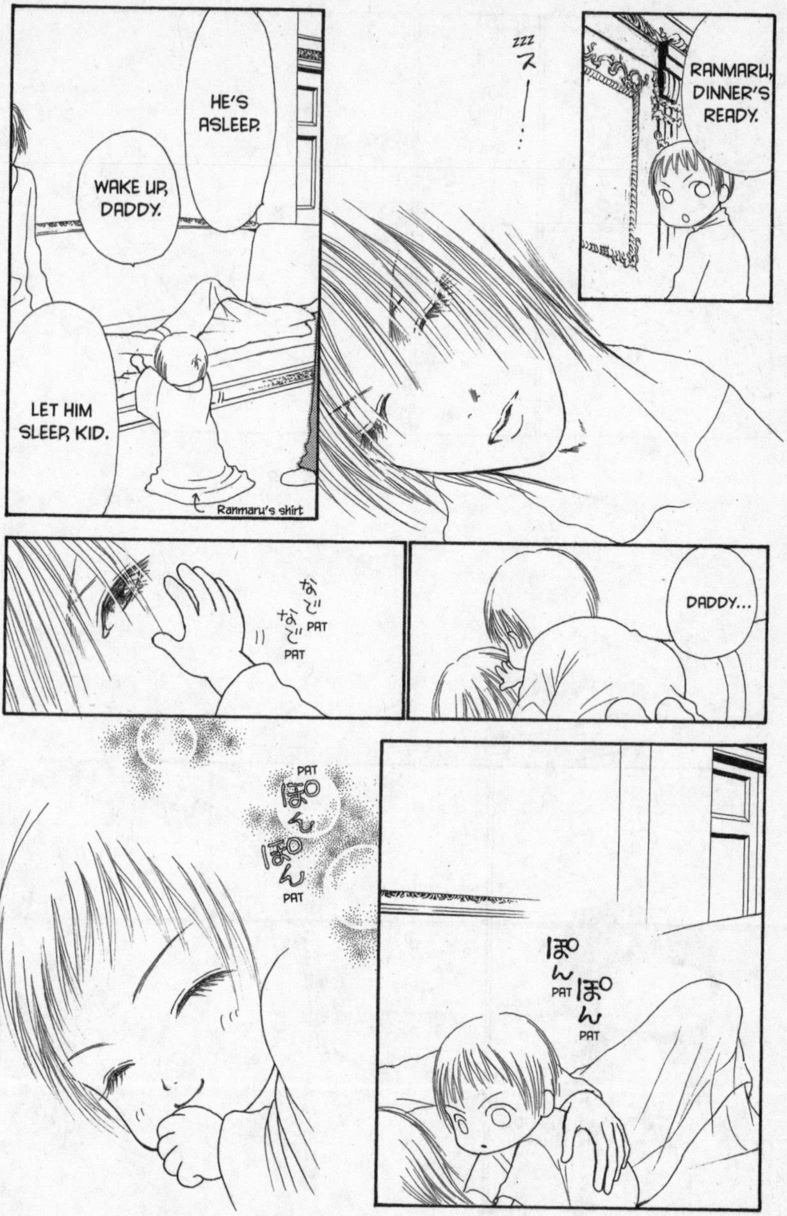
RANMARU, DINNER'S READY.
zzz
ス—!!
HE'S ASLEEP.
WAKE UP, DADDY.
LET HIM SLEEP, KID.
Ranmaru's shirt
DADDY...
なで PAT
なで PAT
ぽん PAT
ぽん PAT
ぽん PAT
ぽん PAT

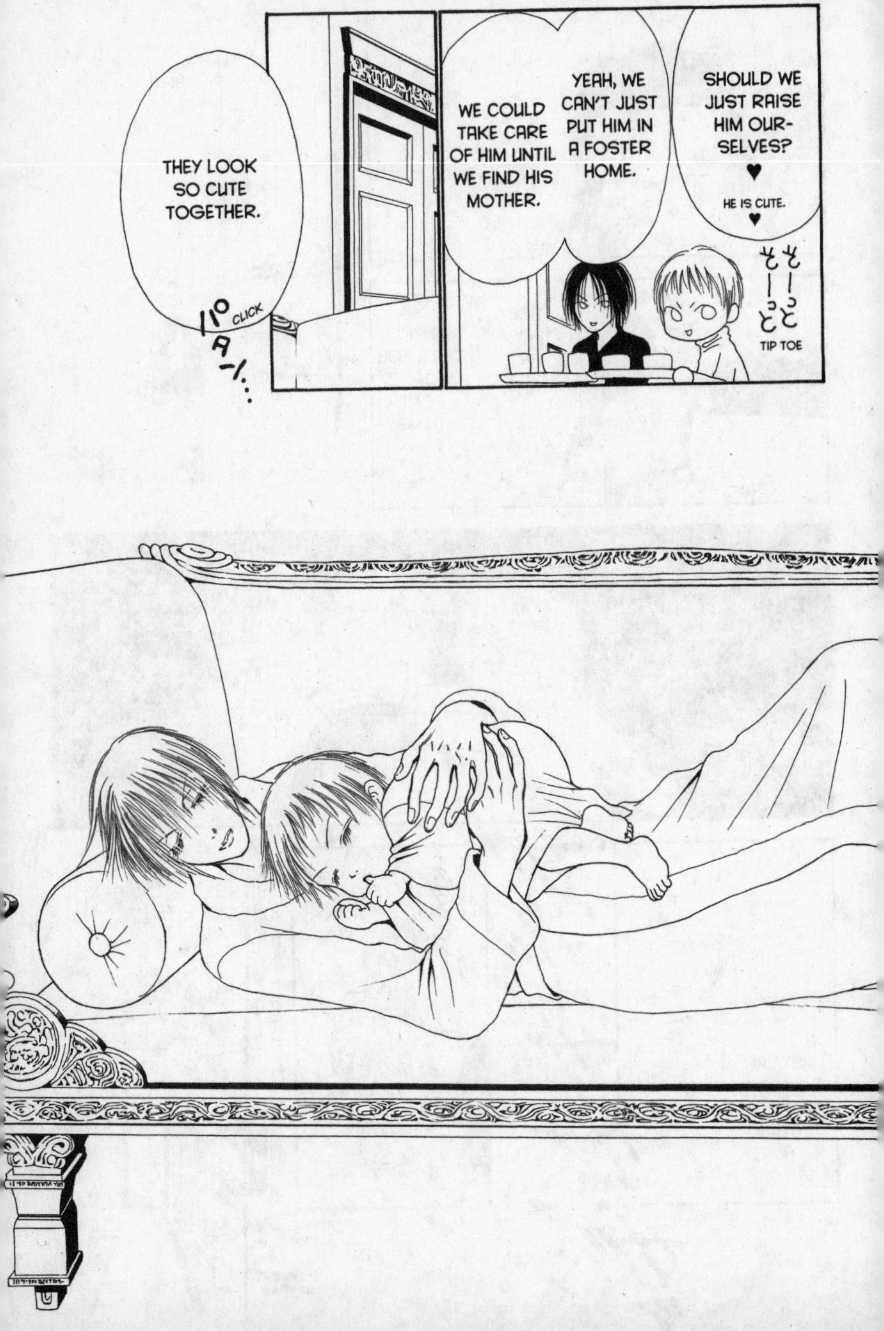
SHOULD WE JUST RAISE HIM OURSELVES? ♥
HE IS CUTE. ♥
YEAH, WE CAN'T JUST PUT HIM IN A FOSTER HOME.
WE COULD TAKE CARE OF HIM UNTIL WE FIND HIS MOTHER.
そーっと そーっと
TIP TOE
THEY LOOK SO CUTE TOGETHER.
パターン…
CLICK

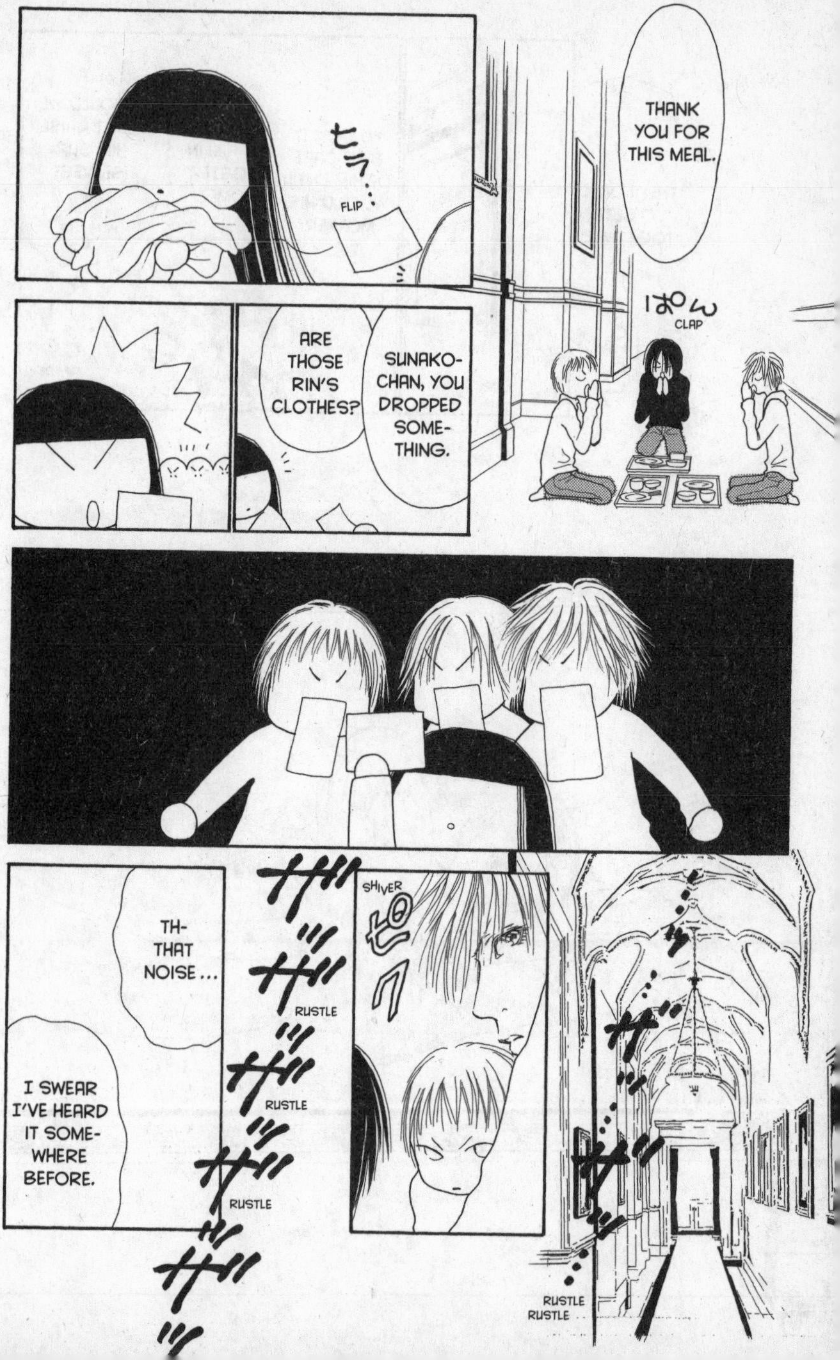
THANK YOU FOR THIS MEAL.
ぱん
CLAP
ヒラ…
FLIP
SUNAKO-CHAN, YOU DROPPED SOMETHING.
ARE THOSE RIN'S CLOTHES?
RUSTLE
RUSTLE
SHIVER
RUSTLE
RUSTLE
RUSTLE
TH-THAT NOISE…
I SWEAR I'VE HEARD IT SOMEWHERE BEFORE.

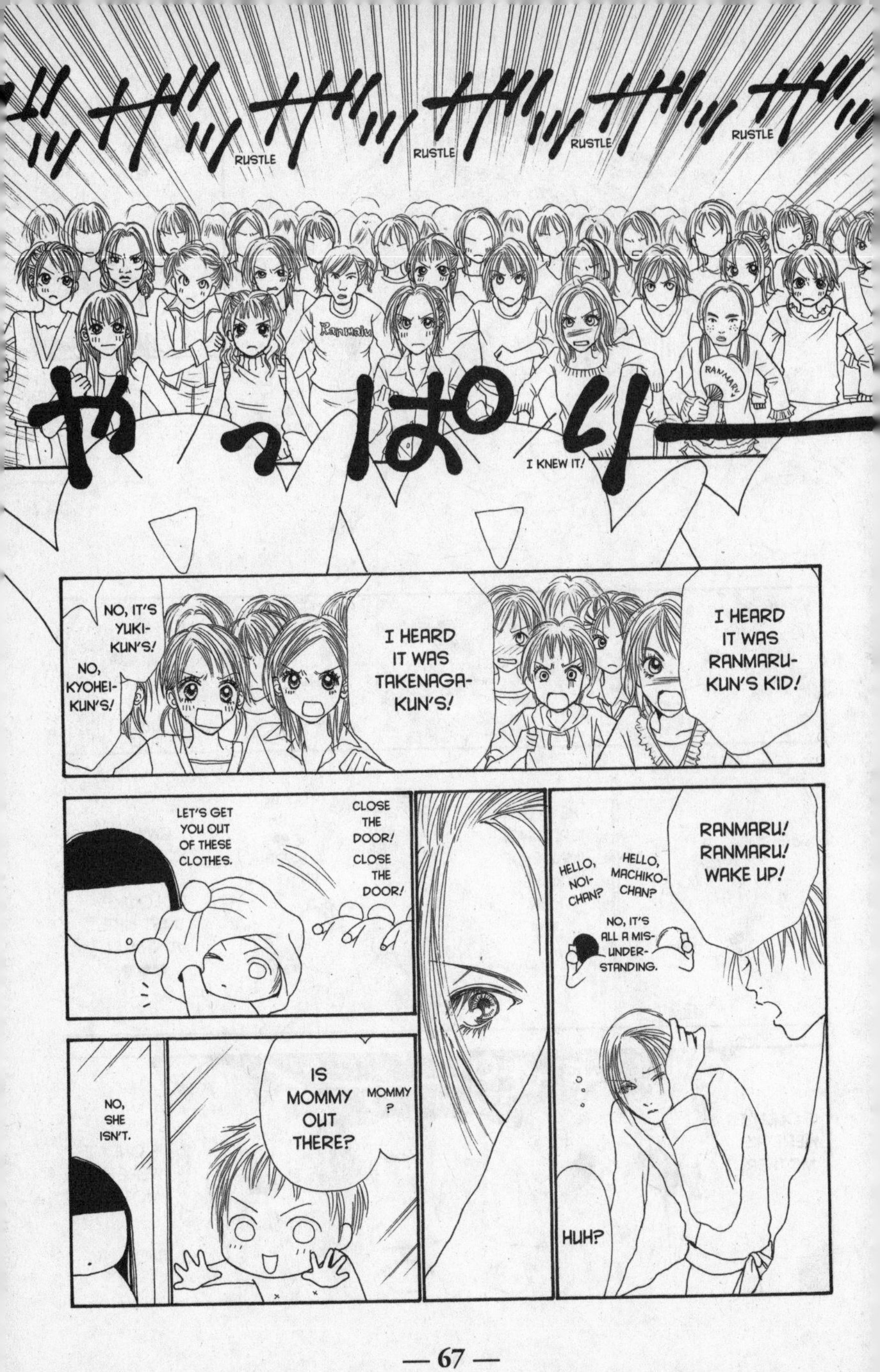

ザッザッザッザッザッザッ
RUSTLE
RUSTLE
RUSTLE
RUSTLE
やっぱりー
I KNEW IT!
I HEARD IT WAS RANMARU-KUN'S KID!
I HEARD IT WAS TAKENAGA-KUN'S!
NO, IT'S YUKI-KUN'S!
NO, KYOHEI-KUN'S!
RANMARU! RANMARU! WAKE UP!
HELLO, MACHIKO-CHAN?
HELLO, NOI-CHAN?
NO, IT'S ALL A MIS-UNDER-STANDING.
HUH?
CLOSE THE DOOR!
CLOSE THE DOOR!
LET'S GET YOU OUT OF THESE CLOTHES.
MOMMY?
IS MOMMY OUT THERE?
NO, SHE ISN'T.

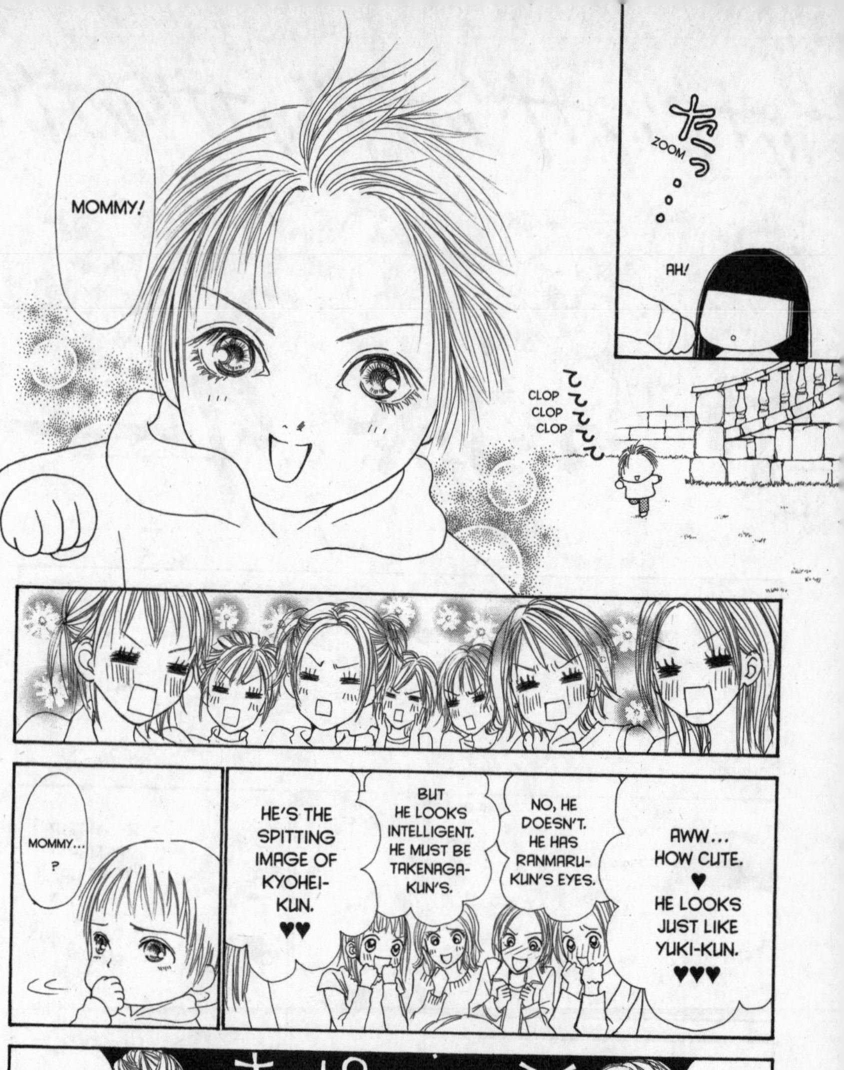
たっ
ZOOM
AH!
てててて
CLOP
CLOP
CLOP
MOMMY!
AWW... HOW CUTE. ♥ HE LOOKS JUST LIKE YUKI-KUN. ♥♥♥
NO, HE DOESN'T. HE HAS RANMARU-KUN'S EYES.
BUT HE LOOKS INTELLIGENT. HE MUST BE TAKENAGA-KUN'S.
HE'S THE SPITTING IMAGE OF KYOHEI-KUN. ♥♥
MOMMY... ?
IF ONLY I WERE HIS MOTHER...
キュピーーン
TWINKLE
MOMMY...
IF ONLY I WERE HIS MOTHER...

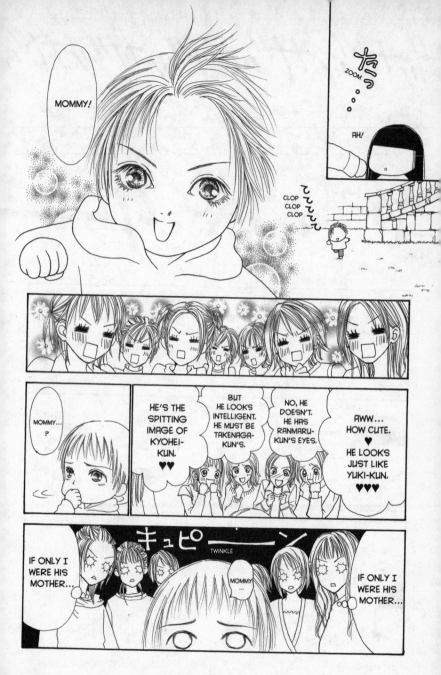

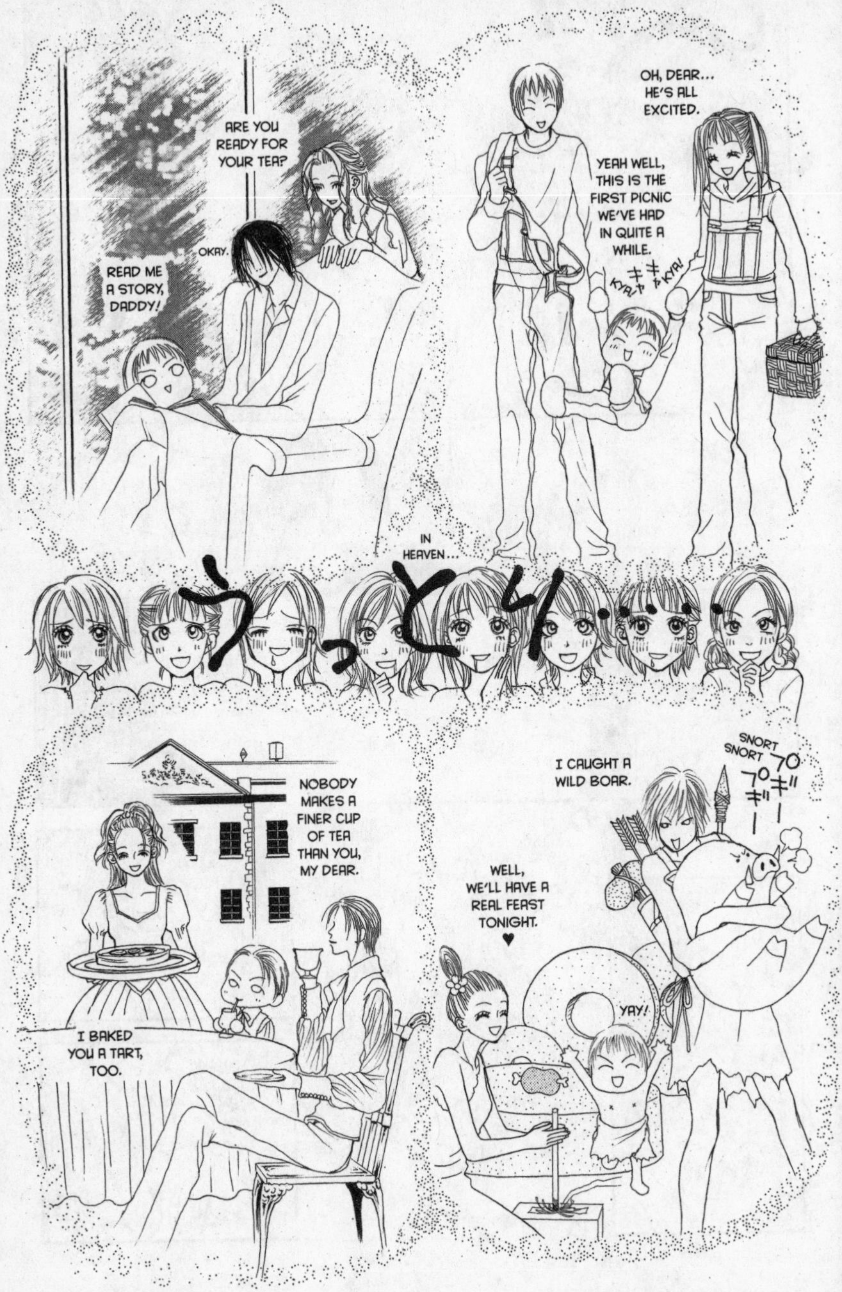
OH, DEAR... HE'S ALL EXCITED.
YEAH WELL, THIS IS THE FIRST PICNIC WE'VE HAD IN QUITE A WHILE.
キャ キャ KYA! KYA!
ARE YOU READY FOR YOUR TEA?
OKAY.
READ ME A STORY, DADDY!
IN HEAVEN...
うっとり…
SNORT SNORT プギー プギー
I CAUGHT A WILD BOAR.
WELL, WE'LL HAVE A REAL FEAST TONIGHT. ♥
YAY!
NOBODY MAKES A FINER CUP OF TEA THAN YOU, MY DEAR.
I BAKED YOU A TART, TOO.

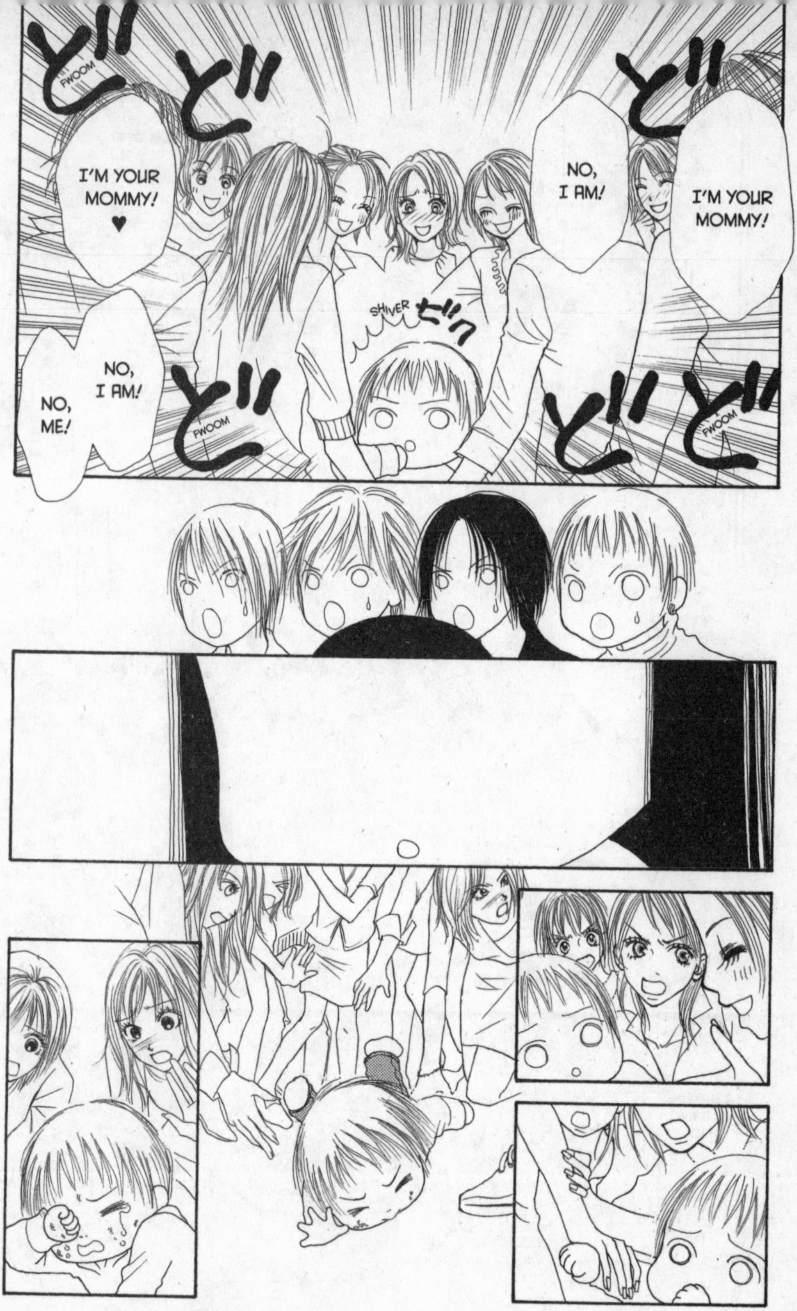
I'M YOUR MOMMY!
NO, I AM!
FWOOM
I'M YOUR MOMMY! ♥
FWOOM
SHIVER
NO, I AM!
NO, ME!
FWOOM

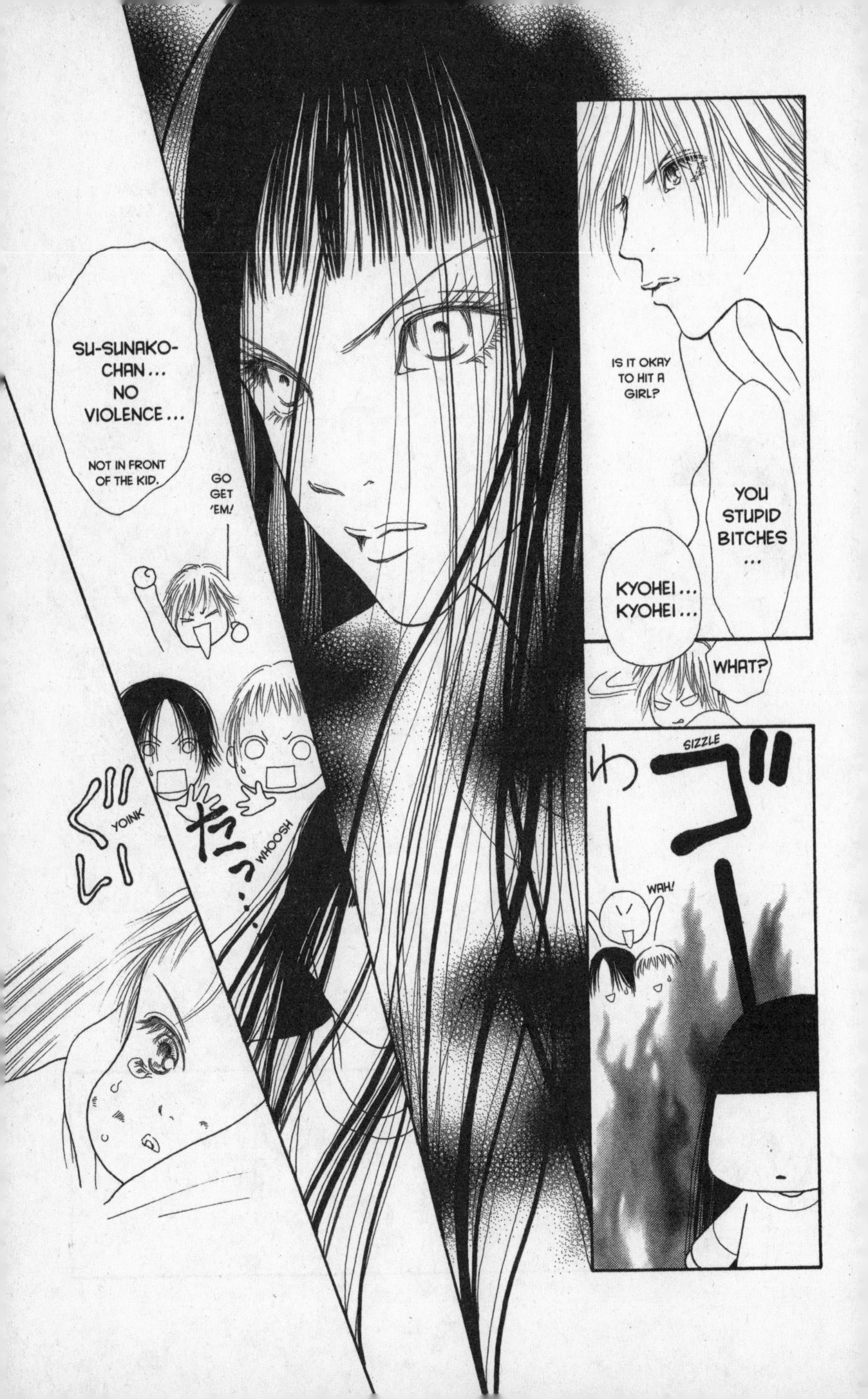
IS IT OKAY TO HIT A GIRL?
YOU STUPID BITCHES ...
KYOHEI... KYOHEI...
WHAT?
SIZZLE
WAH!
SU-SUNAKO-CHAN... NO VIOLENCE...
NOT IN FRONT OF THE KID.
GO GET 'EM!
WHOOSH
YOINK

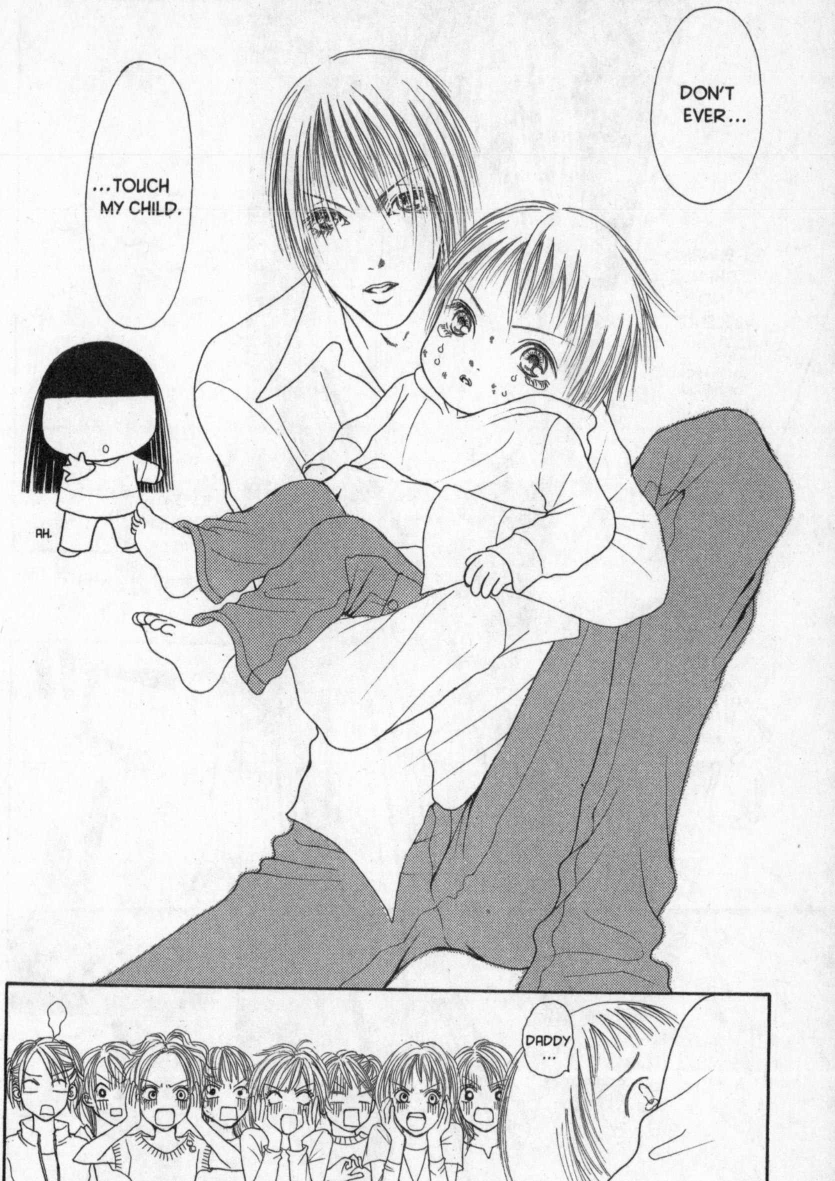
DON'T EVER...
...TOUCH MY CHILD.
AH.
DADDY ...

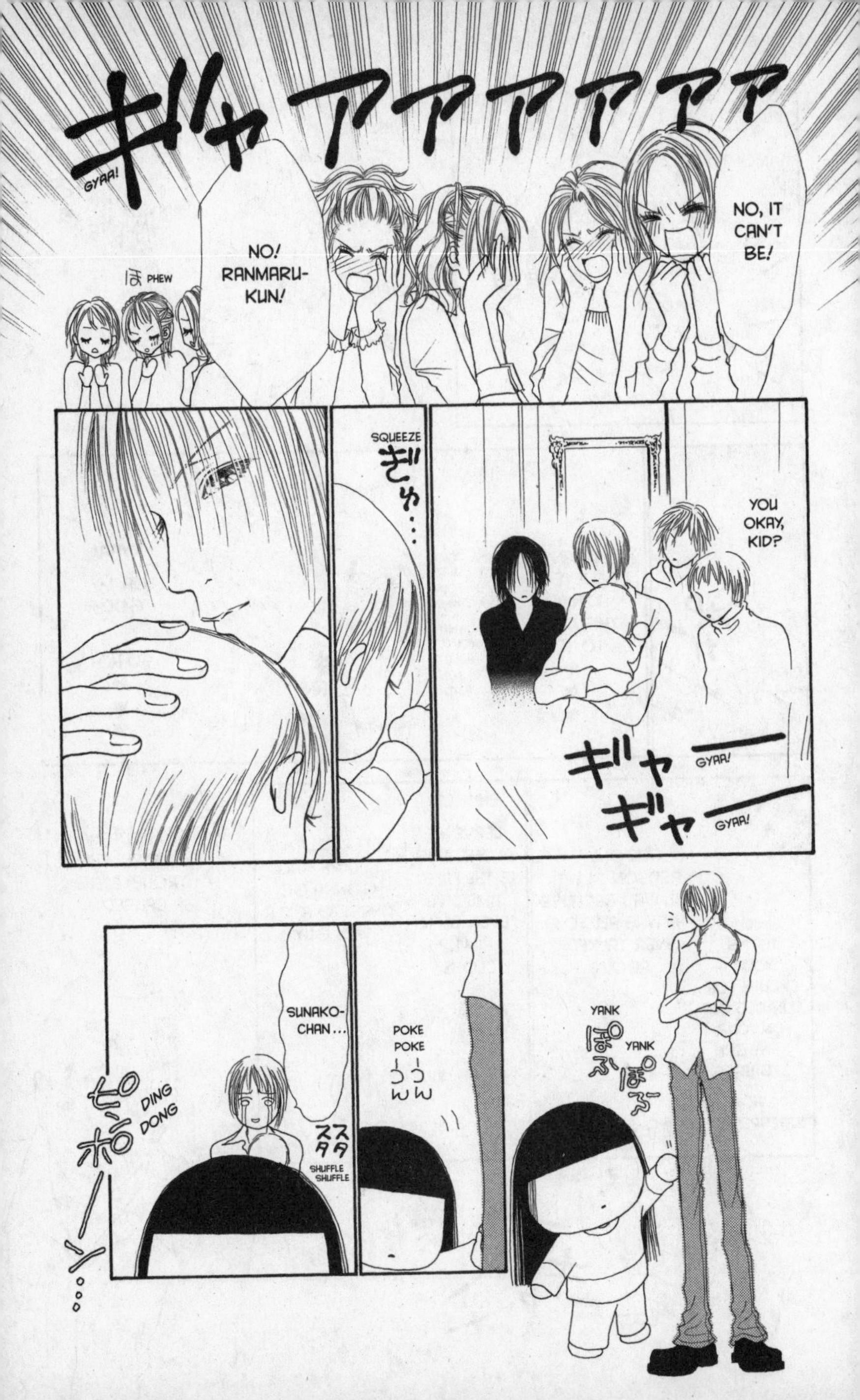
ギャァァァァァ
GYAA!
NO, IT CAN'T BE!
NO! RANMARU-KUN!
ほ PHEW
YOU OKAY, KID?
ギャー GYAA!
ギャー GYAA!
SQUEEZE
ぎゅ…
YANK
ぽふ
YANK
ぽふー
POKE POKE
つんつん
SUNAKO-CHAN…
スタスタ
SHUFFLE SHUFFLE
ピンポーン…
DING DONG

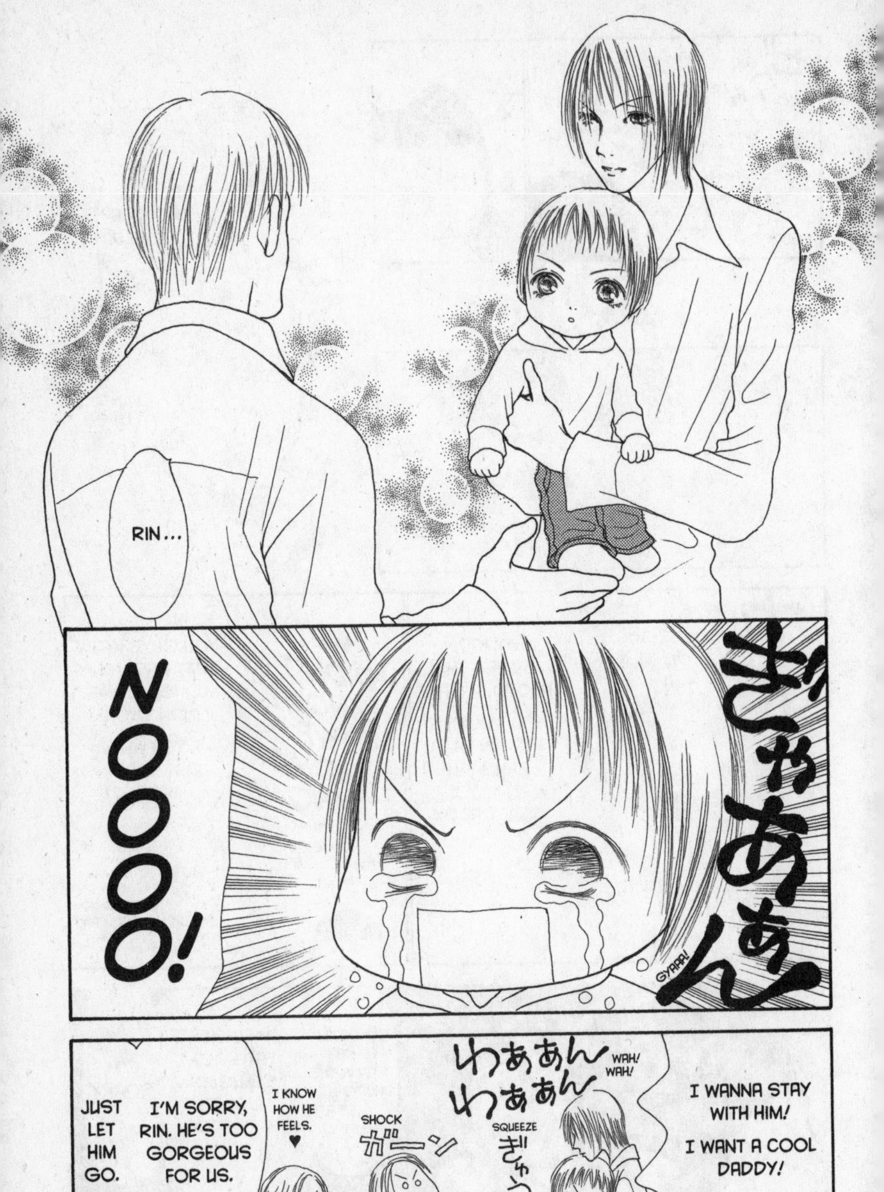
RIN...
ぎゃああん
GYAAA!
NOOOO!
I WANNA STAY WITH HIM!
I WANT A COOL DADDY!
わぁあん わぁあん
WAH! WAH!
SQUEEZE
ぎゅううう
SHOCK
ガーン
I KNOW HOW HE FEELS. ♥
I'M SORRY, RIN. HE'S TOO GORGEOUS FOR US.
JUST LET HIM GO.

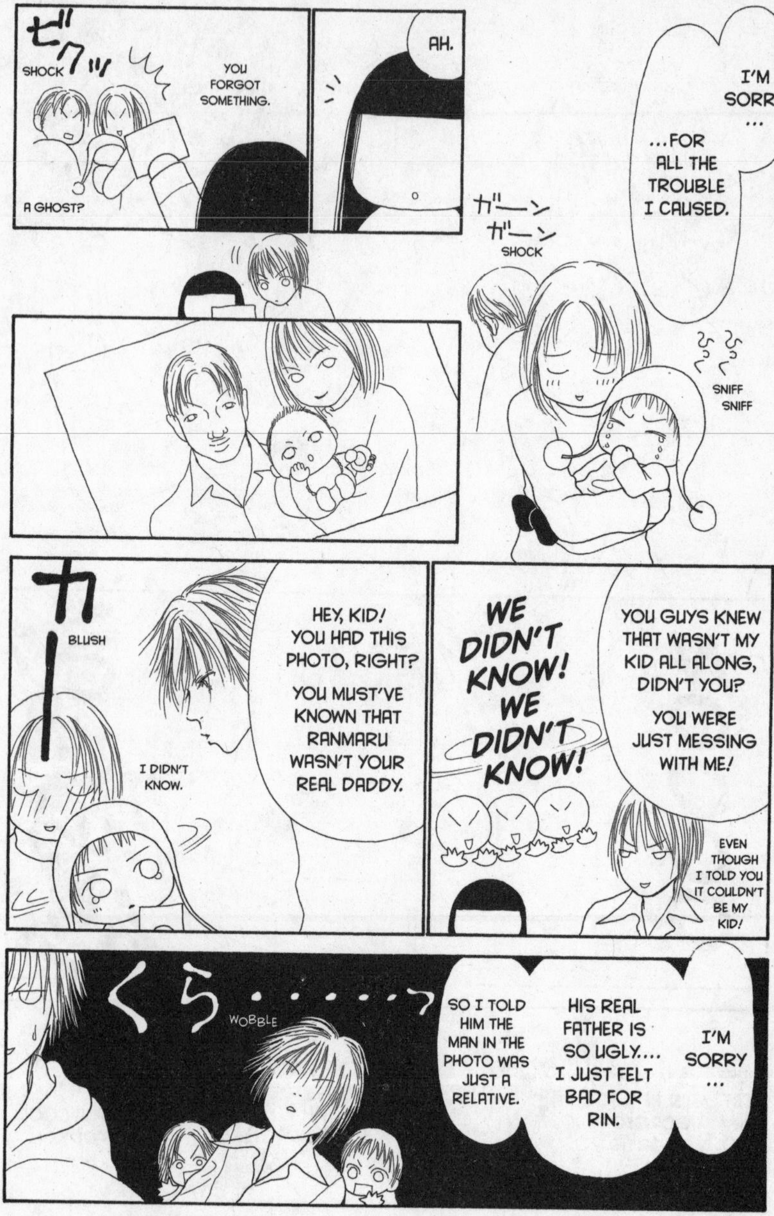

I'M SORRY...
...FOR ALL THE TROUBLE I CAUSED.
ガーン ガーン
SHOCK
SNIFF SNIFF
AH.
ギクッ
SHOCK
YOU FORGOT SOMETHING.
A GHOST?
YOU GUYS KNEW THAT WASN'T MY KID ALL ALONG, DIDN'T YOU?
YOU WERE JUST MESSING WITH ME!
WE DIDN'T KNOW! WE DIDN'T KNOW!
EVEN THOUGH I TOLD YOU IT COULDN'T BE MY KID!
HEY, KID! YOU HAD THIS PHOTO, RIGHT?
YOU MUST'VE KNOWN THAT RANMARU WASN'T YOUR REAL DADDY.
カー
BLUSH
I DIDN'T KNOW.
I'M SORRY...
HIS REAL FATHER IS SO UGLY.... I JUST FELT BAD FOR RIN.
SO I TOLD HIM THE MAN IN THE PHOTO WAS JUST A RELATIVE.
くら......
WOBBLE

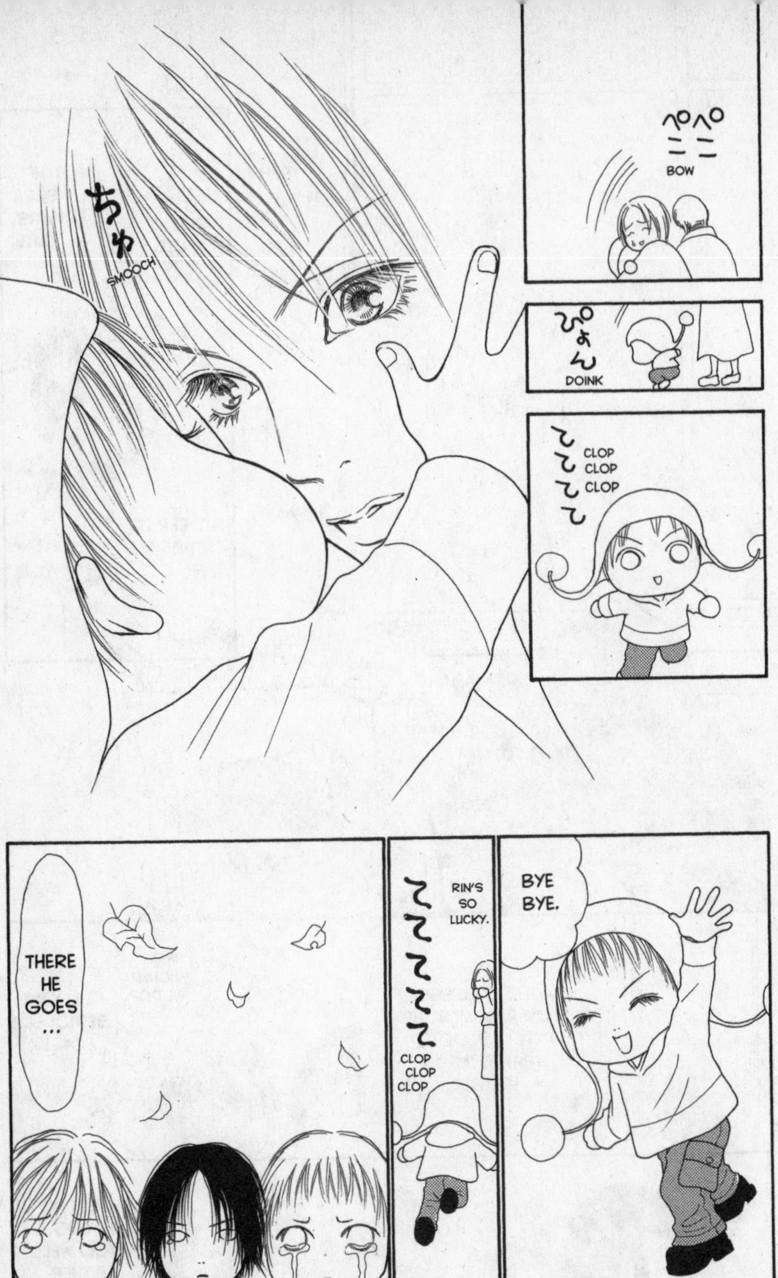
ぺこぺこ
BOW
ぴょん
DOINK
てててて
CLOP CLOP CLOP
ちゅ
SMOOCH
BYE BYE.
RIN'S SO LUCKY.
てててて
CLOP CLOP CLOP
THERE HE GOES...

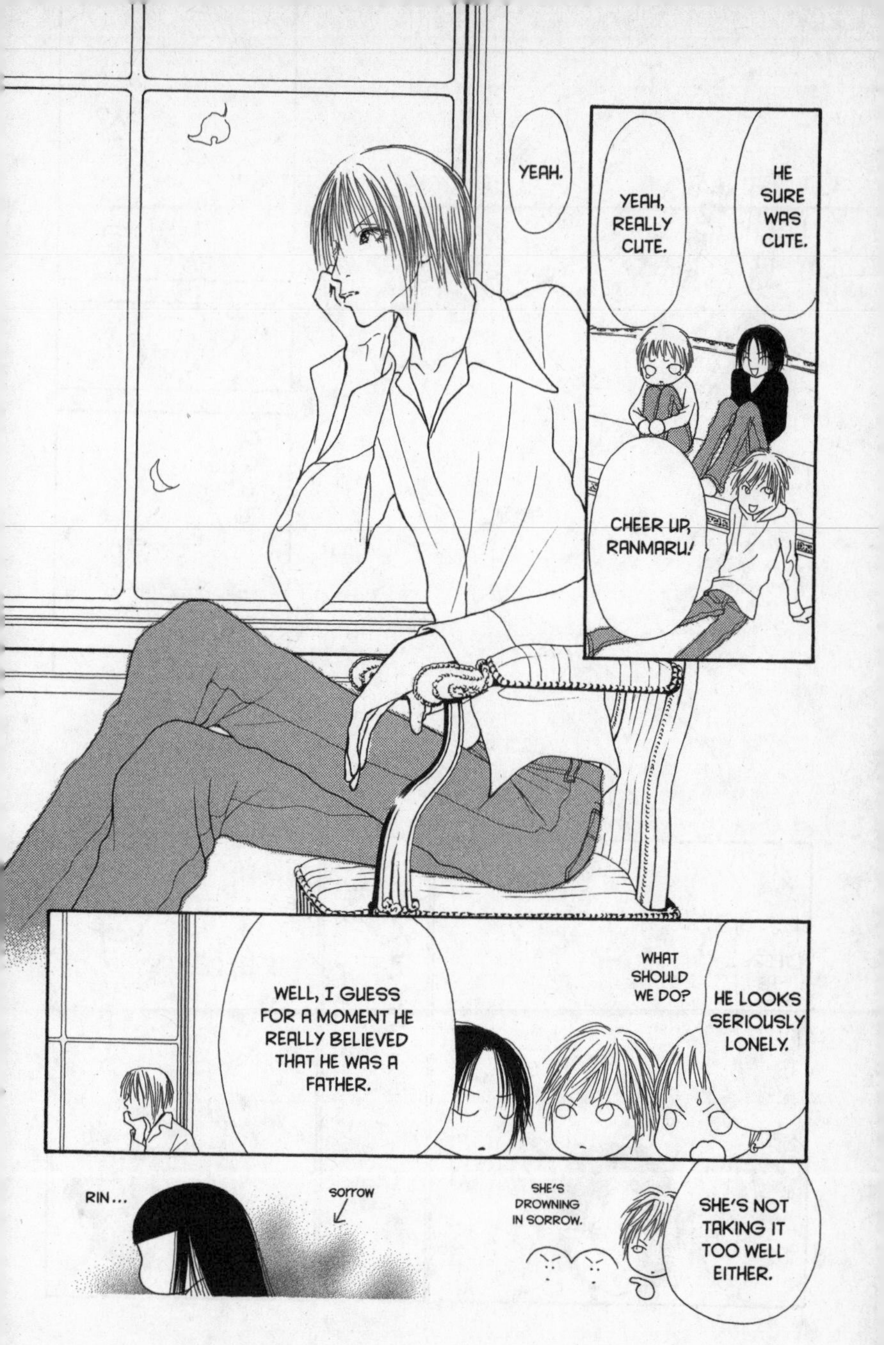
HE SURE WAS CUTE.
YEAH, REALLY CUTE.
CHEER UP, RANMARU!
YEAH.
HE LOOKS SERIOUSLY LONELY.
WHAT SHOULD WE DO?
WELL, I GUESS FOR A MOMENT HE REALLY BELIEVED THAT HE WAS A FATHER.
SHE'S NOT TAKING IT TOO WELL EITHER.
SHE'S DROWNING IN SORROW.
SORROW
RIN...

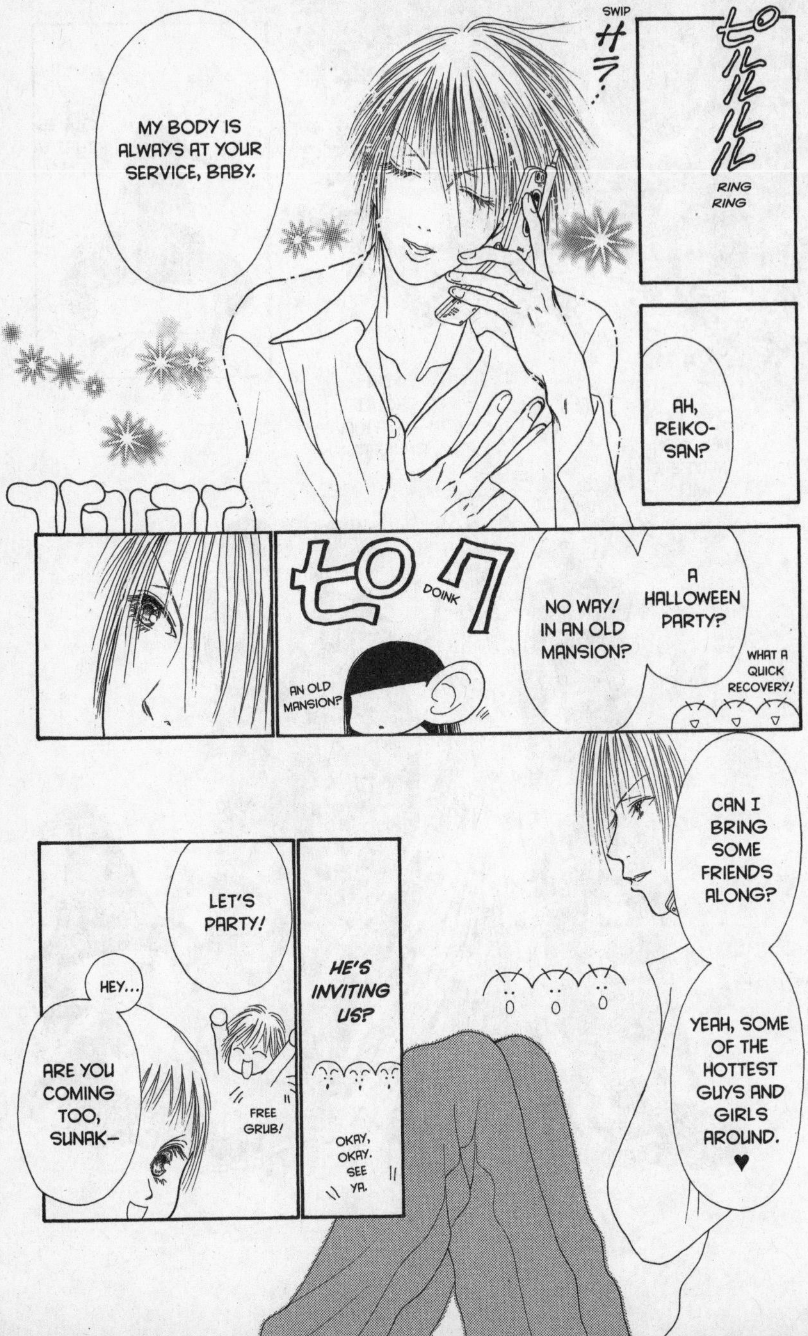
ピルルル
RING RING
AH, REIKO-SAN?
サラ…
SWIP
MY BODY IS ALWAYS AT YOUR SERVICE, BABY.
A HALLOWEEN PARTY?
NO WAY! IN AN OLD MANSION?
WHAT A QUICK RECOVERY!
ピク
DOINK
AN OLD MANSION?
CAN I BRING SOME FRIENDS ALONG?
YEAH, SOME OF THE HOTTEST GUYS AND GIRLS AROUND. ♥
HE'S INVITING US?
OKAY, OKAY. SEE YA.
LET'S PARTY!
FREE GRUB!
HEY...
ARE YOU COMING TOO, SUNAK-

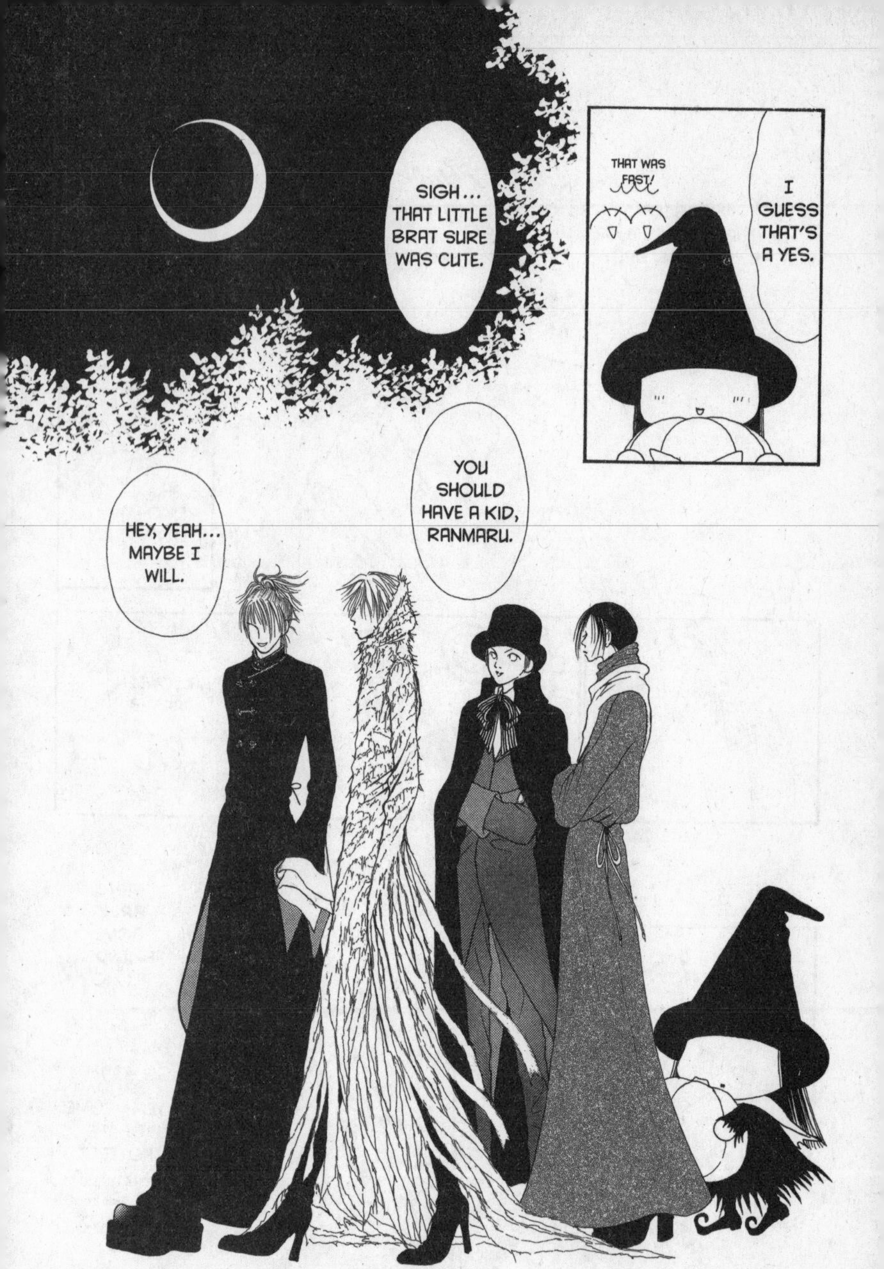
I GUESS THAT'S A YES.
THAT WAS FAST!
SIGH... THAT LITTLE BRAT SURE WAS CUTE.
YOU SHOULD HAVE A KID, RANMARU.
HEY, YEAH... MAYBE I WILL.

Chapter 29
The Strongest Women in the World

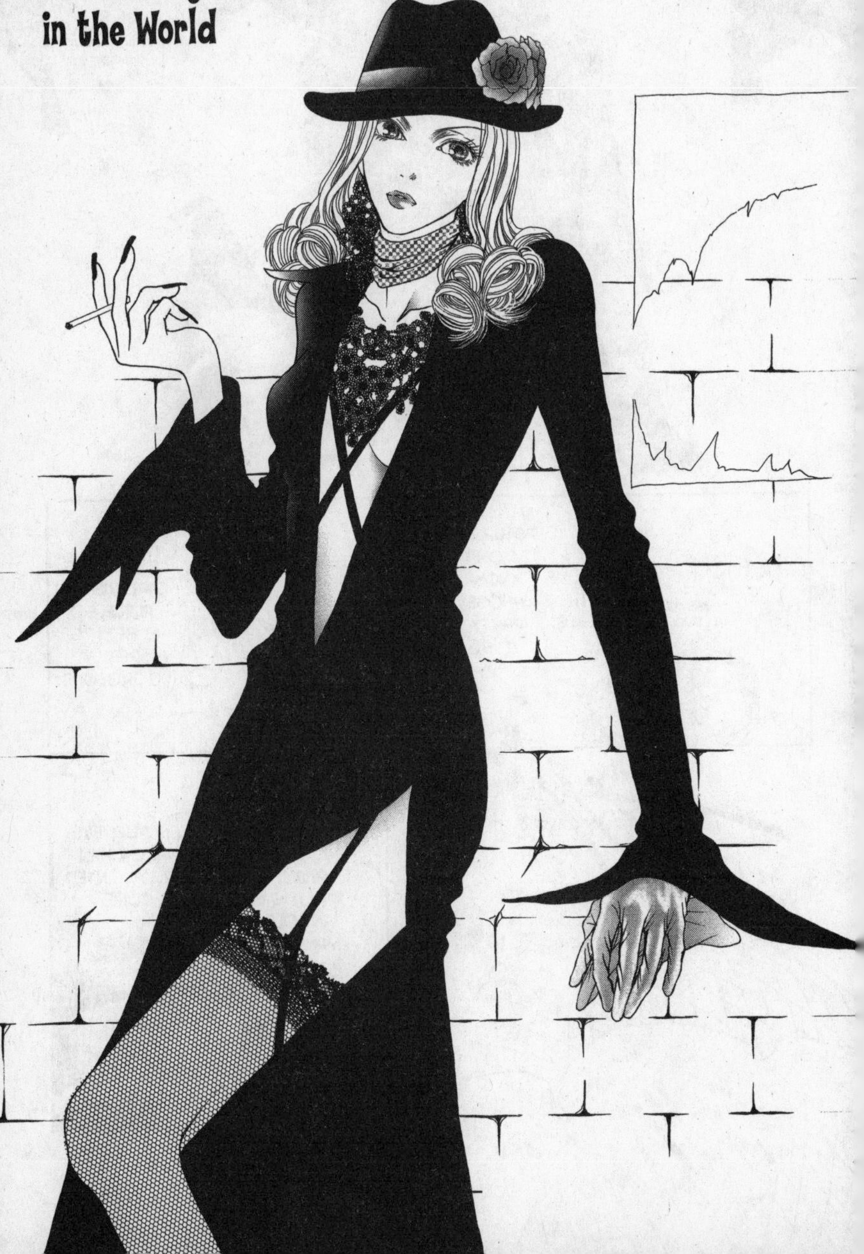

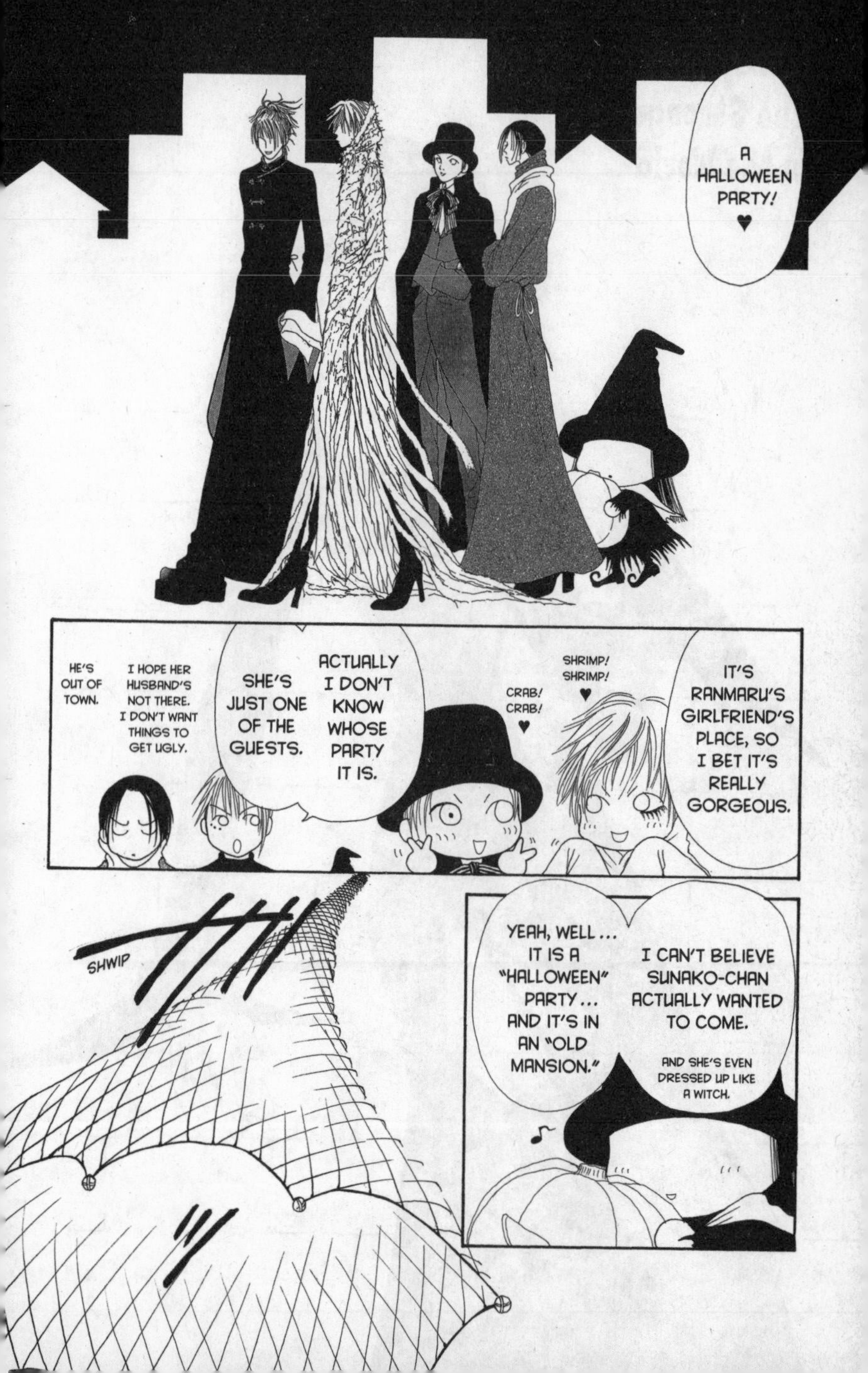
A HALLOWEEN PARTY! ♥
IT'S RANMARU'S GIRLFRIEND'S PLACE, SO I BET IT'S REALLY GORGEOUS.
SHRIMP! SHRIMP! ♥
CRAB! CRAB! ♥
ACTUALLY I DON'T KNOW WHOSE PARTY IT IS.
SHE'S JUST ONE OF THE GUESTS.
I HOPE HER HUSBAND'S NOT THERE. I DON'T WANT THINGS TO GET UGLY.
HE'S OUT OF TOWN.
I CAN'T BELIEVE SUNAKO-CHAN ACTUALLY WANTED TO COME.
AND SHE'S EVEN DRESSED UP LIKE A WITCH.
YEAH, WELL ... IT IS A "HALLOWEEN" PARTY ... AND IT'S IN AN "OLD MANSION."
SHWIP

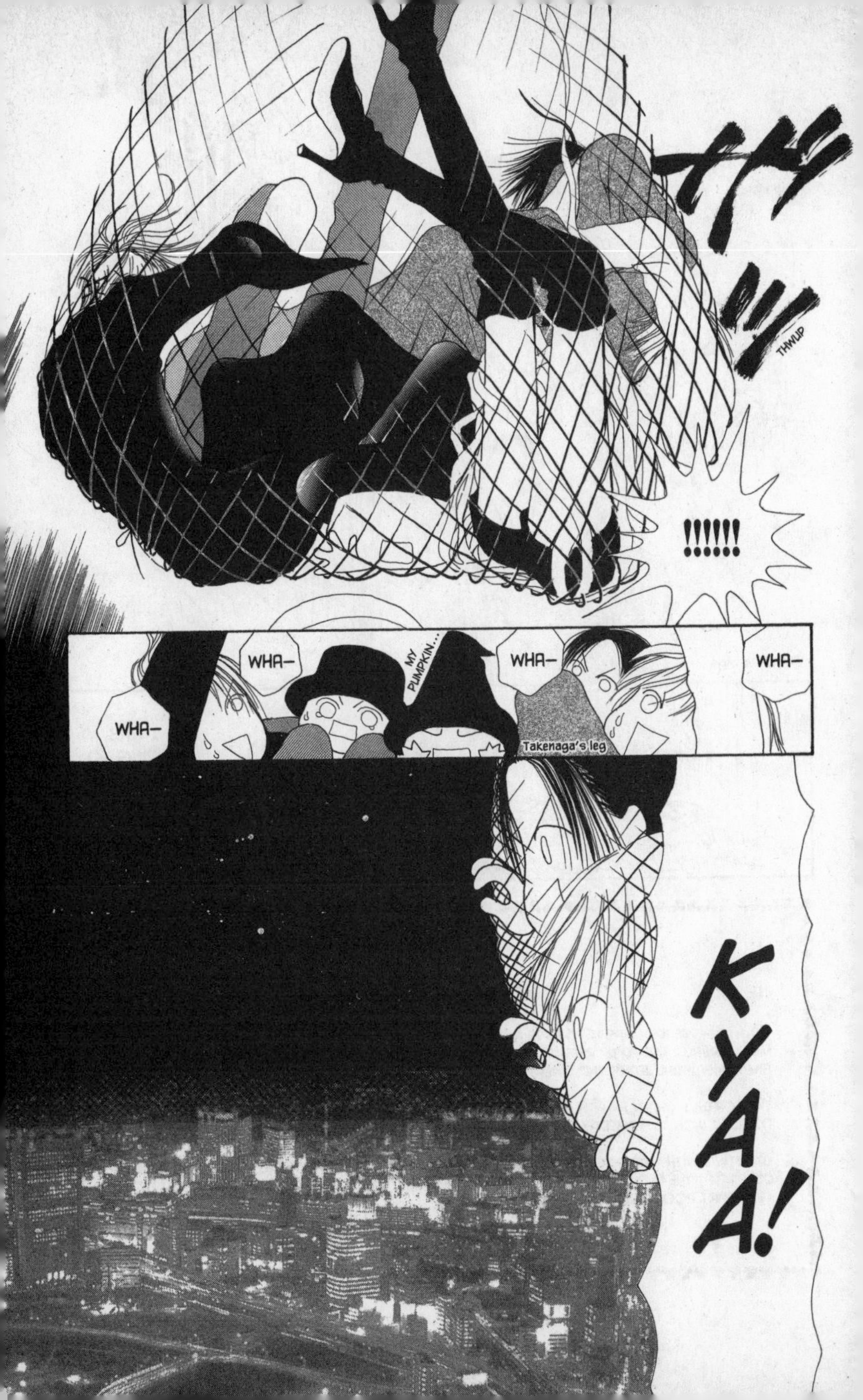
THWUP
!!!!!!
WHA–
WHA–
Takenaga's leg
MY PUMPKIN...
WHA–
WHA–
KYAA!

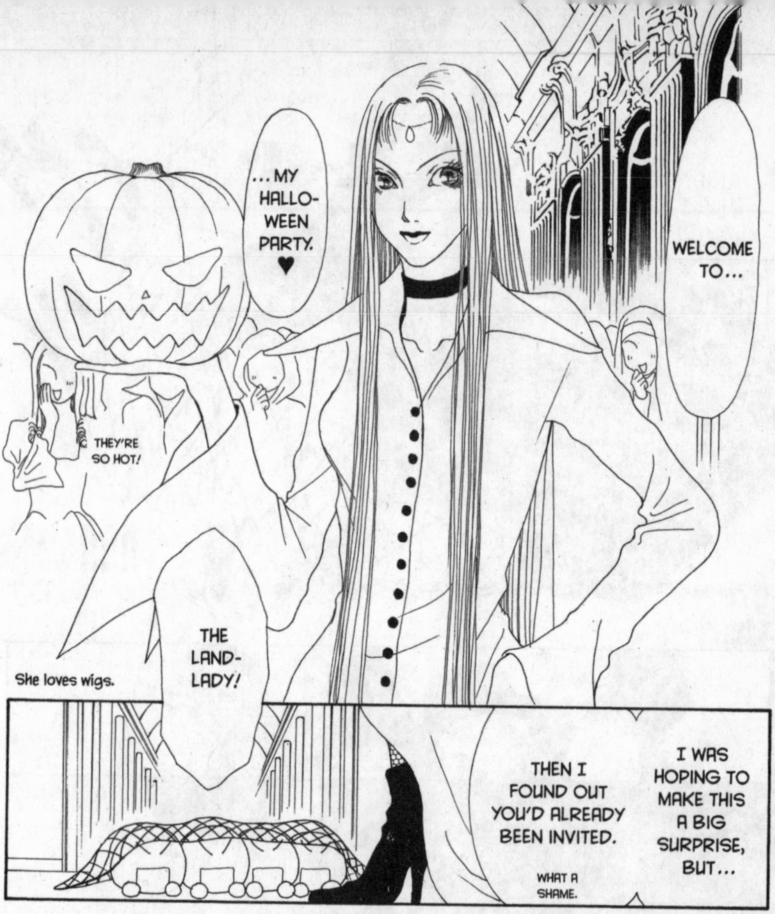
WELCOME TO...
...MY HALLOWEEN PARTY. ♥
THEY'RE SO HOT!
THE LANDLADY!
She loves wigs.
I WAS HOPING TO MAKE THIS A BIG SURPRISE, BUT...
THEN I FOUND OUT YOU'D ALREADY BEEN INVITED.
WHAT A SHAME.

BEHIND THE SCENES

WAIT...WHOSE IDEA WAS IT TO HAVE A COSPLAY ACTION ADVENTURE STORY? OH YEAH, IT WAS MINE. I REALLY ENDED UP REGRETTING THE OUTFIT I GAVE KYOHEI. I SHOULD'VE JUST DRESSED HIM IN HIS USUAL JEANS AND SWEATSHIRT.

THE TORTURE CHAMBER WAS AWESOME. I'D LOVE TO DRAW IT AGAIN IF I GET THE CHANCE. ♥ (...BUT I WON'T.) SOMEDAY I'D LIKE TO SEE A REAL LIVE "IRON MAIDEN." ♥♥♥

STARTING WITH THIS BOOK, I GOT TO HIRE FULL TIME ASSISTANTS. YAHOO! ♥ I'LL GIVE YOU THE DETAILS AT THE END OF THE BOOK!...SORRY TO MAKE YOU GUYS WORK SO HARD RIGHT FROM THE START. POOR ARAKI-KUN & YOSHII.

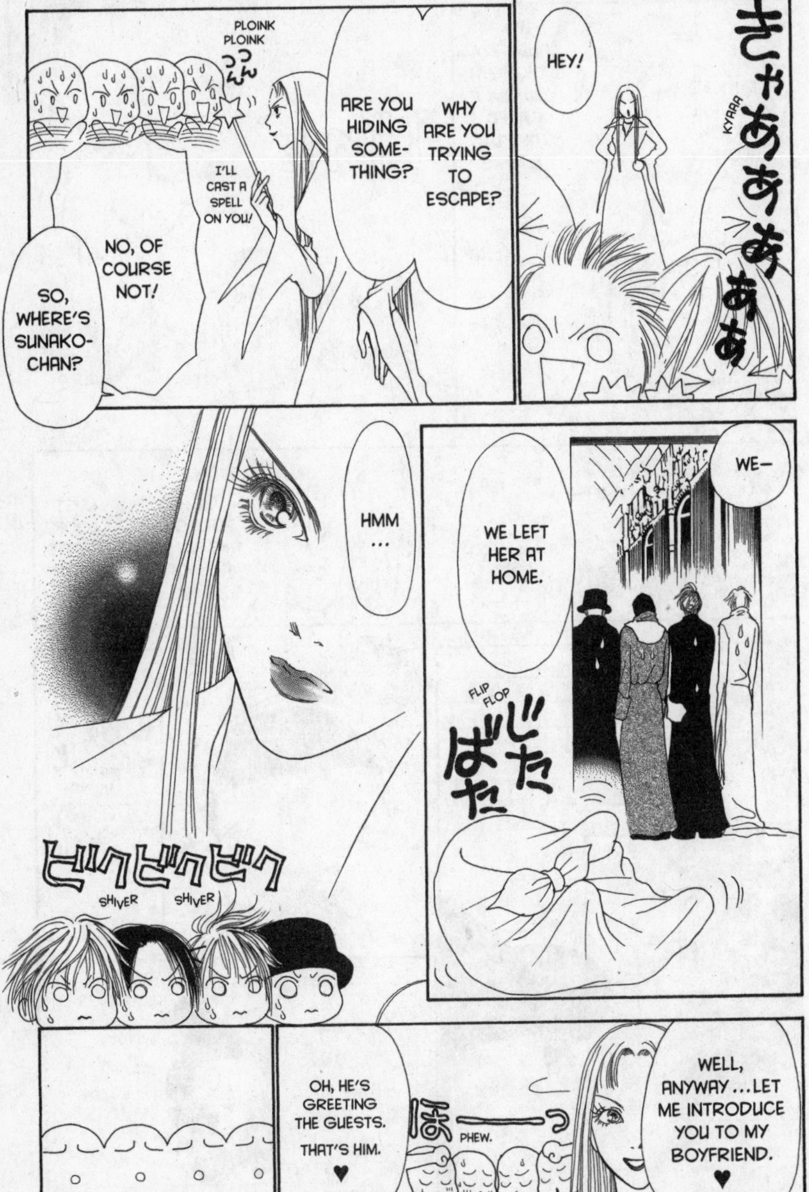
きゃあああ
KYAAA
HEY!
WHY ARE YOU TRYING TO ESCAPE?
ARE YOU HIDING SOME-THING?
PLOINK PLOINK
つんつん
I'LL CAST A SPELL ON YOU!
NO, OF COURSE NOT!
SO, WHERE'S SUNAKO-CHAN?
WE-
WE LEFT HER AT HOME.
じたばた
FLIP FLOP
HMM...
ビクビクビク
SHIVER SHIVER
WELL, ANYWAY...LET ME INTRODUCE YOU TO MY BOYFRIEND. ♥
ほーっ
PHEW.
OH, HE'S GREETING THE GUESTS. THAT'S HIM. ♥

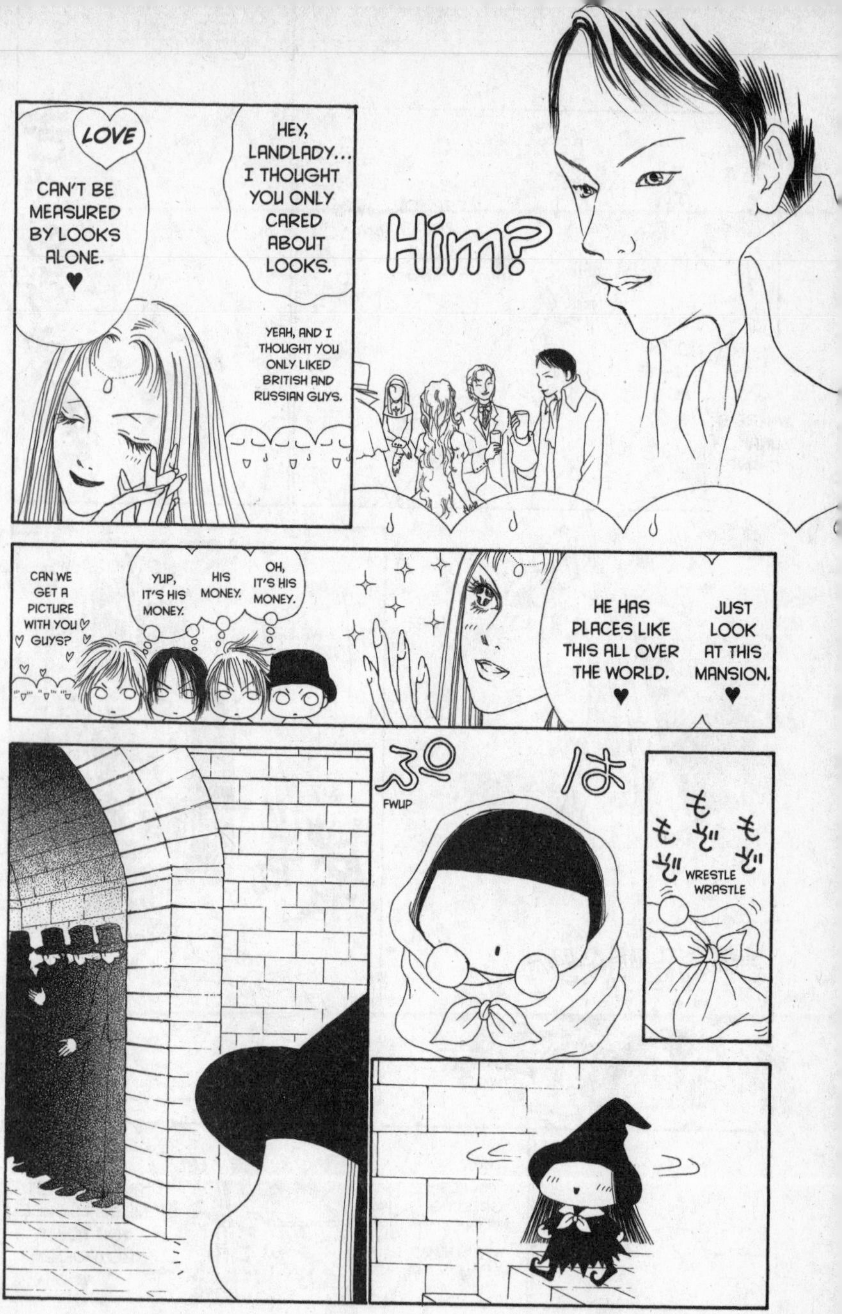
Him?
HEY, LANDLADY... I THOUGHT YOU ONLY CARED ABOUT LOOKS.
LOVE CAN'T BE MEASURED BY LOOKS ALONE. ♥
YEAH, AND I THOUGHT YOU ONLY LIKED BRITISH AND RUSSIAN GUYS.
JUST LOOK AT THIS MANSION. ♥
HE HAS PLACES LIKE THIS ALL OVER THE WORLD. ♥
OH, IT'S HIS MONEY.
HIS MONEY.
YUP, IT'S HIS MONEY.
CAN WE GET A PICTURE WITH YOU GUYS?
もぞもぞもぞ
WRESTLE WRASTLE
ぷは
FWUP

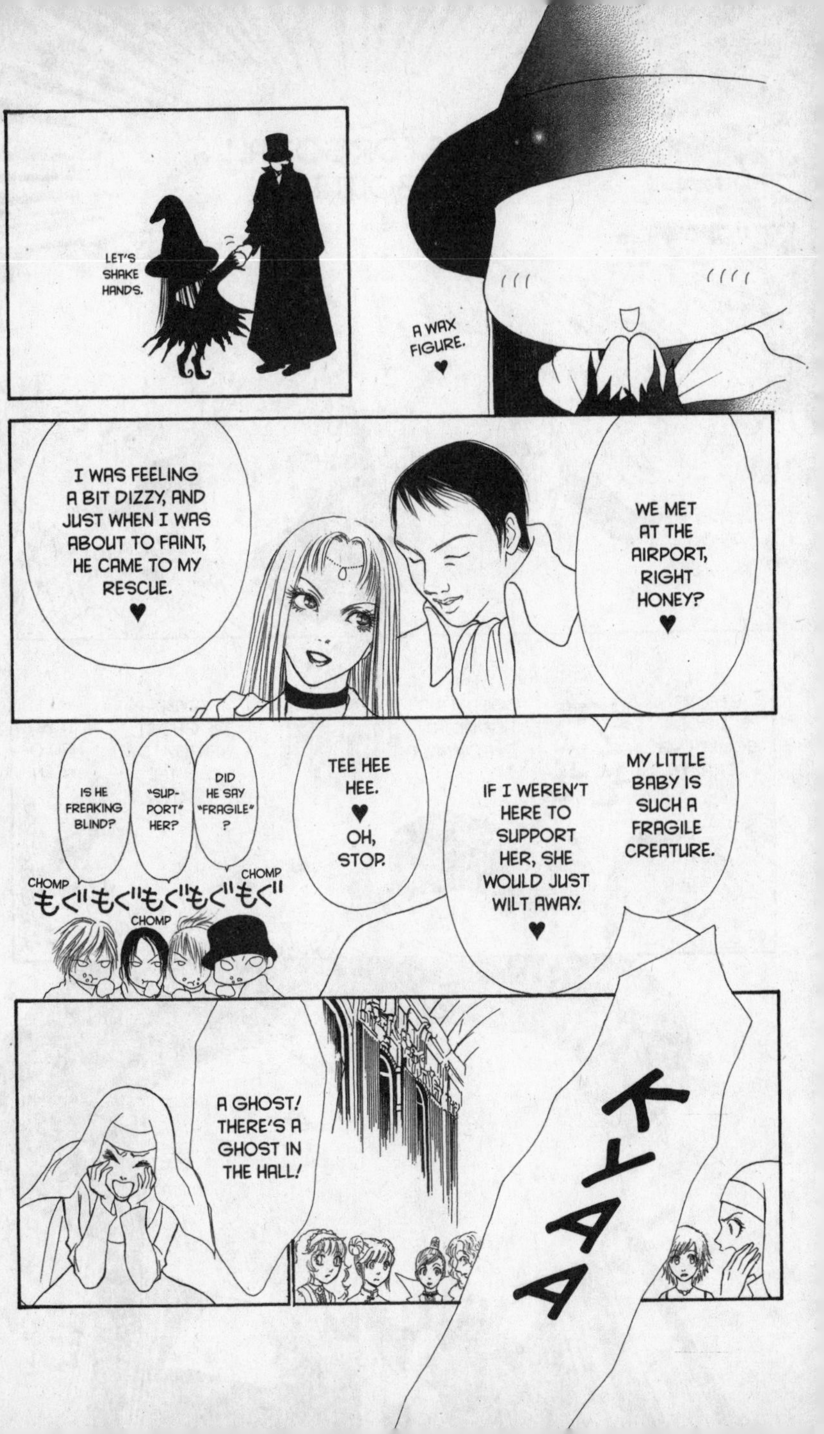
A WAX FIGURE. ♥
LET'S SHAKE HANDS.
WE MET AT THE AIRPORT, RIGHT HONEY? ♥
I WAS FEELING A BIT DIZZY, AND JUST WHEN I WAS ABOUT TO FAINT, HE CAME TO MY RESCUE. ♥
MY LITTLE BABY IS SUCH A FRAGILE CREATURE.
IF I WEREN'T HERE TO SUPPORT HER, SHE WOULD JUST WILT AWAY. ♥
TEE HEE HEE. ♥ OH, STOP.
DID HE SAY "FRAGILE"?
"SUP-PORT" HER?
IS HE FREAKING BLIND?
CHOMP
もぐもぐもぐもぐもぐ
CHOMP
CHOMP
KYAAA
A GHOST! THERE'S A GHOST IN THE HALL!

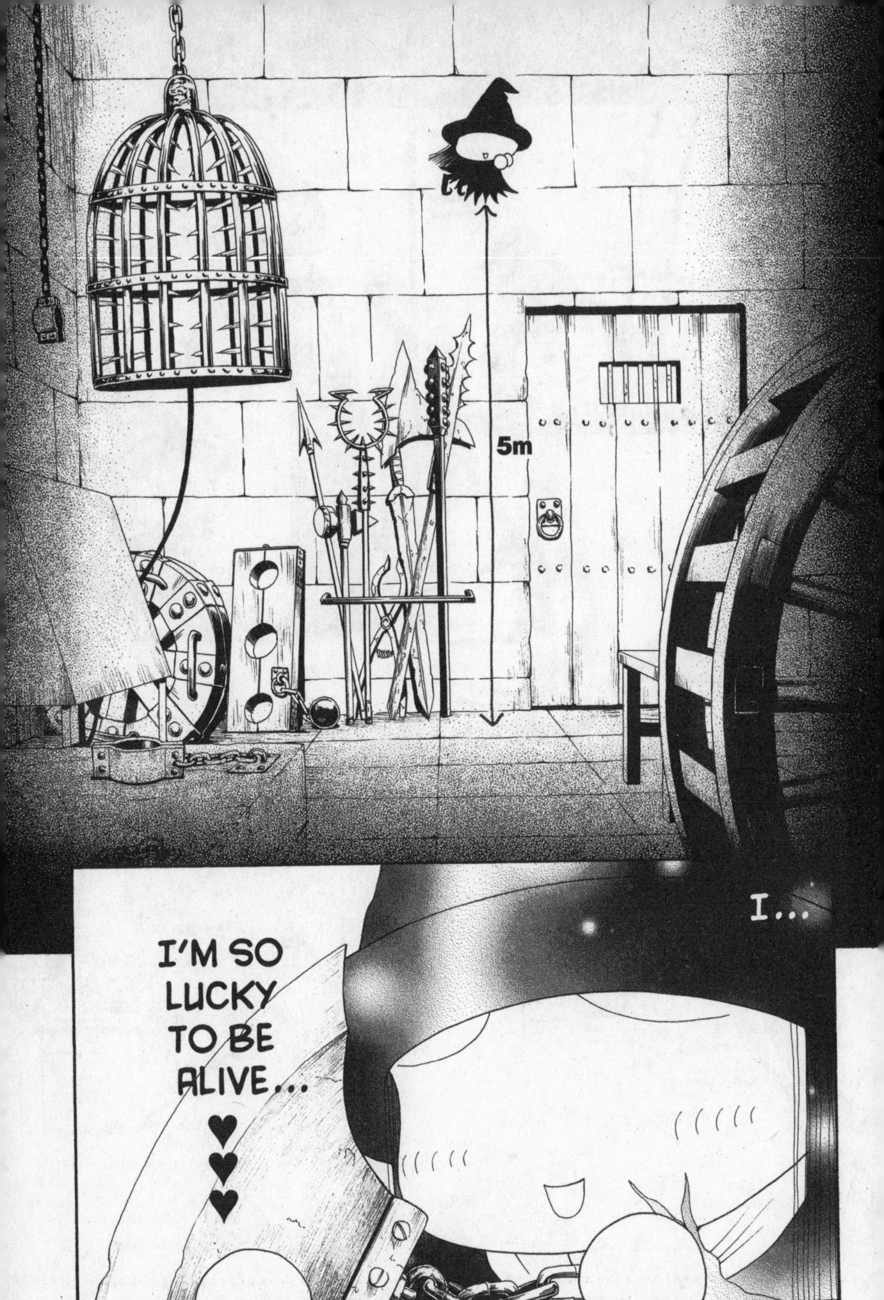
5m
I...
I'M SO LUCKY TO BE ALIVE...

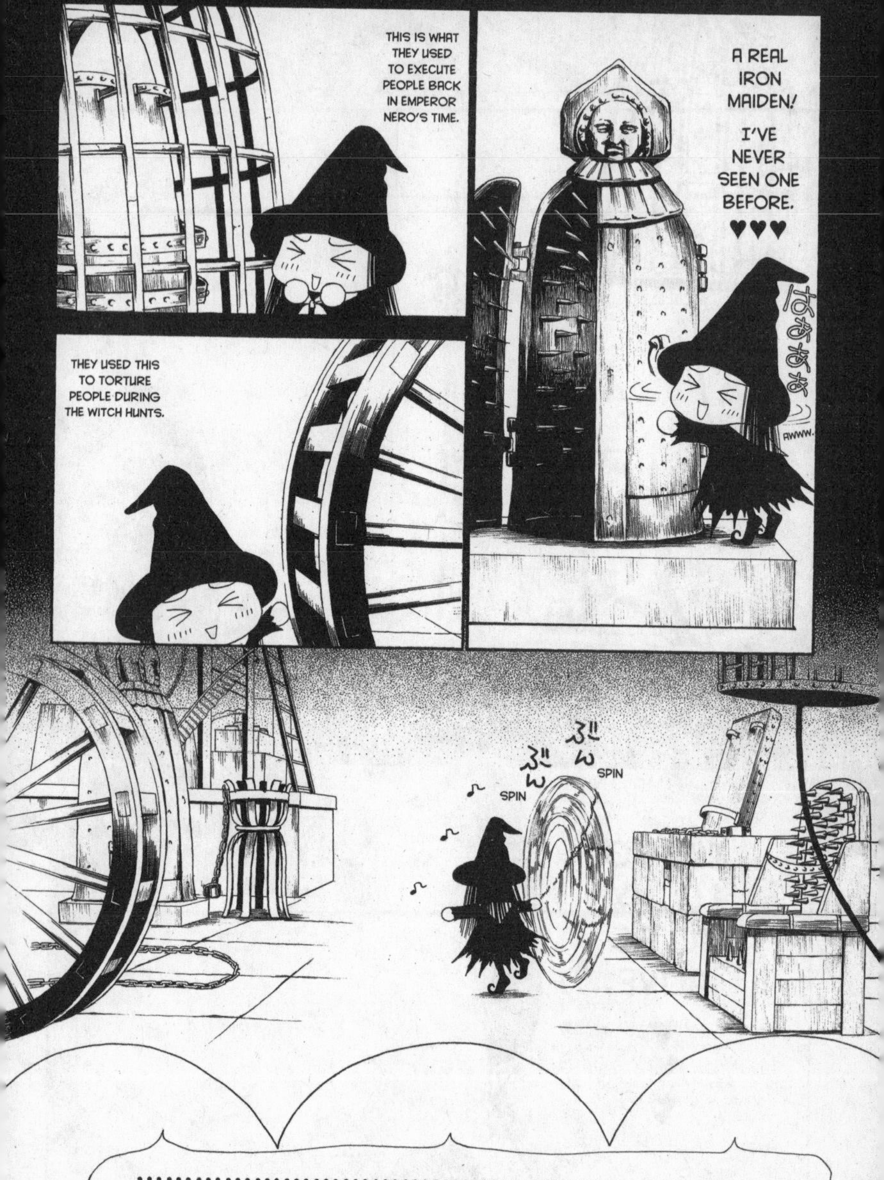
A REAL IRON MAIDEN!
I'VE NEVER SEEN ONE BEFORE. ♥♥♥
はあああ
AWWW.
THIS IS WHAT THEY USED TO EXECUTE PEOPLE BACK IN EMPEROR NERO'S TIME.
THEY USED THIS TO TORTURE PEOPLE DURING THE WITCH HUNTS.
ぶぃん
SPIN
ぶぃん
SPIN
....

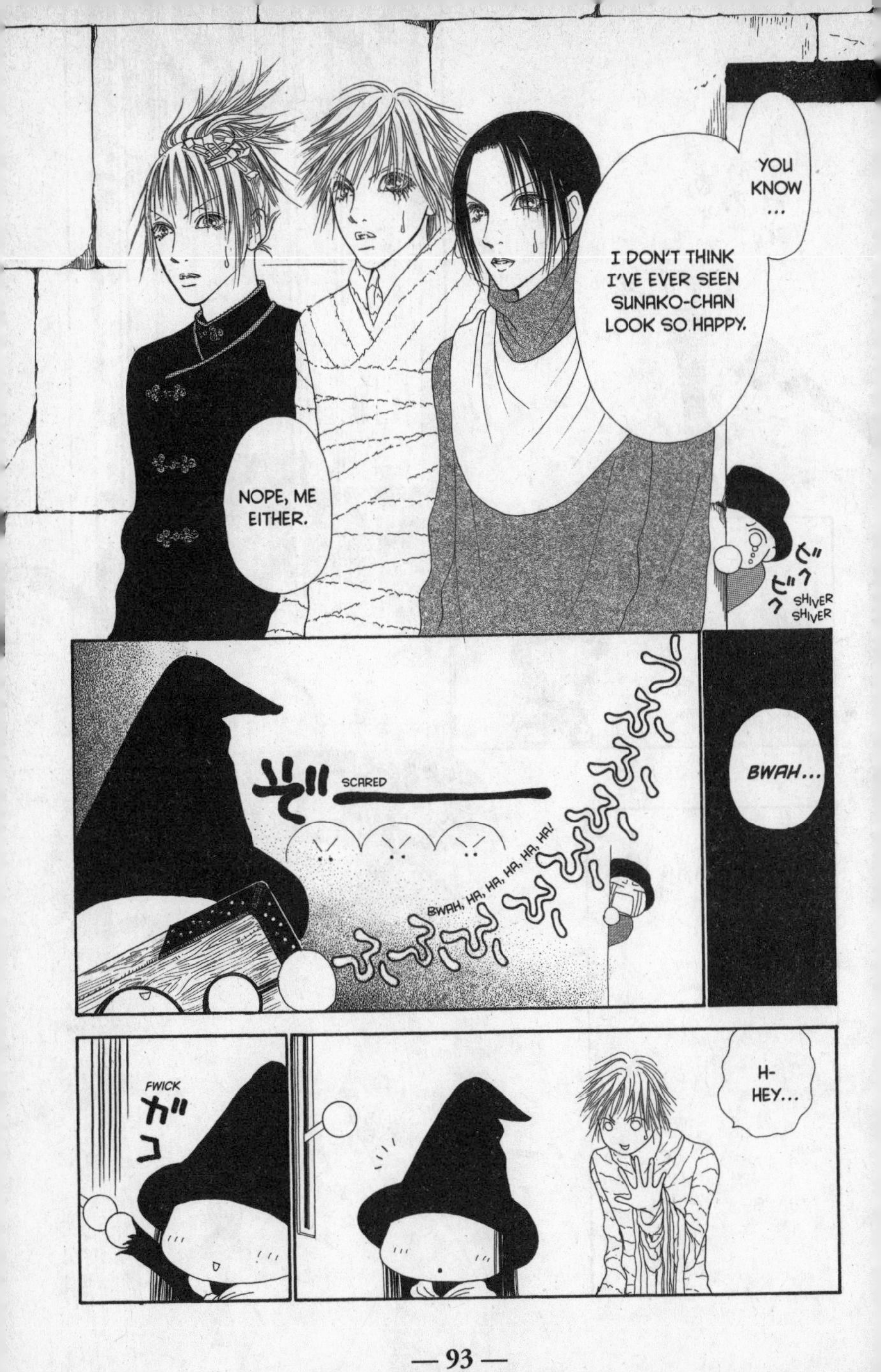
YOU KNOW ...
I DON'T THINK I'VE EVER SEEN SUNAKO-CHAN LOOK SO HAPPY.
NOPE, ME EITHER.
ビクビク SHIVER SHIVER
BWAH...
ふふふふふふふふ
BWAH, HA, HA, HA, HA, HA!
ぞ SCARED
H- HEY...
ガコ FWICK

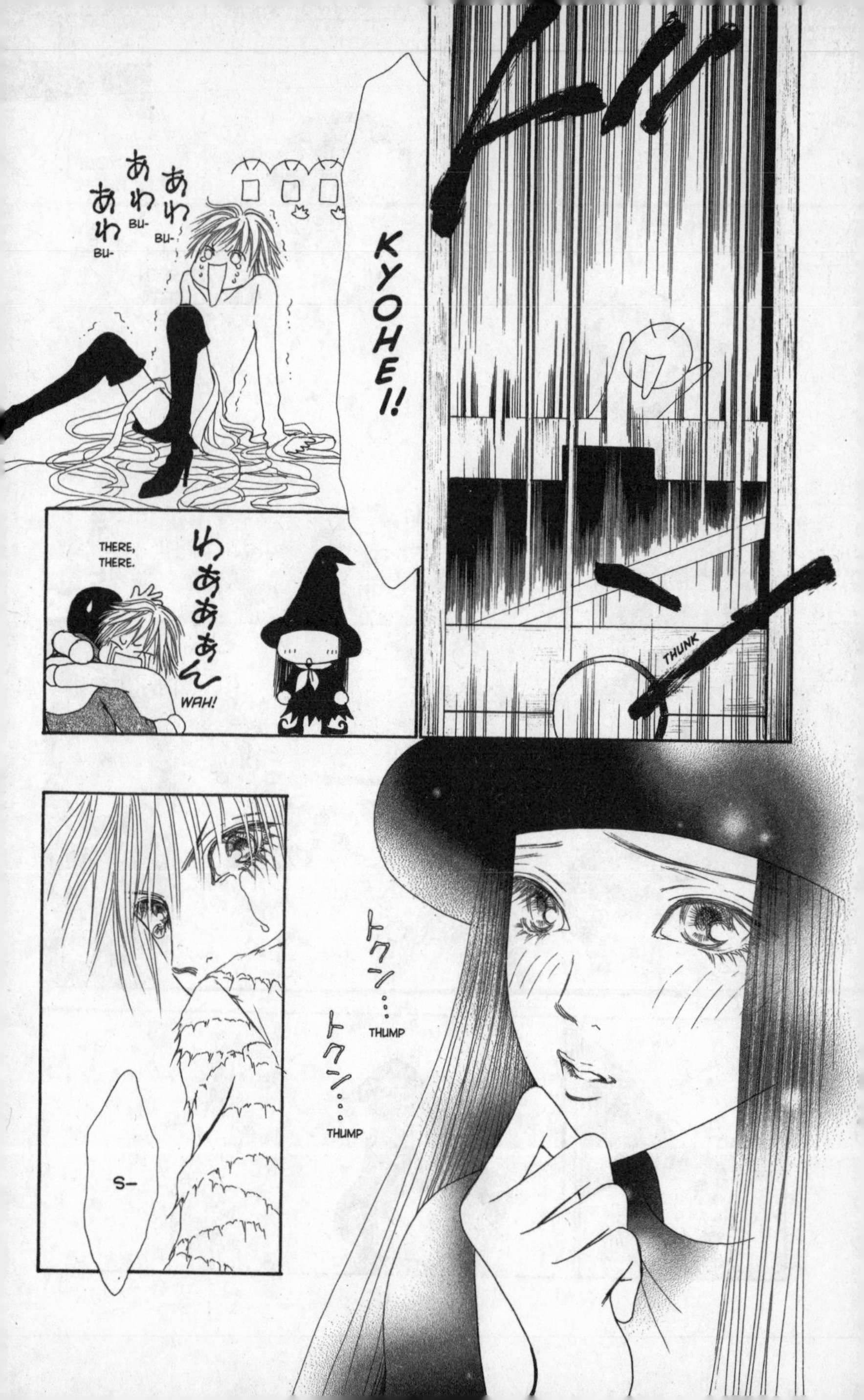
THUNK
KYOHE!!
あわ
BU-
あわ
BU-
わあああん
WAH!
THERE, THERE.
トクン…
THUMP
トクン…
THUMP
S–

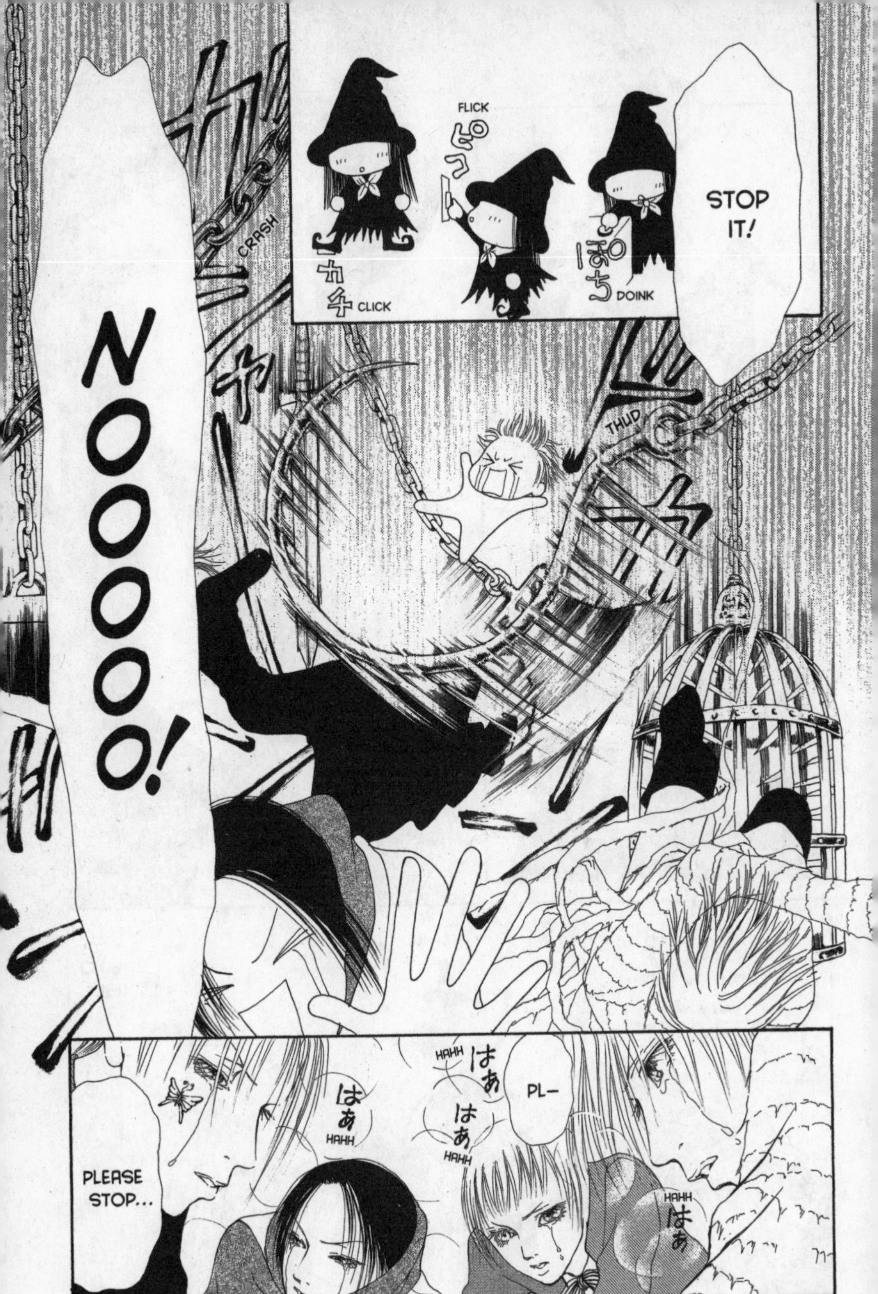
STOP IT!
DOINK
FLICK
CLICK
THUD
CRASH
NOOOOOO!
PL–
HAHH
HAHH
HAHH
HAHH
PLEASE STOP...

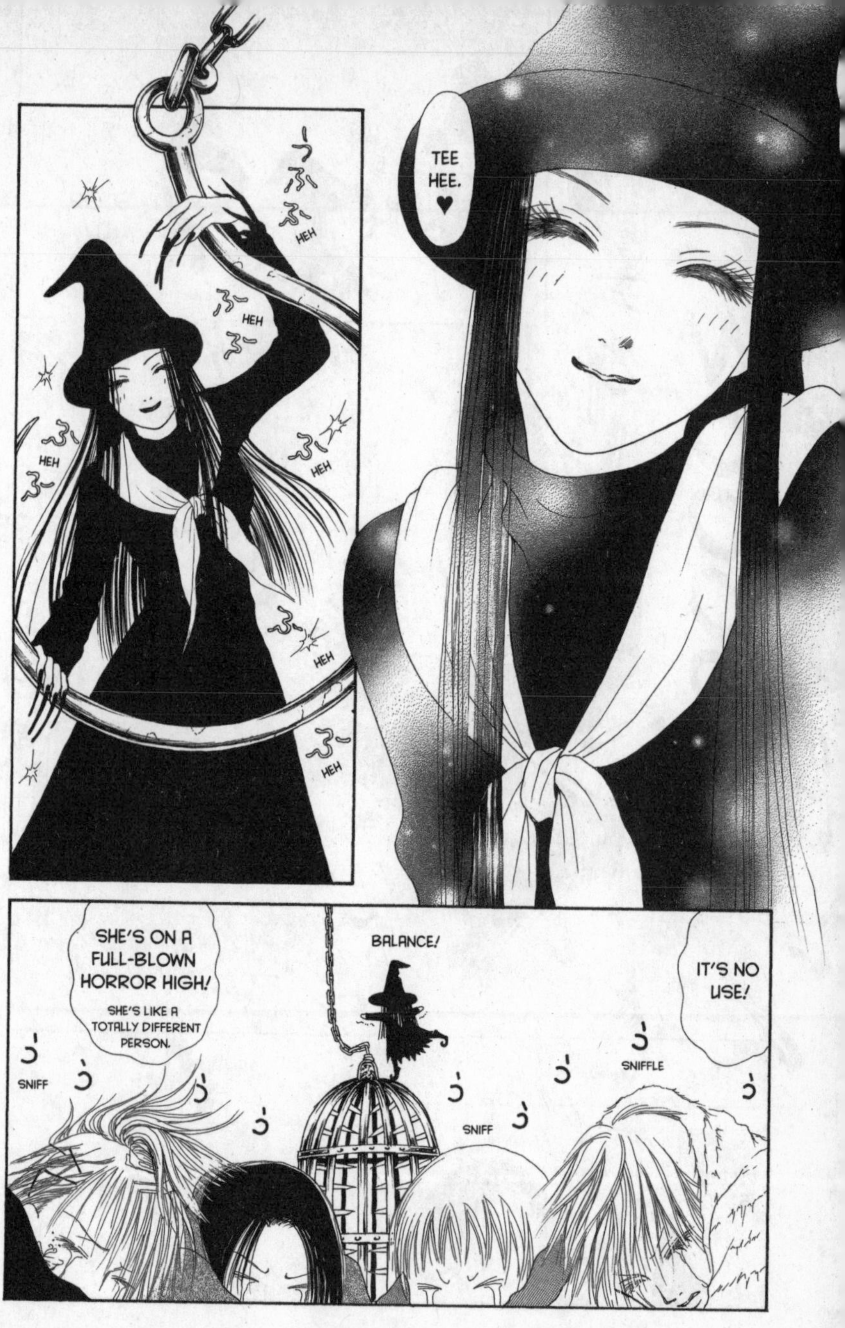
TEE HEE. ♥
HEH
HEH
HEH
HEH
HEH
HEH
IT'S NO USE!
SNIFFLE
SNIFF
BALANCE!
SHE'S ON A FULL-BLOWN HORROR HIGH!
SHE'S LIKE A TOTALLY DIFFERENT PERSON.
SNIFF

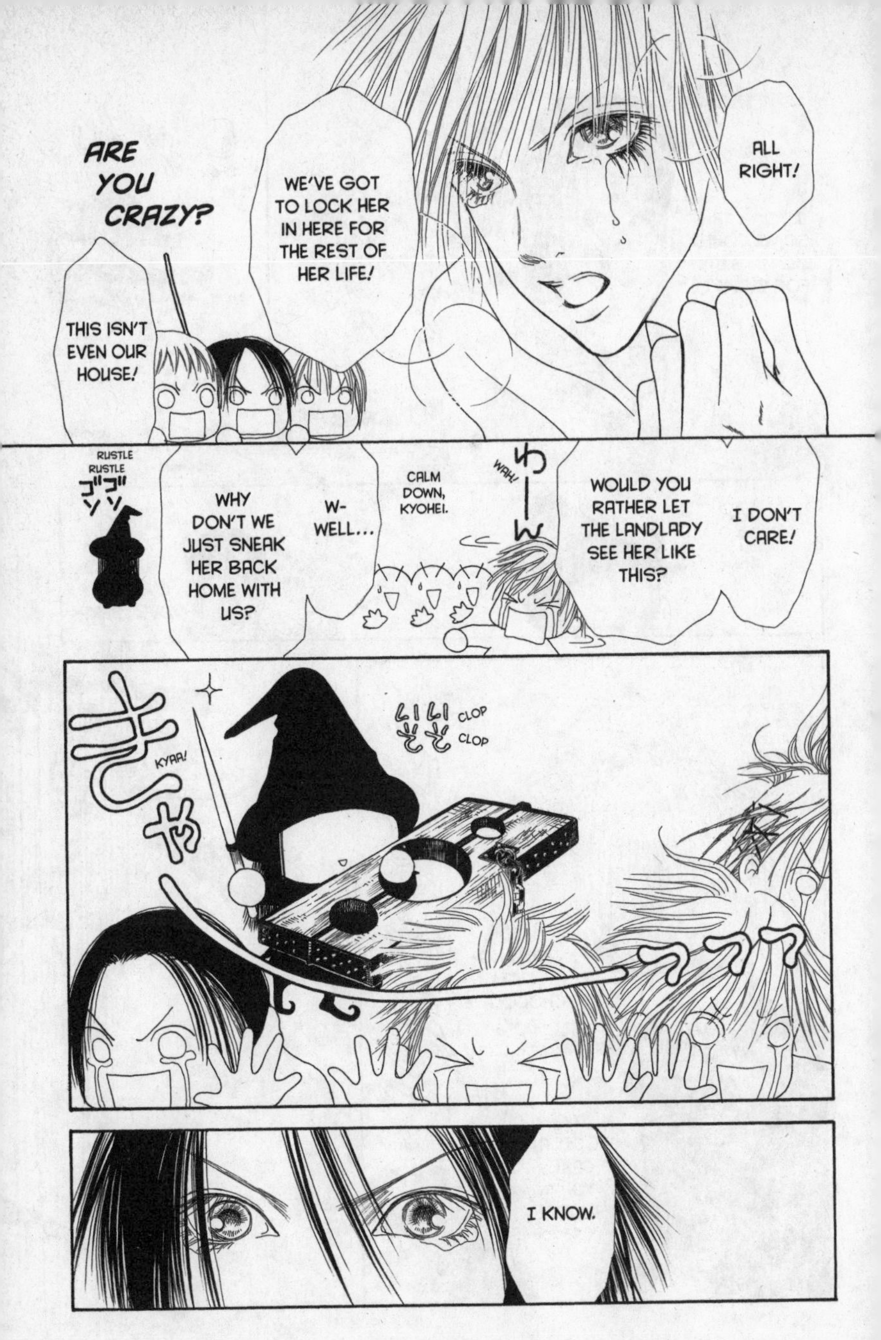
ALL RIGHT!
WE'VE GOT TO LOCK HER IN HERE FOR THE REST OF HER LIFE!
ARE YOU CRAZY?
THIS ISN'T EVEN OUR HOUSE!
I DON'T CARE!
WOULD YOU RATHER LET THE LANDLADY SEE HER LIKE THIS?
WAH!
CALM DOWN, KYOHEI.
W-WELL...
WHY DON'T WE JUST SNEAK HER BACK HOME WITH US?
RUSTLE RUSTLE
CLOP CLOP
KYAA!
I KNOW.

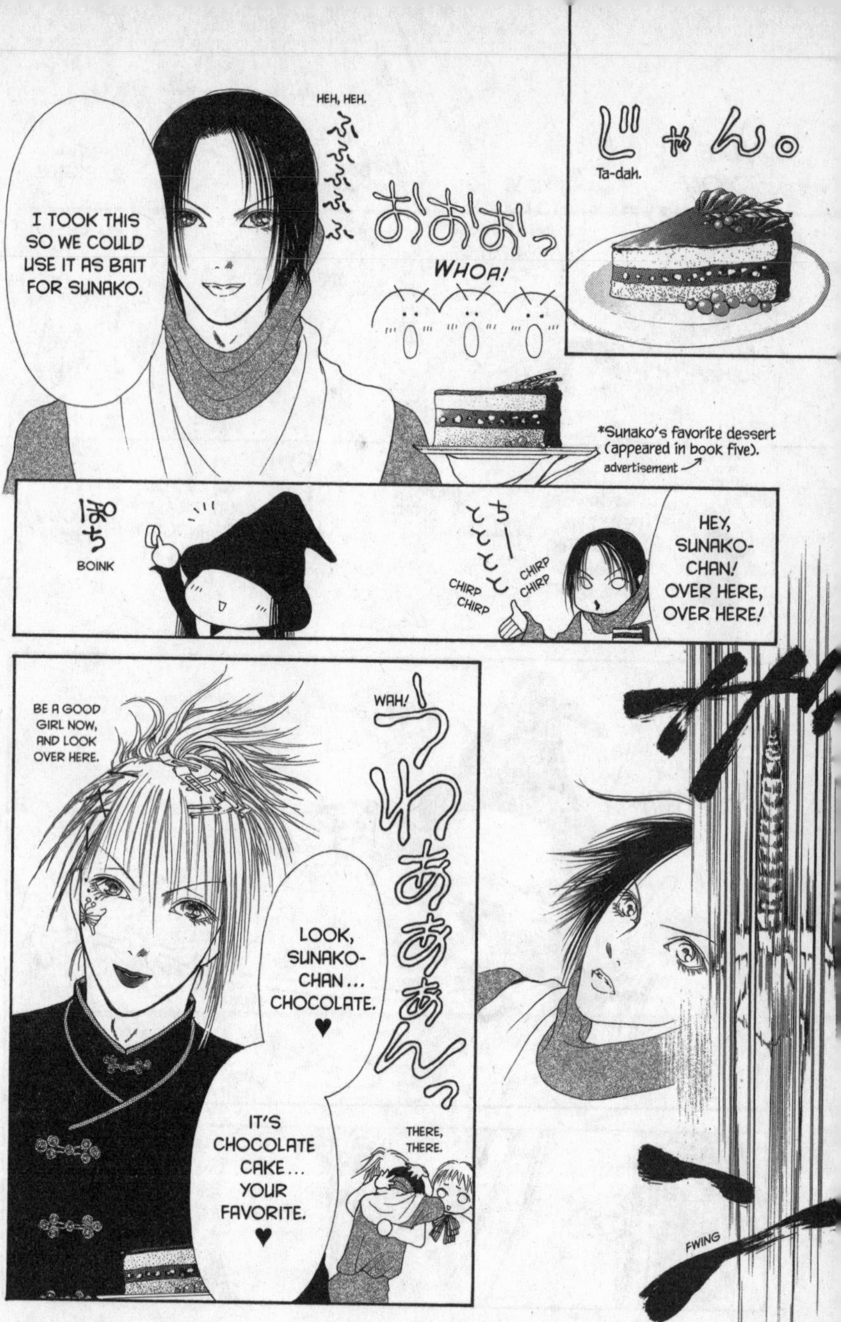
じゃん。
Ta-dah.
おおおっ
WHOA!
HEH, HEH.
ふふふふふ
I TOOK THIS SO WE COULD USE IT AS BAIT FOR SUNAKO.
*Sunako's favorite dessert (appeared in book five).
advertisement
HEY, SUNAKO-CHAN! OVER HERE, OVER HERE!
ちーととと
CHIRP CHIRP
CHIRP CHIRP
ぽち
BOINK
FWING
うわあああんっ
WAH!
BE A GOOD GIRL NOW, AND LOOK OVER HERE.
LOOK, SUNAKO-CHAN... CHOCOLATE. ♥
IT'S CHOCOLATE CAKE... YOUR FAVORITE. ♥
THERE, THERE.

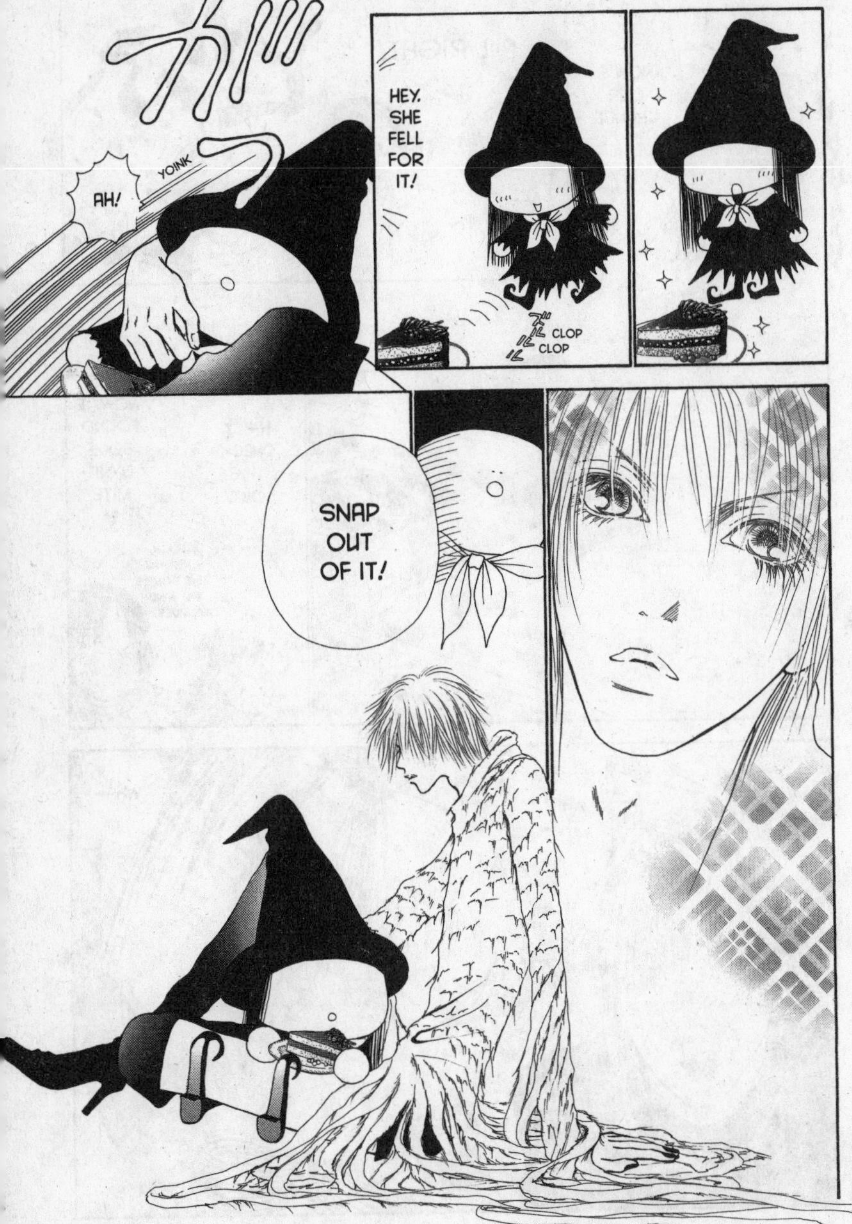
HEY. SHE FELL FOR IT!
CLOP CLOP
AH!
YOINK
SNAP OUT OF IT!

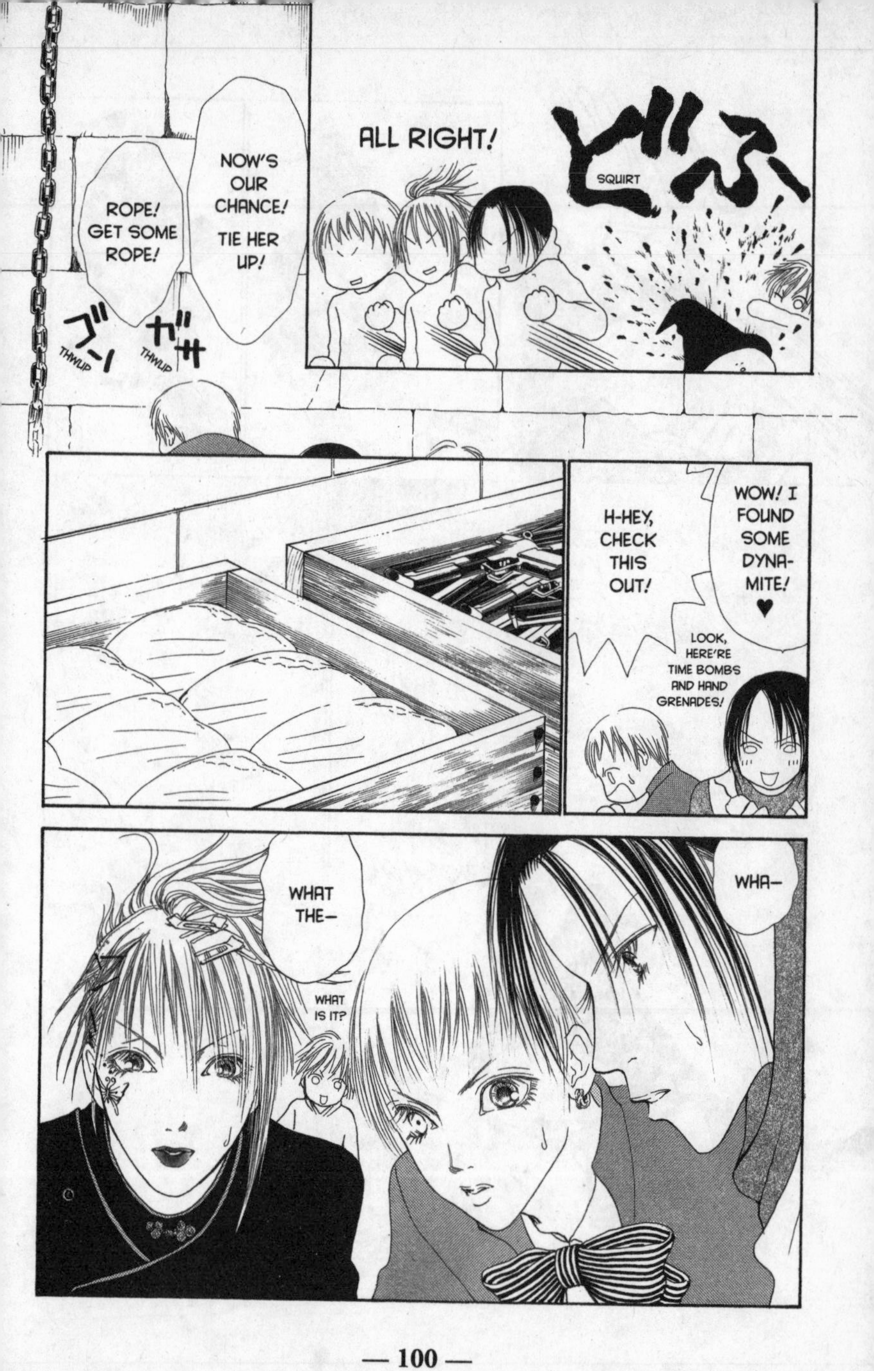
どぷ
SQUIRT
ALL RIGHT!
NOW'S OUR CHANCE! TIE HER UP!
ROPE! GET SOME ROPE!
ザザ
THWUP
ゴーン
THWUP
WOW! I FOUND SOME DYNAMITE! ♥
H-HEY, CHECK THIS OUT!
LOOK, HERE'RE TIME BOMBS AND HAND GRENADES!
WHA-
WHAT THE-
WHAT IS IT?

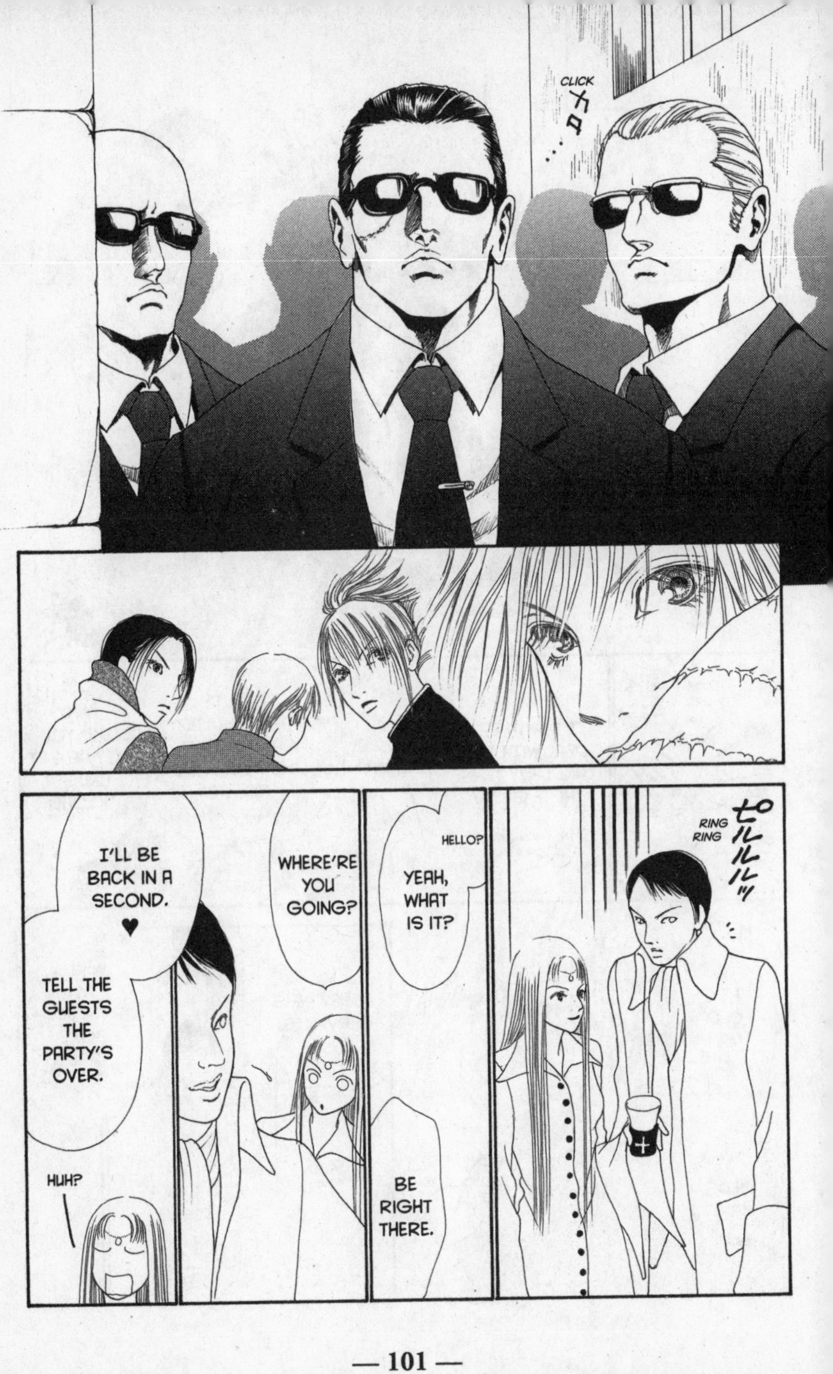
CLICK
カタ…
RING RING
ピルルルッ
HELLO?
YEAH, WHAT IS IT?
BE RIGHT THERE.
WHERE'RE YOU GOING?
I'LL BE BACK IN A SECOND. ♥
TELL THE GUESTS THE PARTY'S OVER.
HUH?

AH.

YOU'RE RIGHT.

YOU IDIOT. YOU IDIOT...

I'D RATHER DEAL WITH THE LANDLADY THAN THESE GUYS!

THEY MIGHT KILL US FOR REAL!

ARE YOU CRAZY?

Sunako

BECAUSE... IF THE LANDLADY SAW SUNAKO LIKE THIS, SHE'D KILL US!

WHY DID YOU LET US GET CAUGHT, KYOHEI?

HEY, OLD MAN!

OLD MAN? GRR...

...MY HONEY PIE'S SERVANTS!

WE'RE NOT SERVANTS!

WHA—? TH-THESE BOYS ARE...

I JUST...

...LOVE WATCHING BEAUTIFUL AND FRAGILE WOMEN CRY AND SCREAM IN TERROR.

HEH...

WHAT'RE YOU DOING HANGING AROUND THE LANDLADY?

HOW COULD YOU SAY SUCH A THING?

ARE YOU TRYING TO TURN HER INTO A CRIMINAL?

!!!!!!

I'VE NEVER TRIED IT WITH A MAN BEFORE, BUT YOU GUYS ARE SO CUTE, IT MIGHT BE FUN. ♥

SOMETIMES, EVEN THE MOST RESERVED WOMAN CAN SURPRISE YOU WITH THE MOST HORRIFYING SCREAM.

THERE IS NO SOUND MORE BEAUTIFUL.

I LOOKED EVERY-WHERE FOR—

OH, THERE YOU ARE.

NO! DON'T COME IN HERE!

HE'S JUST LIKE SUNAKO-CHAN!

NO, BUT HE'S FOR REAL! HE'S A MURDERER!

HE'S A SADIST! A SADIST!

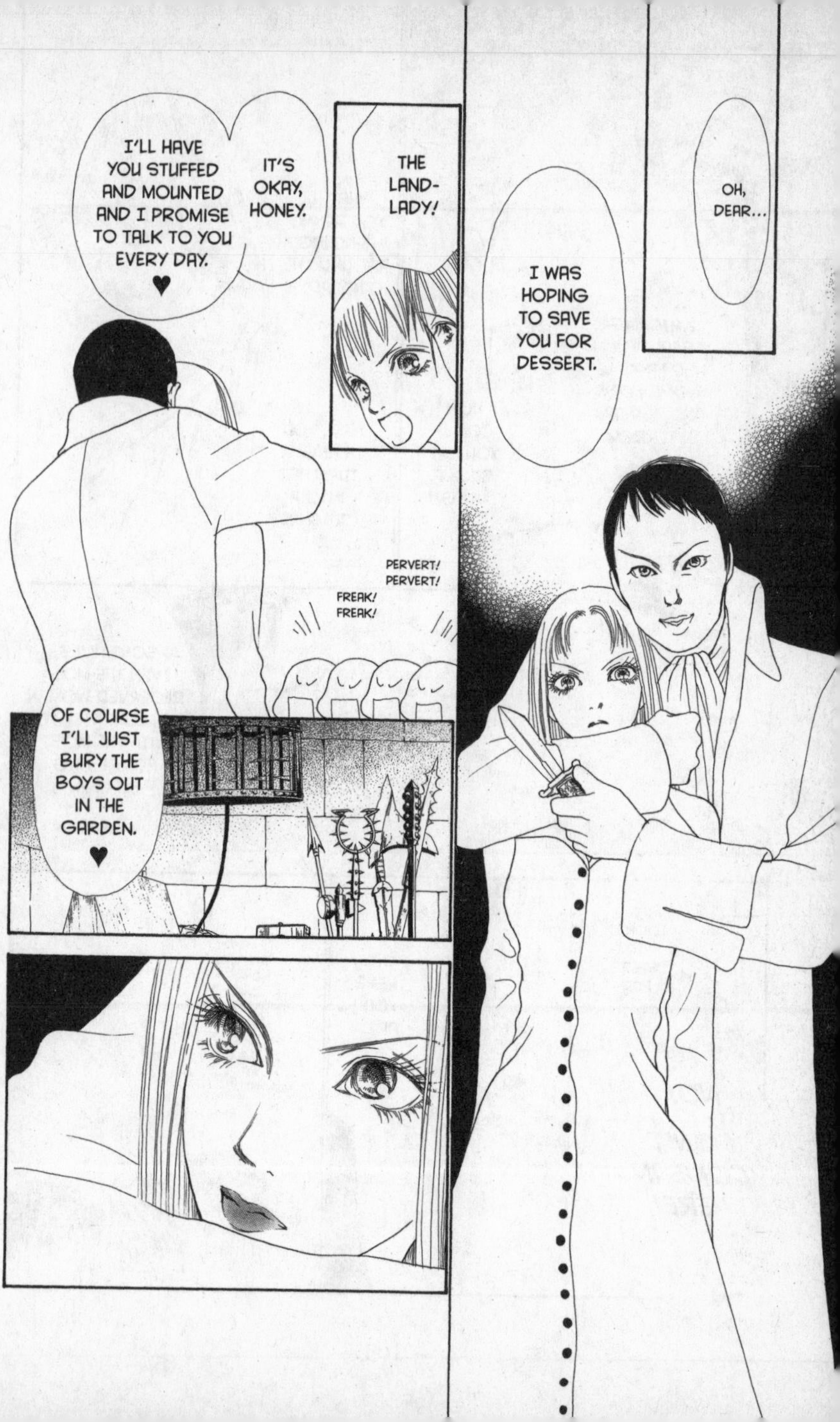
OH, DEAR...
I WAS HOPING TO SAVE YOU FOR DESSERT.
THE LAND-LADY!
IT'S OKAY, HONEY.
I'LL HAVE YOU STUFFED AND MOUNTED AND I PROMISE TO TALK TO YOU EVERY DAY. ♥
PERVERT! PERVERT!
FREAK! FREAK!
OF COURSE I'LL JUST BURY THE BOYS OUT IN THE GARDEN. ♥

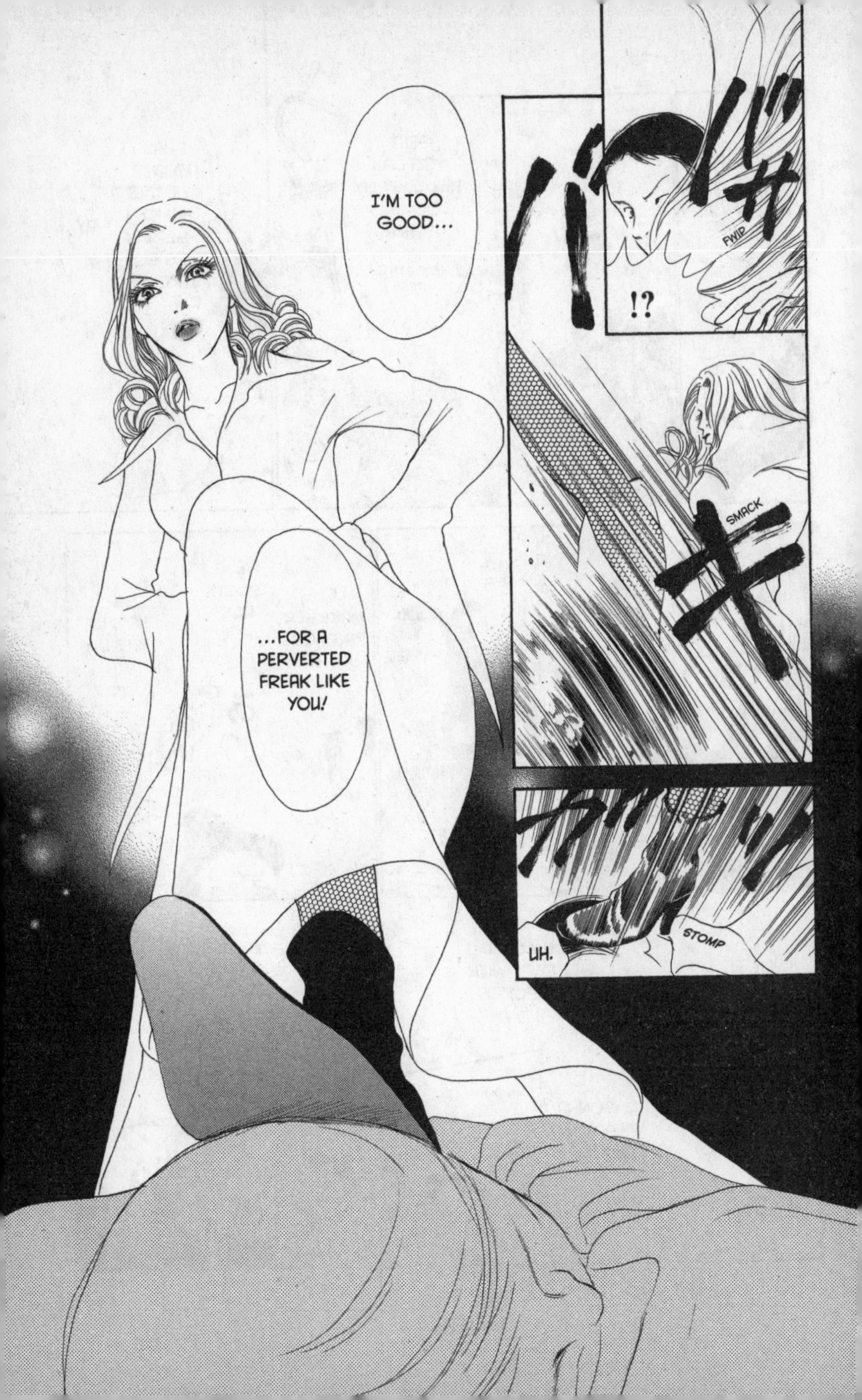
FWIP
!?
SMACK
STOMP
UH.
I'M TOO GOOD...
...FOR A PERVERTED FREAK LIKE YOU!

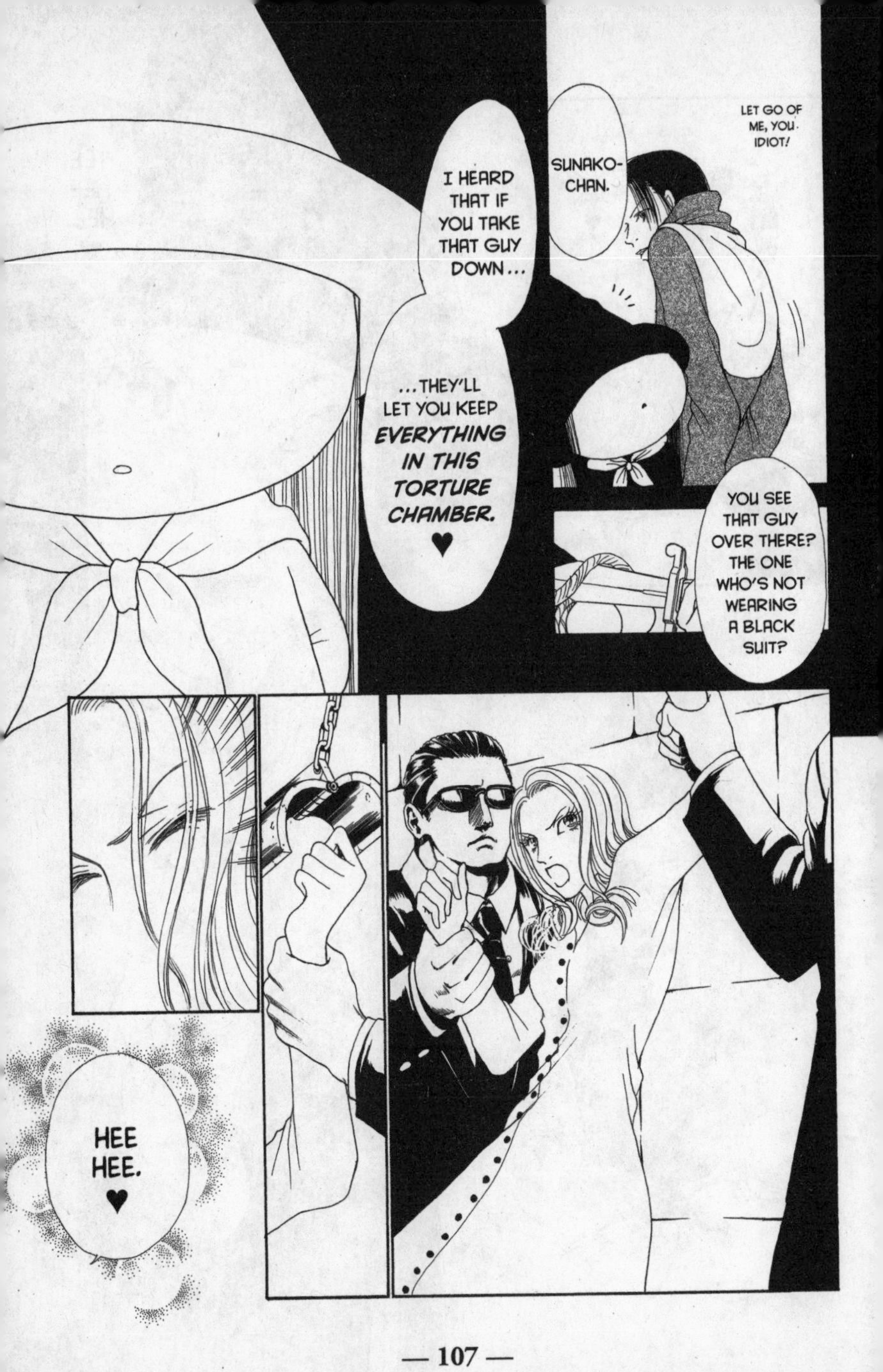
LET GO OF ME, YOU IDIOT!
SUNAKO-CHAN.
YOU SEE THAT GUY OVER THERE? THE ONE WHO'S NOT WEARING A BLACK SUIT?
I HEARD THAT IF YOU TAKE THAT GUY DOWN...
...THEY'LL LET YOU KEEP *EVERYTHING IN THIS TORTURE CHAMBER.* ♥
HEE HEE. ♥

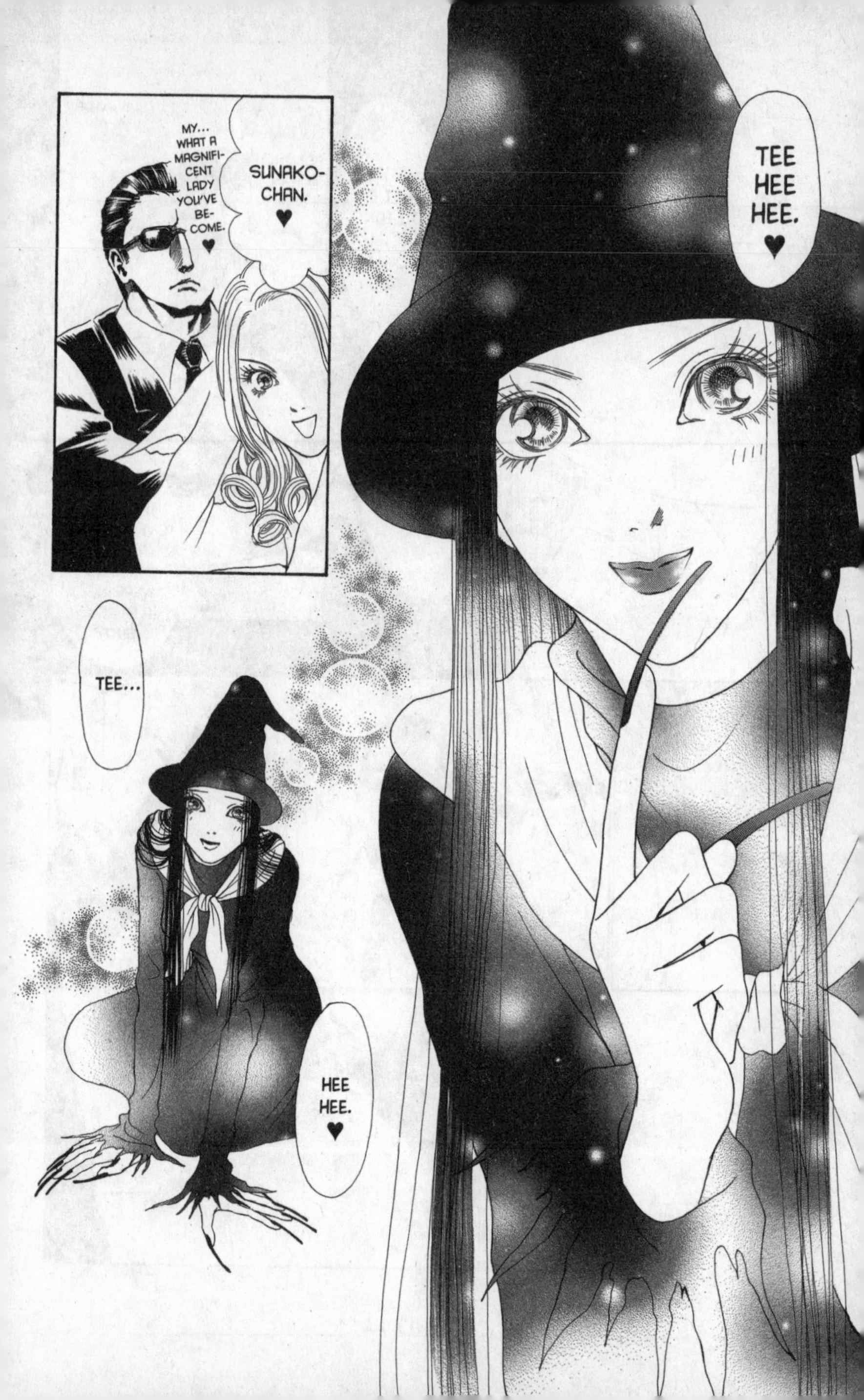
TEE HEE HEE. ♥
SUNAKO-CHAN. ♥
MY... WHAT A MAGNIFI-CENT LADY YOU'VE BE-COME. ♥
TEE...
HEE HEE. ♥

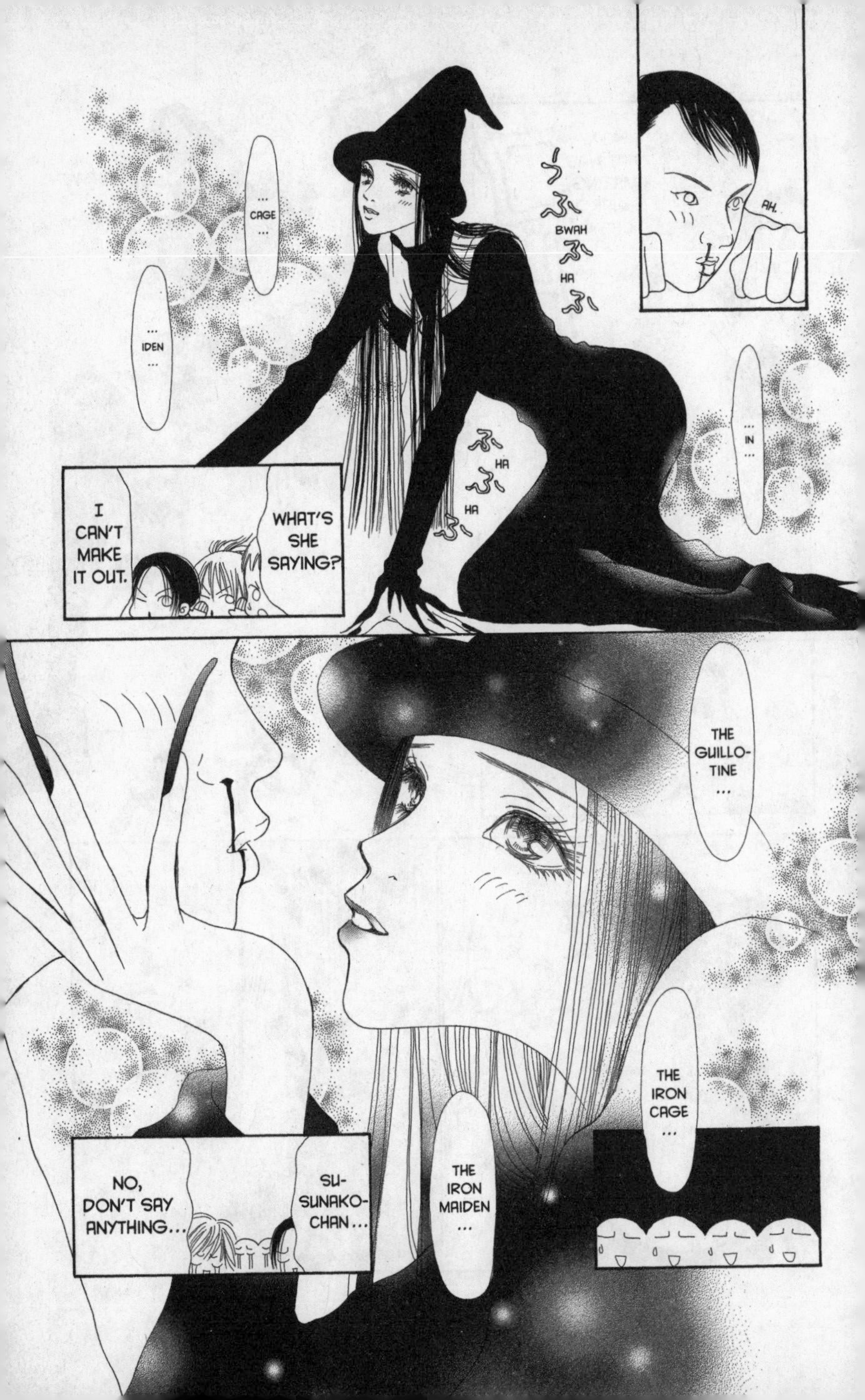
AH.
うふふふ
BWAH HA
...IN...
...CAGE...
...IDEN...
ふふふ
HA HA
WHAT'S SHE SAYING?
I CAN'T MAKE IT OUT.
THE GUILLO-TINE...
THE IRON CAGE...
THE IRON MAIDEN...
SU-SUNAKO-CHAN...
NO, DON'T SAY ANYTHING...

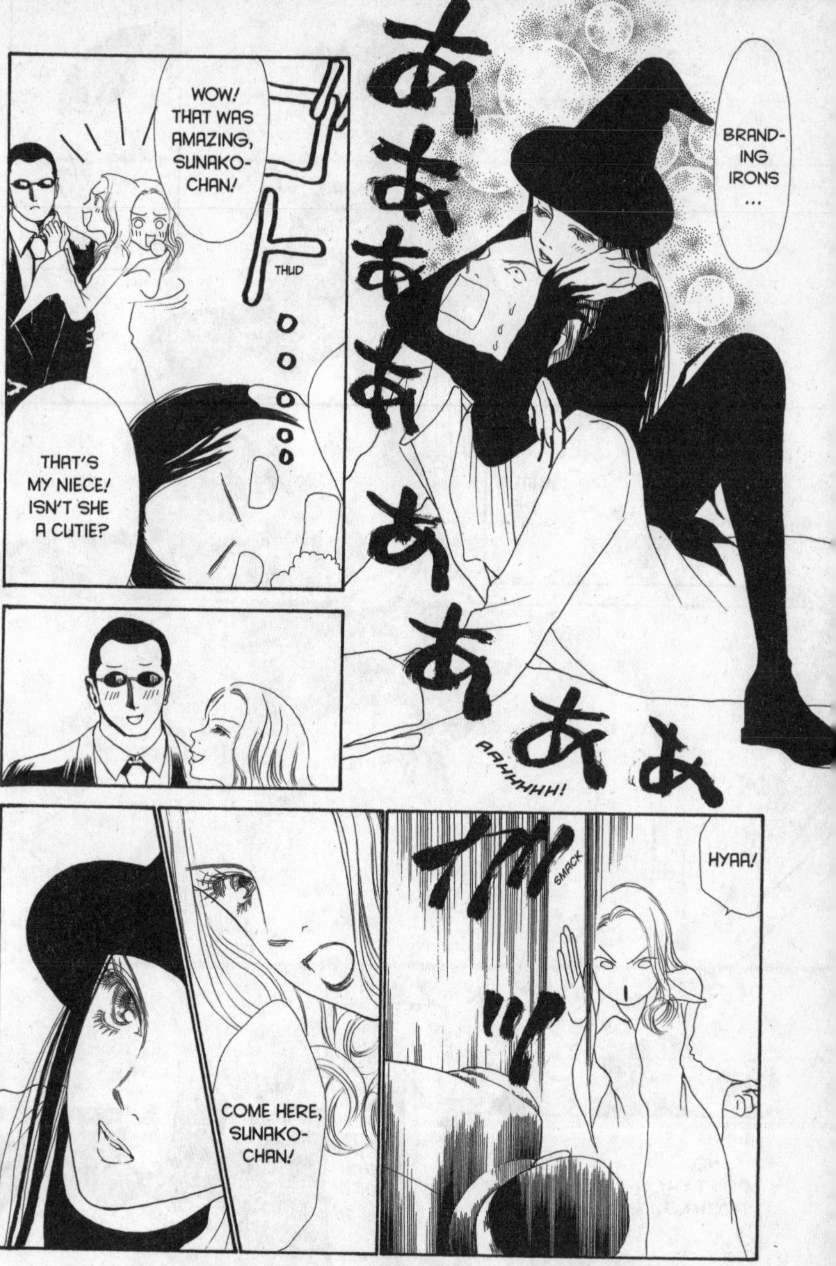
BRAND-ING IRONS...
AAHHHHH!
WOW! THAT WAS AMAZING, SUNAKO-CHAN!
THUD
THAT'S MY NIECE! ISN'T SHE A CUTIE?
HYAA!
SMACK
COME HERE, SUNAKO-CHAN!

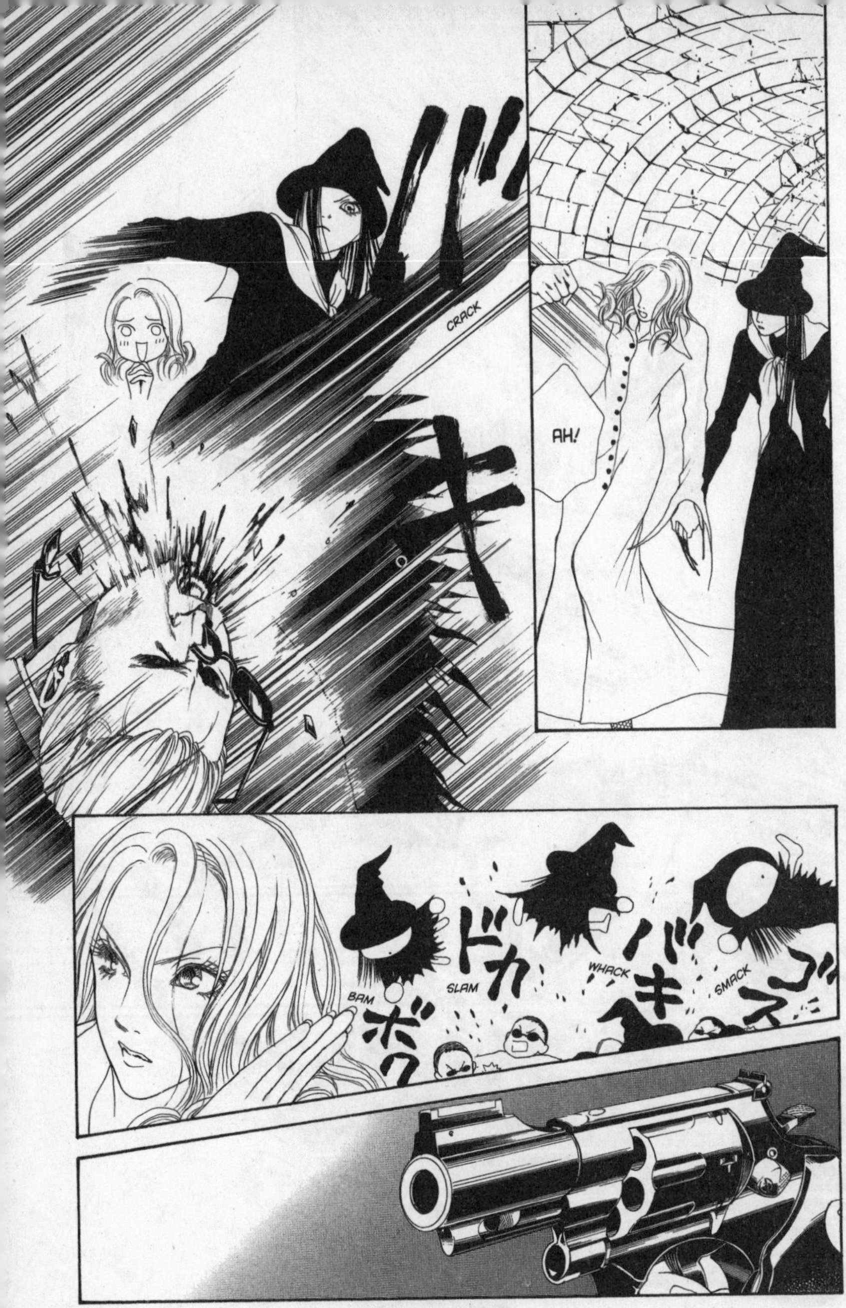
AH!
CRACK
ゴス
SMACK
バキ
WHACK
ドカ
SLAM
ボク
BAM

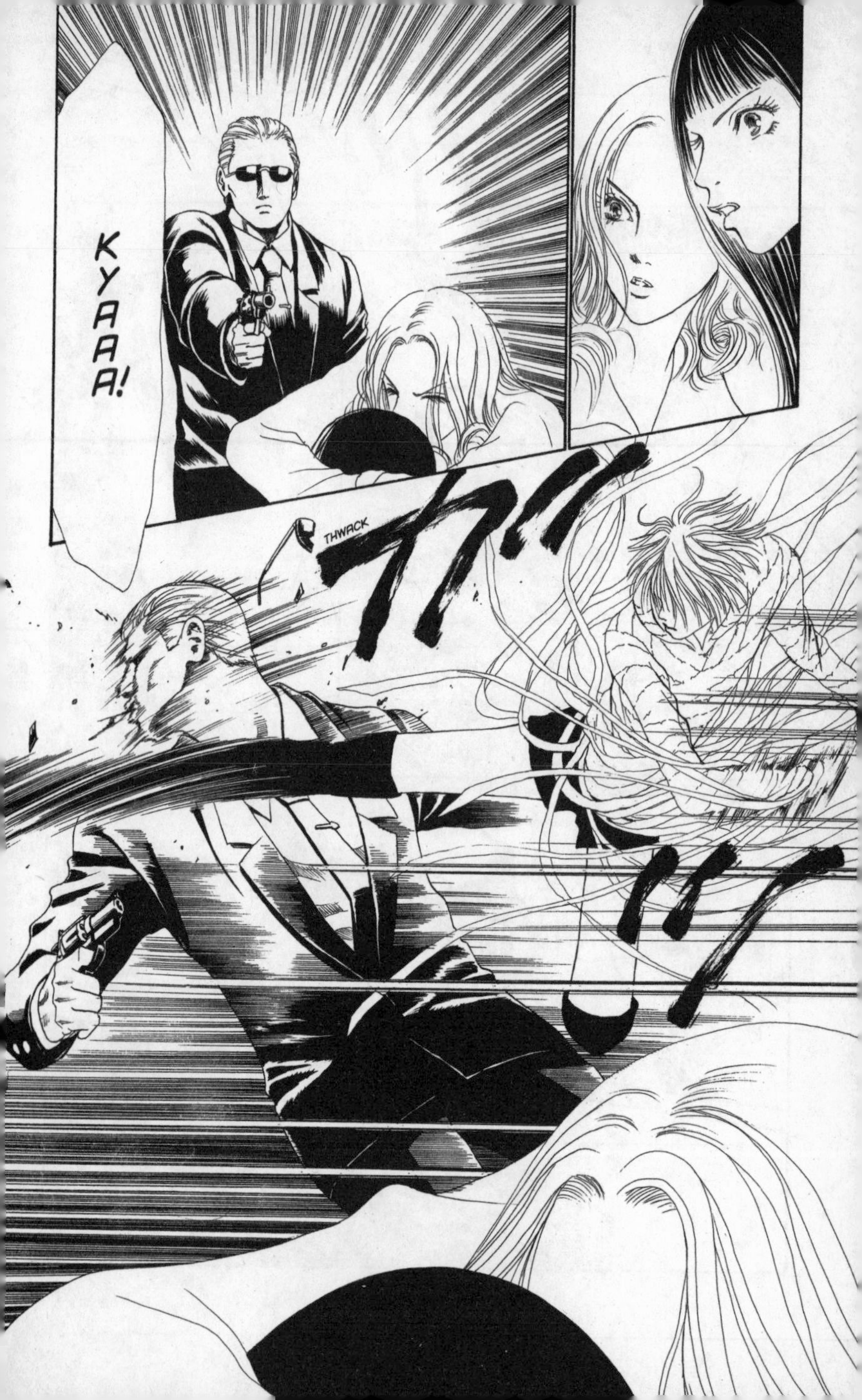
KYAAAA!
THWACK

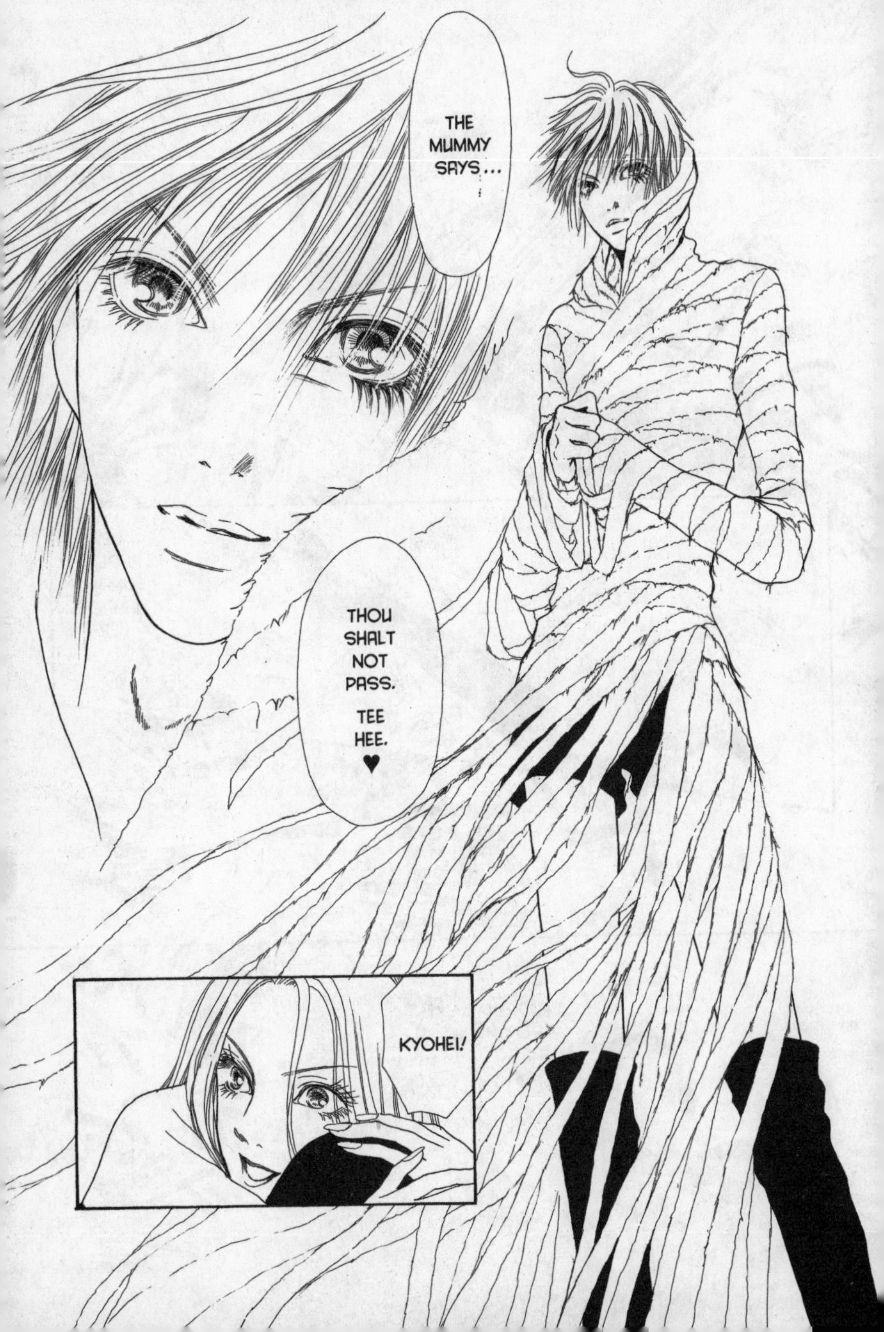
THE MUMMY SAYS...
THOU SHALT NOT PASS. TEE HEE. ♥
KYOHEI!

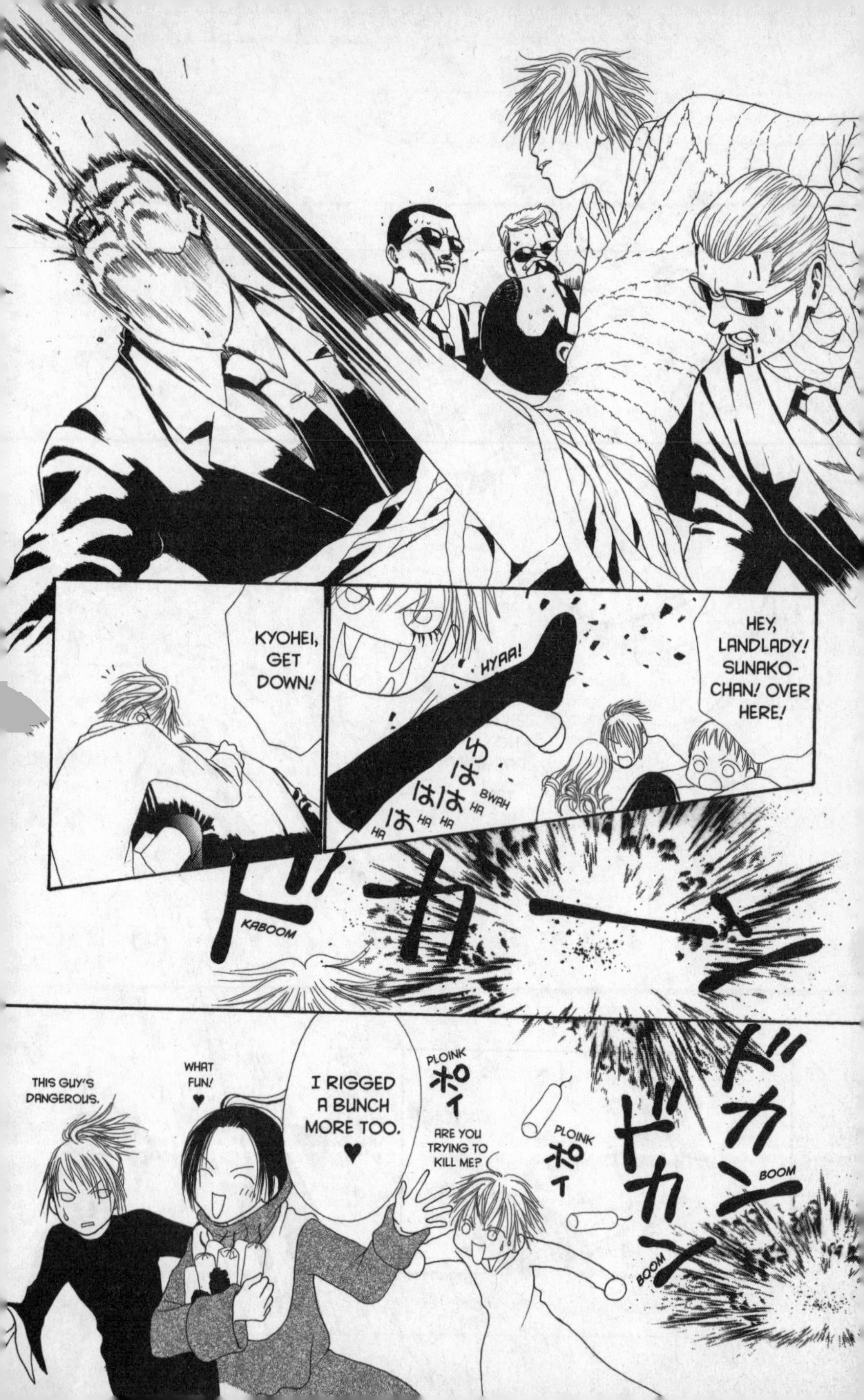
HEY, LANDLADY! SUNAKO-CHAN! OVER HERE!
HYAA!
ゆはははは
BWAH HA HA HA HA
KYOHEI, GET DOWN!
ドカーン
KABOOM
ドカン
BOOM
ドカン
BOOM
ポイ
PLOINK
ARE YOU TRYING TO KILL ME?
ポイ
PLOINK
I RIGGED A BUNCH MORE TOO. ♥
WHAT FUN! ♥
THIS GUY'S DANGEROUS.

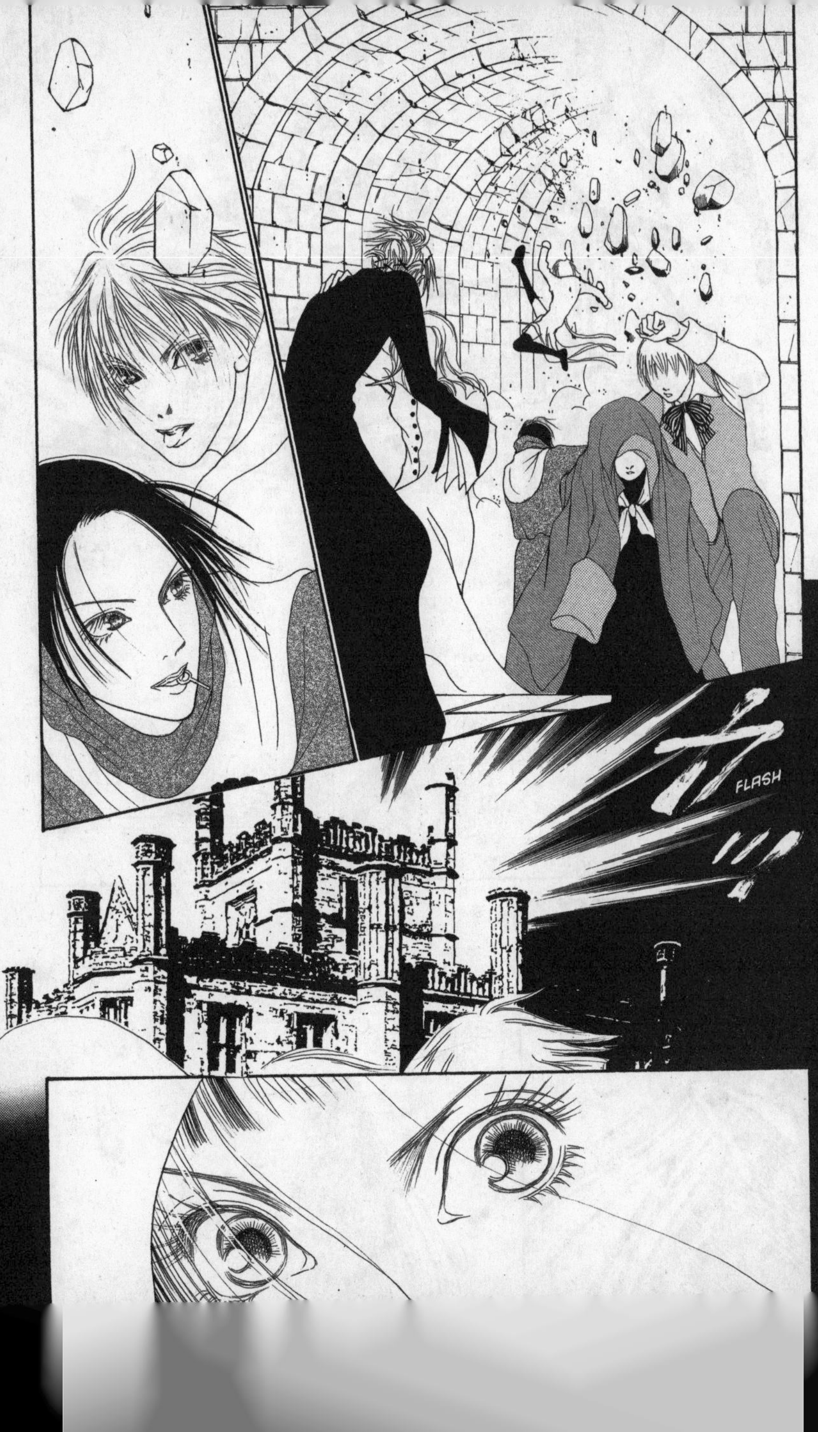
FLASH

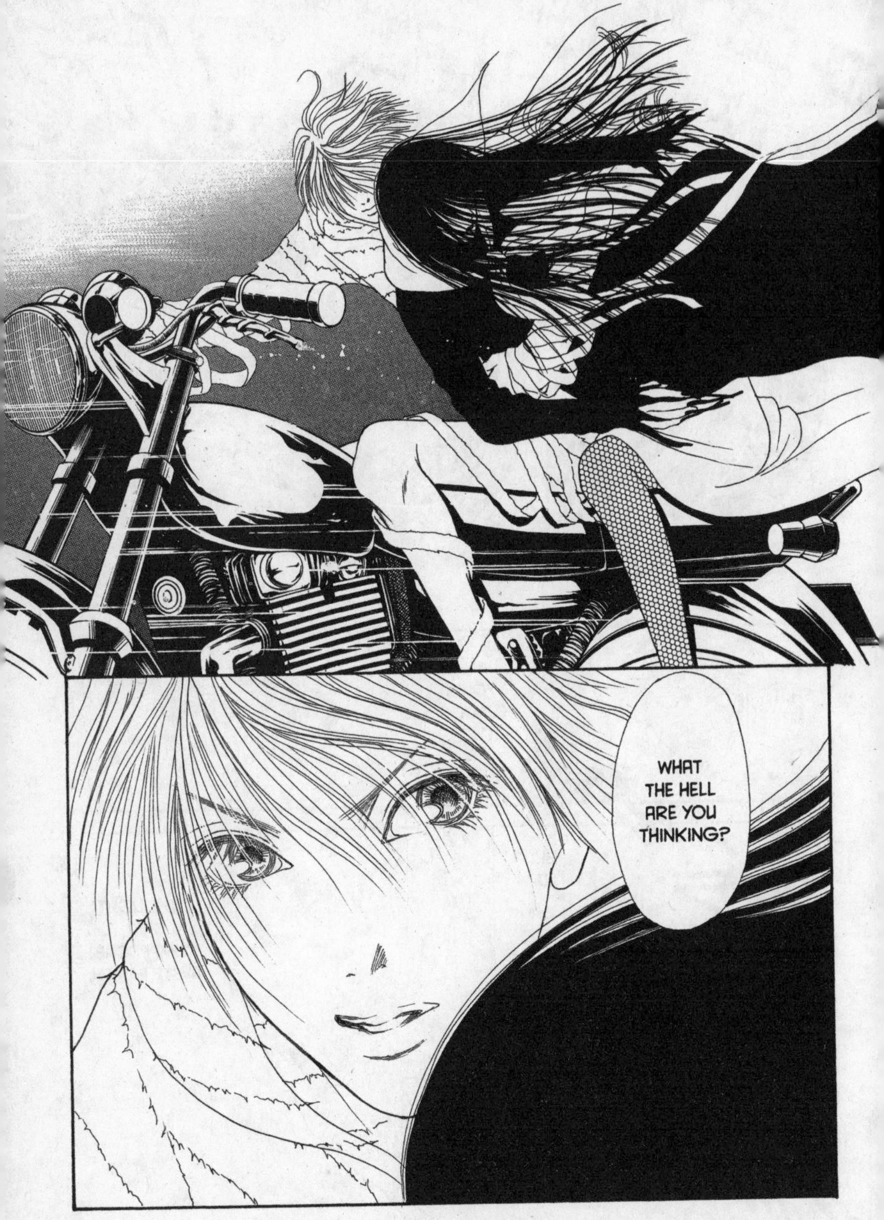
WHAT THE HELL ARE YOU THINKING?

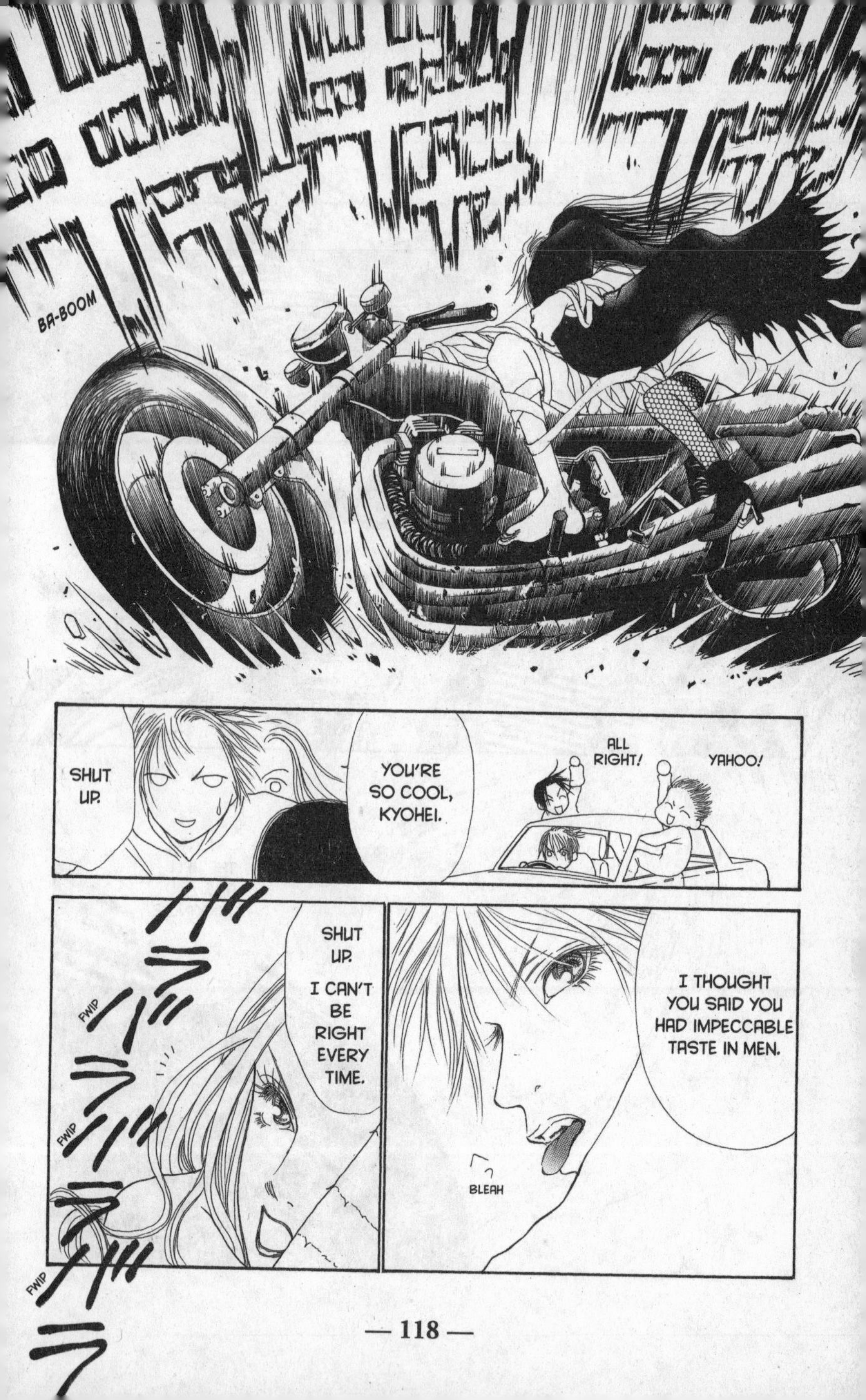
BA-BOOM
YAHOO!
ALL RIGHT!
YOU'RE SO COOL, KYOHEI.
SHUT UP.
I THOUGHT YOU SAID YOU HAD IMPECCABLE TASTE IN MEN.
BLEAH
SHUT UP.
I CAN'T BE RIGHT EVERY TIME.
FWIP
FWIP
FWIP

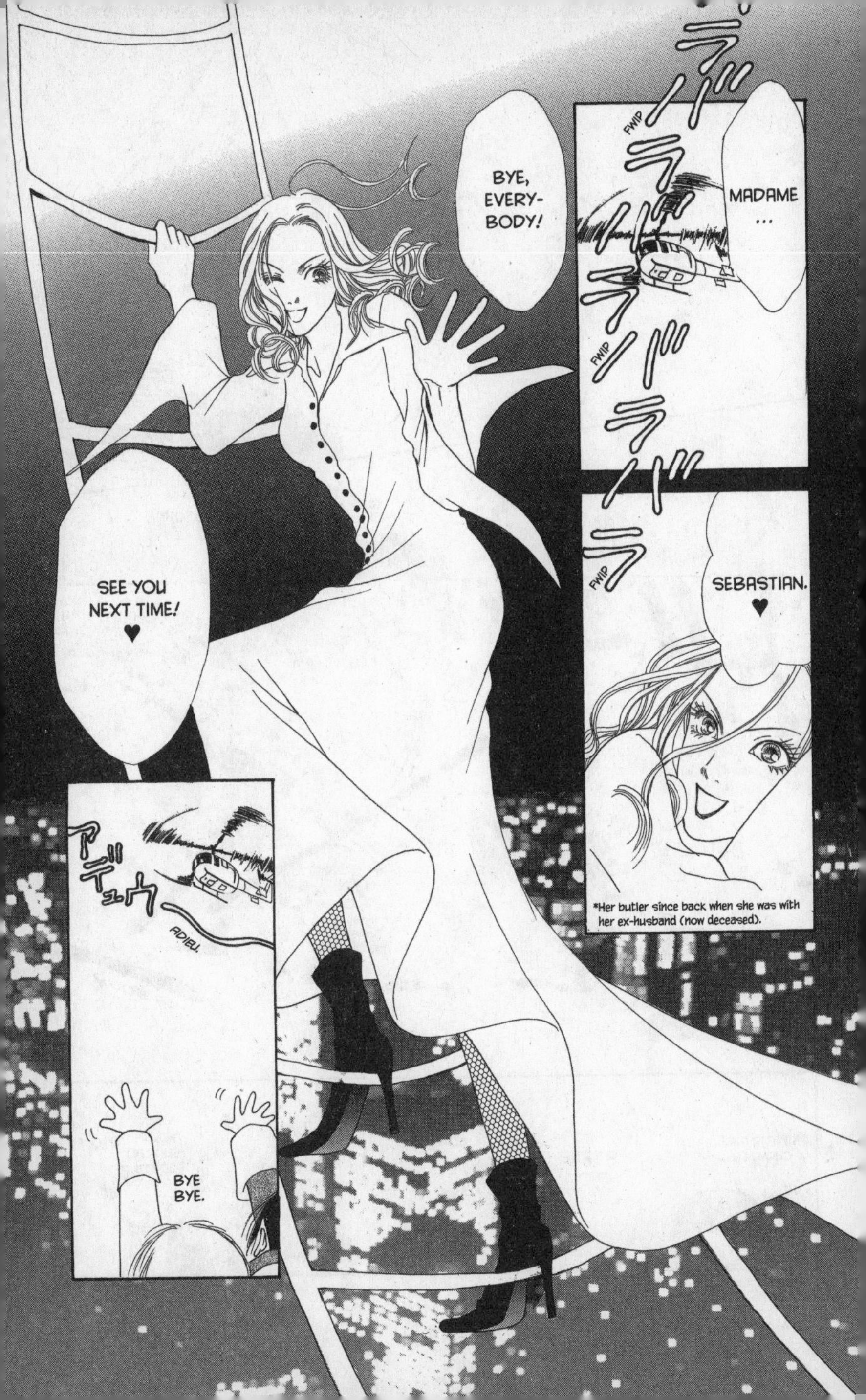
MADAME ...
FWIP
FWIP
FWIP
SEBASTIAN. ♥
*Her butler since back when she was with her ex-husband (now deceased).
BYE, EVERY-BODY!
SEE YOU NEXT TIME! ♥
アデュウ
ADIEU.
BYE BYE.

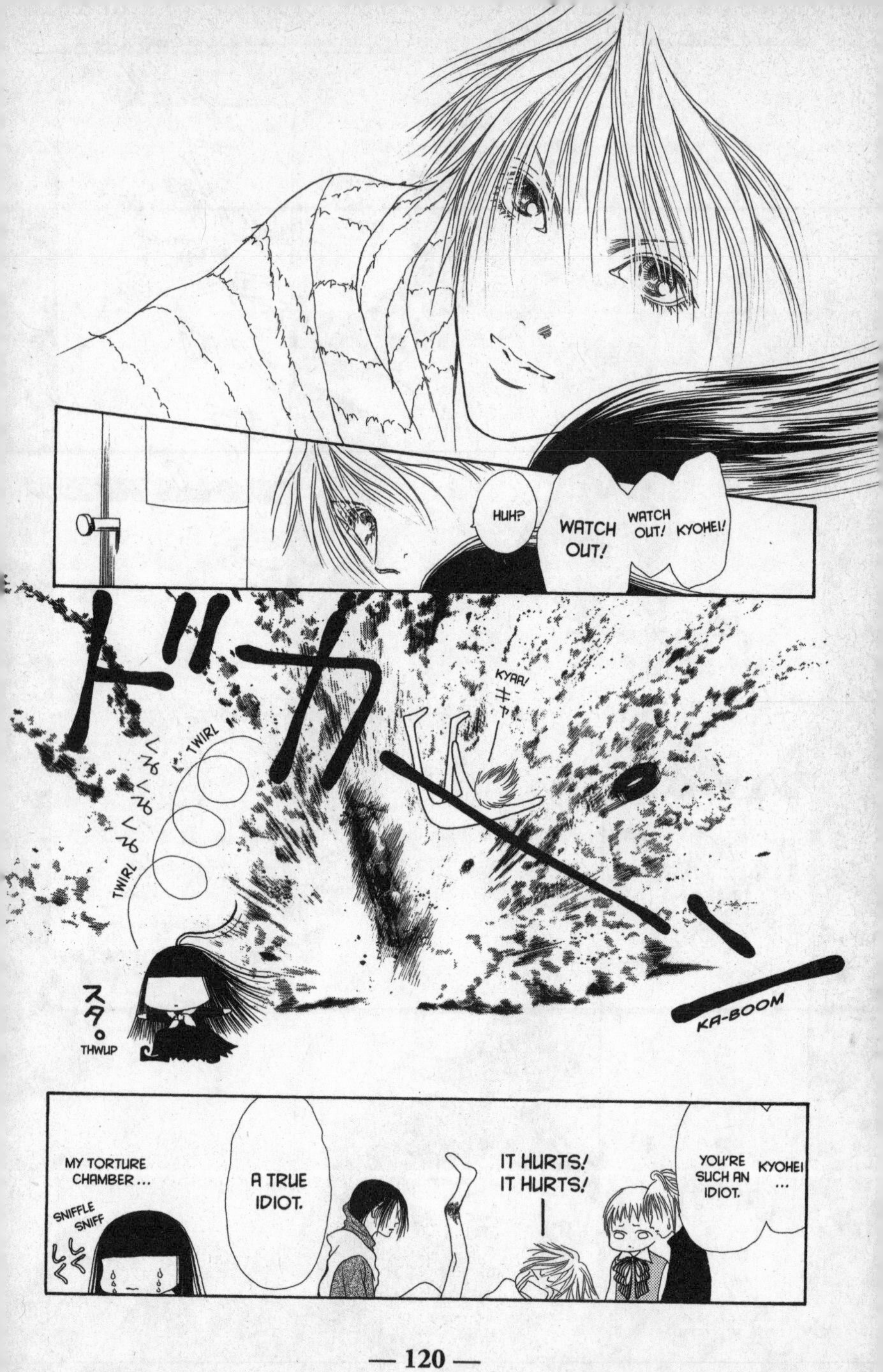
WATCH OUT! KYOHEI!
WATCH OUT!
HUH?
ドカーン
KA-BOOM
キャー
KYAA!
くるくるくる
TWIRL
TWIRL
スタ。
THWUP
KYOHEI ...
YOU'RE SUCH AN IDIOT.
IT HURTS! IT HURTS!
A TRUE IDIOT.
MY TORTURE CHAMBER ...
しくしく
SNIFFLE SNIFF

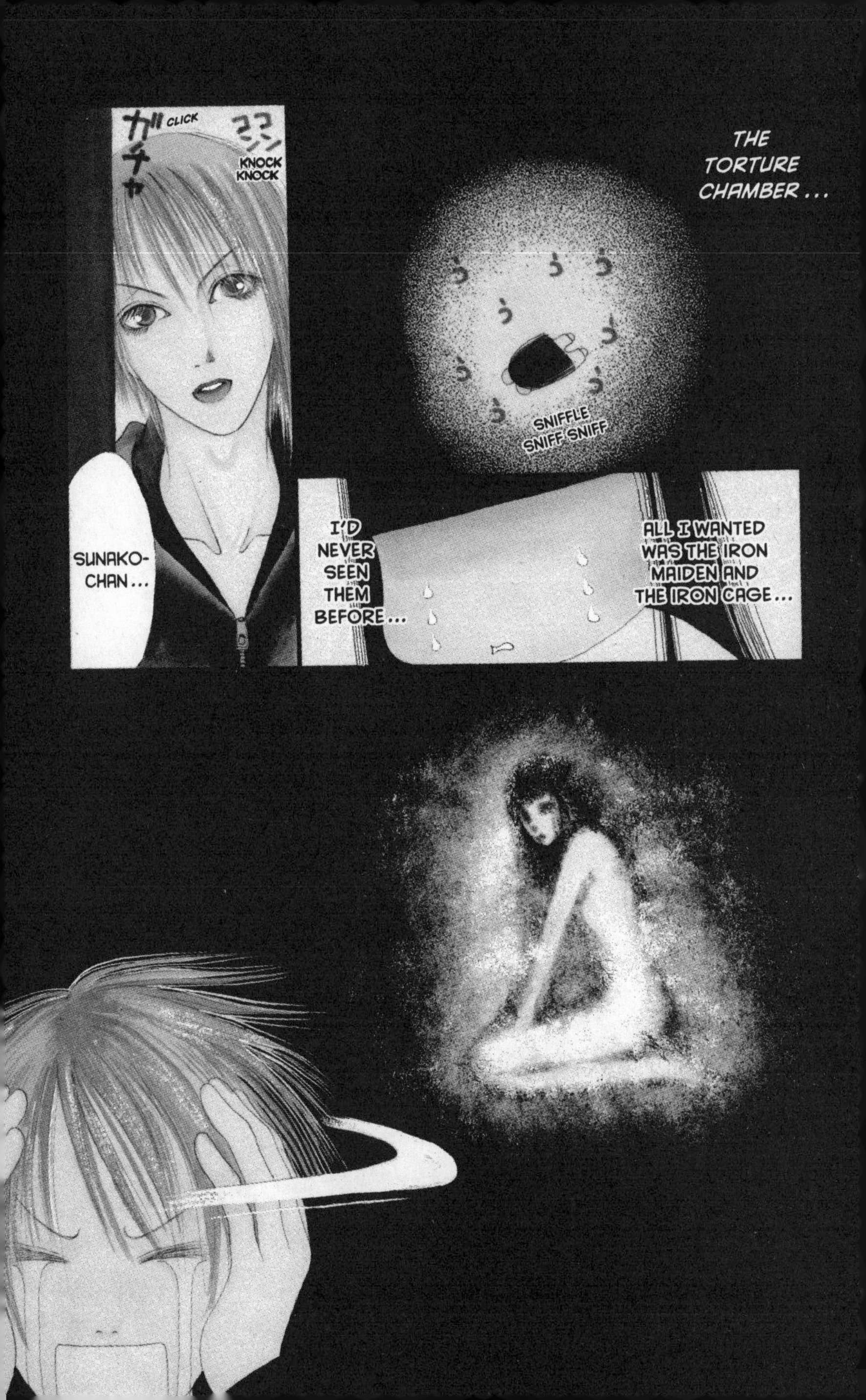
THE TORTURE CHAMBER ...
SNIFFLE SNIFF SNIFF
ALL I WANTED WAS THE IRON MAIDEN AND THE IRON CAGE ...
I'D NEVER SEEN THEM BEFORE ...
KNOCK KNOCK
CLICK
SUNAKO-CHAN ...

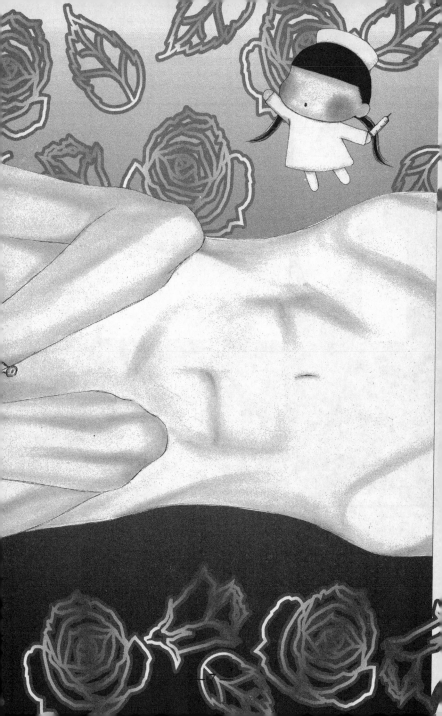

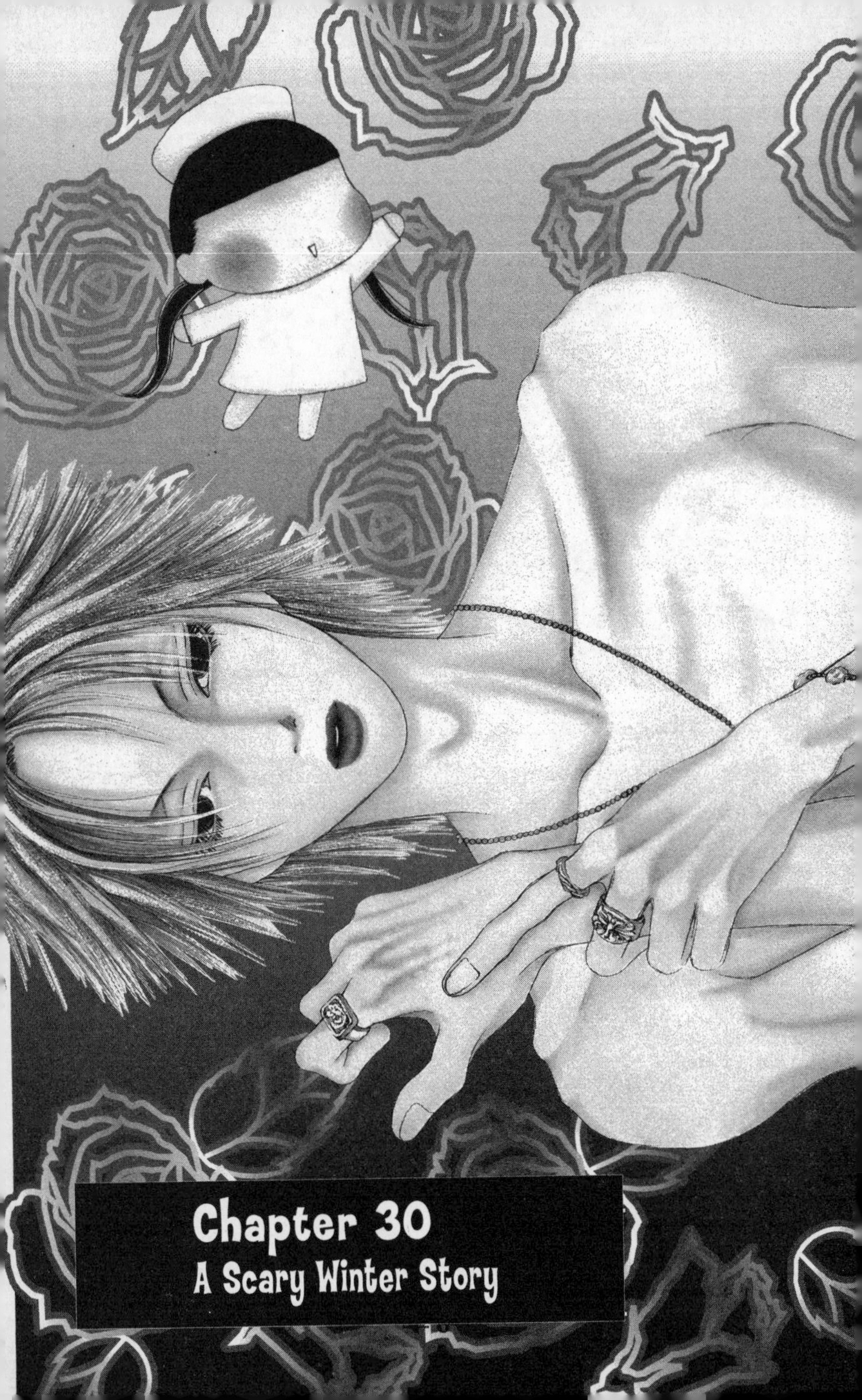

Chapter 30
A Scary Winter Story

WEIRD PEOPLE I FOUND IN THE CITY

LIVE COMEDY ②

I OVERHEARD A CONVERSATION BETWEEN A COUPLE (?).

WOW! THE HAMBURGER PLATE IS ONLY 580 YEN! THAT'S SO CHEAP. ♥

I'M GETTING THAT! ♥

A LONG TIME AGO, WHEN I WAS HAVING DINNER AT A DINER IN MEGURO... (I WAS LIVING IN MEGURO AT THE TIME.)

MY HAIR WAS BLACK AND I HAD A PERM.

YOU WOULD MAKE SUCH A CUTE KITTY.

ENNUI ↓

BLEAH

I...

...WANT TO BE A CAT IN MY NEXT LIFE.

UM, HELLO... YOU GUYS... THIS IS A PUBLIC PLACE!

WOULD YOU BE MY MASTER?

FWAH

IF I WERE BORN AS A CAT...

THEY WERE PERFECT FOR EACH OTHER.

BLUSH

FWAH

FOREVER.

BOTH OF THEM WERE KIND OF AVERAGE-LOOKING.

LIVE COMEDY ①

AND THAT'S WHEN I SAW...

I WANT AN OMELET OVER RICE!

ONE DAY AFTER MIDNIGHT, I WENT TO A CERTAIN RESTAURANT IN KOMAZAWA WITH ARAKI-KUN AND IYU KOZAKURA. THE TWO OF THEM HAD COME OVER TO HELP ME WORK ON MY MANGA.

(I WAS LIVING IN KOMAZAWA AT THAT TIME.)

IYU KOZAKURA

ARAKI-KUN

KNOW WHAT I'M SAYING, HONEY? BLAH, BLAH, BLAH... SO THEN I SAID...

HE WAS TALKING TO SOME (POSEUR-LOOKING) ROCKER CHICK.

...THIS GUY IN THE ENTERTAINMENT BIZ WHO LOOKED AS IF HE'D WALKED STRAIGHT OUT OF A COMEDY SKIT...!

BROWN HAIR

HE HAD SHOULDER-LENGTH HAIR, DARK SKIN, AND A MUSTACHE.

IT WOULD'VE BEEN PERFECT IF HE HAD HIS SWEATSHIRT LIKE THIS!

TALKING VERY LOUD

SO... DO YOU STILL THINK ABOUT YOUR FANS EVEN THOUGH YOU'VE LEFT THE BUSINESS?

ALL I CARE ABOUT IS SINGING, YOU KNOW...

THEY WERE SO FUNNY THAT ARAKI-KUN AND I COULDN'T STOP STARING.

SUPPOSEDLY, SHE WAS SOME (FAMOUS) SINGER. I DIDN'T RECOGNIZE HER FACE. I WONDER WHO SHE WAS....

PASSIONATE COMEDIC CONVERSATION

I JUST CAN'T STAND BEING SCREWED BY THE RECORD COMPANIES ANYMORE!

BUT WHAT'S GONNA HAPPEN TO ALL YOUR FANS?

SERIOUSLY, I THOUGHT THEY WERE IN SOME KIND OF PRANK SHOW OR SOMETHING. I WAS LOOKING AROUND FOR A HIDDEN CAMERA.

?

ONE TIME, I SAW A GIRL SINGING OUT LOUD WHILE WAITING IN LINE AT A RAMEN RESTAURANT IN SETAGAYA. MAYBE IT WAS THE SAME GIRL ...(SHE WAS WITH A GUY TOO.) ↳ THE SONG SHE WAS SINGING WAS ♪ MEOW, MEOW, MEOW ♪

DID YOU FORGET THAT KYOHEI'S IN THE HOSPITAL?

?

YOU KNOW, THE UNIVERSITY HOSPITAL.

JUST DON'T LOOK.

JUST DON'T LOOK AT HER.

HE SAID HE REALLY WANTED TO EAT ONE OF YOUR OMELETS... AND SOME OF YOUR FRIED SHRIMP TOO.

I-I'LL GO BRING KYOHEI A CHANGE OF CLOTHES, SO...

WILL YOU MAKE A BENTO FOR HIM?

BEHIND THE SCENES

FOR A LONG TIME, I'VE WANTED TO DRAW A STORY ABOUT A "FRAGILE BISHONEN BOY," SINCE THE FOUR MAIN CHARACTERS ARE SO TOUGH. IT WAS REALLY HARD TO COME UP WITH A GOOD HAIRSTYLE FOR HIM. HEH, HEH.

WHEN I WAS DRAWING THE NAKED PICTURE OF KYOHEI FOR THE SPLASH PAGE, I NEEDED A MODEL, SO I MADE A FRIEND OF MINE, WHO JUST HAPPENED TO BE VISITING, STRIP DOWN ... THEN I TOOK A PHOTO. MY POOR FRIEND....I'M SORRY....YOU WERE JUST IN THE WRONG PLACE AT THE WRONG TIME.

NO WAY!

CLICK CLICK

TAKE THEM OFF.

YOUR JEANS ARE IN THE WAY.

THE DEADLINE FOR THIS STORY WAS THE SAME DAY AS THE BAROKKU CONCERT. (WHY IS IT ALWAYS THE SAME DAY?)

I'LL TALK MORE ABOUT THAT DAY IN THE BONUS MANGA AT THE END OF THE BOOK.

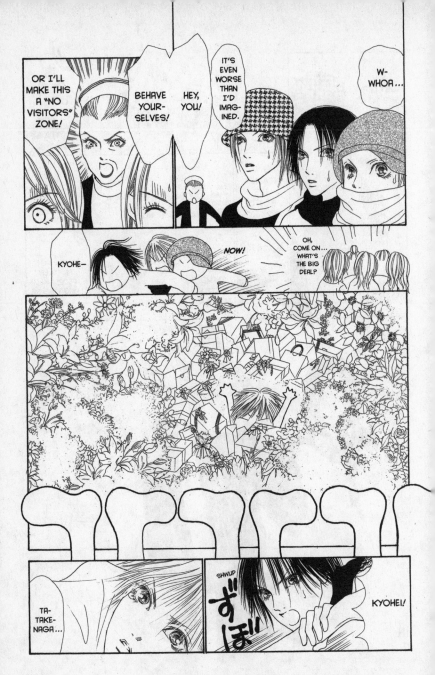

WAIT!

FINALLY, I CAN RELAX AND ENJOY MY FOOD.

FINALLY...

WELL THEN, I'LL JUST BE—

YUM ♥ YUM ♥

SNIFFLE SNIFF SNIFF

I NEED YOU TO STAY HERE AND DRIVE AWAY THE EVIL SPIRITS!

NO THANKS.

YEAH? SO WHAT?

YOU CAN'T LEAVE ME ALONE IN HERE.

THERE'S SOMETHING CREEPY ABOUT THIS ROOM.

BWAH

KYAA! A GHOST!

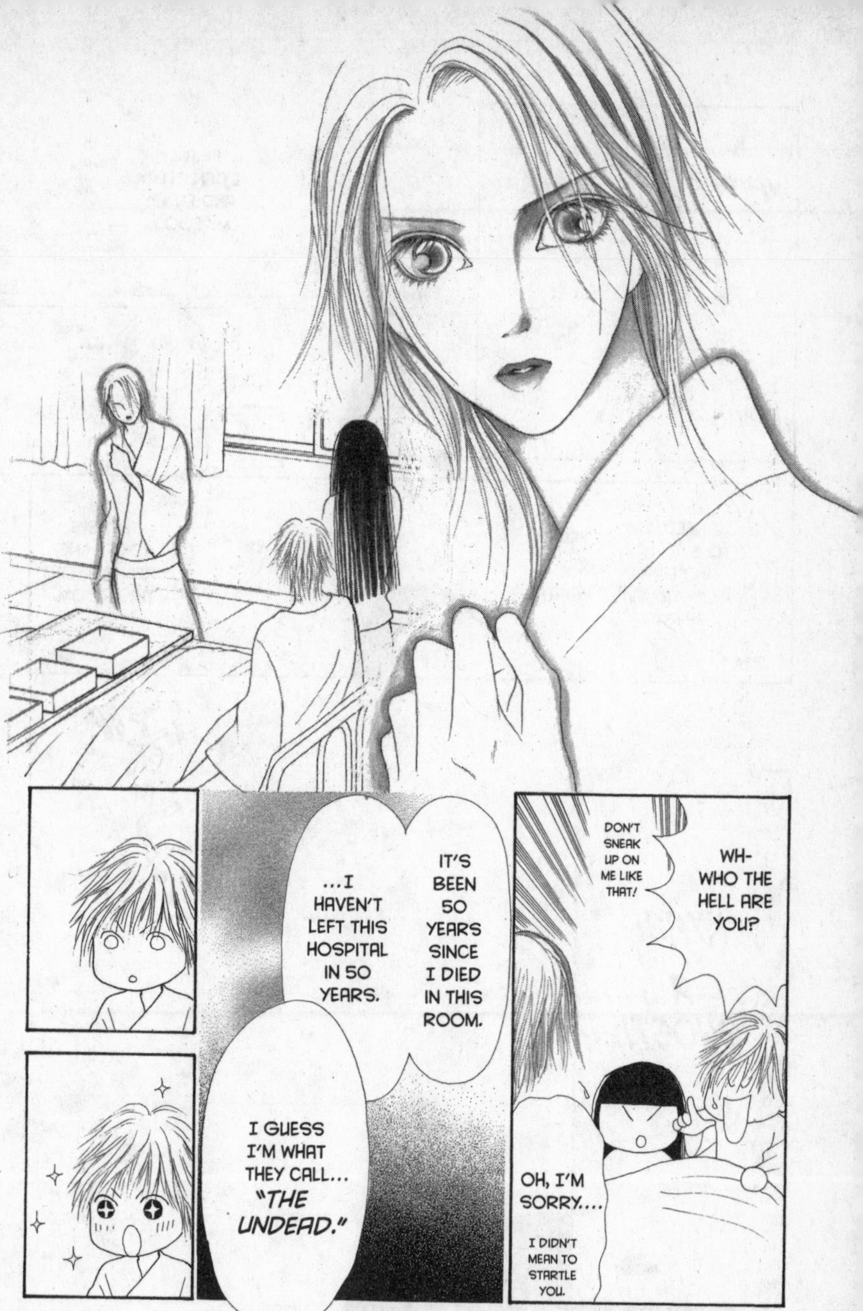
WH- WHO THE HELL ARE YOU?
DON'T SNEAK UP ON ME LIKE THAT!
OH, I'M SORRY....
I DIDN'T MEAN TO STARTLE YOU.
IT'S BEEN 50 YEARS SINCE I DIED IN THIS ROOM.
...I HAVEN'T LEFT THIS HOSPITAL IN 50 YEARS.
I GUESS I'M WHAT THEY CALL... "THE UNDEAD."

WOW...

I'VE NEVER MET A MORTAL...

IT MUST BE THANKS TO HER POWER.

...WHO CAN ACTUALLY SEE ME AND TALK TO ME.

YOU'RE WAY SCARIER THAN THIS GUY.

ARE YOU AFRAID OF GHOSTS?

GYA, HA, HA, HA! WOW!

SLAP SLAP

WHAT?

EVEN A REAL GHOST CAN'T BELIEVE IT.

HA, HA, HA, HA! THAT'S TOO FUNNY!

GYA, HA, HA!

Y-YOU MEAN SHE'S A REGULAR PERSON?

I'M TAMA. NICE TO MEET YOU.

I'M SO GLAD TO HAVE SOMEONE TO TALK TO.

I'M KYOHEI.

THUD

AH... SUNAKO-CHAN IS PASSED OUT.

HAHH HAHH HAHH HAHH

K-KYOHEI...

TH-THEY'VE ALL GONE HOME.

AH... HE'S GONE.

HEY, TAMA... THESE ARE MY FRIENDS...

...WITH A FACE JUST LIKE A GIRL'S.

HE'S A REAL HOT "BISHONEN BOY"...

A GHOST. ♥

WHO'RE YOU TALKING TO?

GRR

YOU'D BETTER GET SOME TESTS DONE.

MAYBE YOU HAVE A FEVER.

ARE YOU OKAY, KYOHEI?

DON'T JOKE AROUND ABOUT STUFF LIKE THAT.

STOP IT!

YOU ALWAYS SAY THAT.

SHE REALLY IS SCARIER THAN THE REAL THING.

HMM...

CLOP CLOP

ビ SHIVER

むく FWIP

NO! IT'S JUST A PERSON!

AH! A GHOST!

HELP ME, GOD...

MAYBE I'M IMAGINING THINGS.

I FEEL LIKE I JUST SAW SOMETHING HORRIBLY FRIGHTENING.

ポ BOING

SO IF I WERE AN EMPLOYEE, I COULD GET IN...

ONLY EMPLOYEES ARE ALLOWED PAST THIS POINT.

WHAT DO YOU THINK YOU'RE DOING?

OH, SHE'S HUMAN.

AH!

SPARKLE
SPARKLE

YOU REALLY THINK I'M GONNA FALL FOR A BRAT LIKE YOU?

YOU'RE JUST A LITTLE KID.

フン
HMMPH.

THERE IT IS!

ガーン
SHOCK

YOU MUST REALLY CARE ABOUT YOUR PATIENTS.

FEEL BETTER!

GOOD LUCK, RANMARU.

WELL, I GUESS WE'RE GOING.

ガーン
ガーン
ガーン
SHOCK

A BRAT LIKE ME... A BRAT LIKE ME...?

HEY, THERE'S SUNAKO-CHAN!

WE'RE GOING—

— 137 —

SHIVER

HAHH HAHH

I'M LOST...

YEAH.

YOU'RE LOOKING FOR SOMETHING?

THERE WAS A LETTER THAT I WANTED TO GIVE MY GIRLFRIEND, BUT...

I CAN'T REMEMBER WHERE I HID IT.

FIFTY YEARS !?

AND THAT'S WHY YOU'VE BEEN HERE FOR THE PAST 50 YEARS?

YOU'RE STILL GETTING TONS OF LETTERS FROM GIRLS.

WELL, I DON'T KNOW...

...IF THAT'S WHY EXACTLY, BUT...

THEN I'LL WRITE ONE TO YOU, KAYO-CHAN.

YOU'RE SO LUCKY.

I'VE NEVER EVEN GOTTEN A LOVE LETTER BEFORE.

THAT'S WHY I'M GOING TO WRITE ONE TO YOU...

THAT'S WHY—

DON'T BE STUPID. YOU ONLY WRITE LOVE LETTERS WHEN YOU'RE IN LOVE WITH SOMEONE.

YOU PROMISE?

I MEAN, I'M ALREADY DEAD.

IT'S NOT LIKE I COULD GIVE IT TO HER EVEN IF I FOUND IT...

WHOOSH

HEY, YOU!

GRR

AHH... LOVE IN THE SHOWA ERA...

LOVE IS A MANY SPLEN-DORED THING. ♥

CREAK キィ…

B- BEHIND THIS DOOR...

ドキ ドキ THUMP THUMP

ドキ ドキ THUMP THUMP

ばたり。 THUD

HAVE I JUST BEEN WASTING MY TIME?

She was hiding up on the roof.

ガチ SHIVER ガチガチ

ガチガチ SHIVER

う SNIFF

う う う SNIFF

SHIVER SHIVER ビク ビク

TIP TOE そ

GUESS I HAVE NO CHOICE...

YOU IDIOT!

DO YOU KNOW WHERE THEY CARRY OUT THE HUMAN EXPERIMENTS?

DO....

SHY

SHOCK

UH... UM...

.THEN... THEN...

I AT LEAST WANT A SOUVENIR.

I'LL COME WITH YOU SO YOU WON'T GET LOST.

STRAIGHT-FORWARD

THERE AREN'T ANY.

WHAT?

?

?

SHIVER

HE'S GONE.

HE'S HERE.

HE'S HERE.

HE'S GONE.

WOW! LOOK AT ME!

I'M A SPIRITUAL MEDIUM!

YOU MEAN YOU CAN'T SEE ME UNLESS I'M NEXT TO KYOHEI?

SHIVER

I GUESS YOU CAN SENSE MY PRESENCE.

YOU DON'T HAVE TO COME WITH ME!

SHIVER

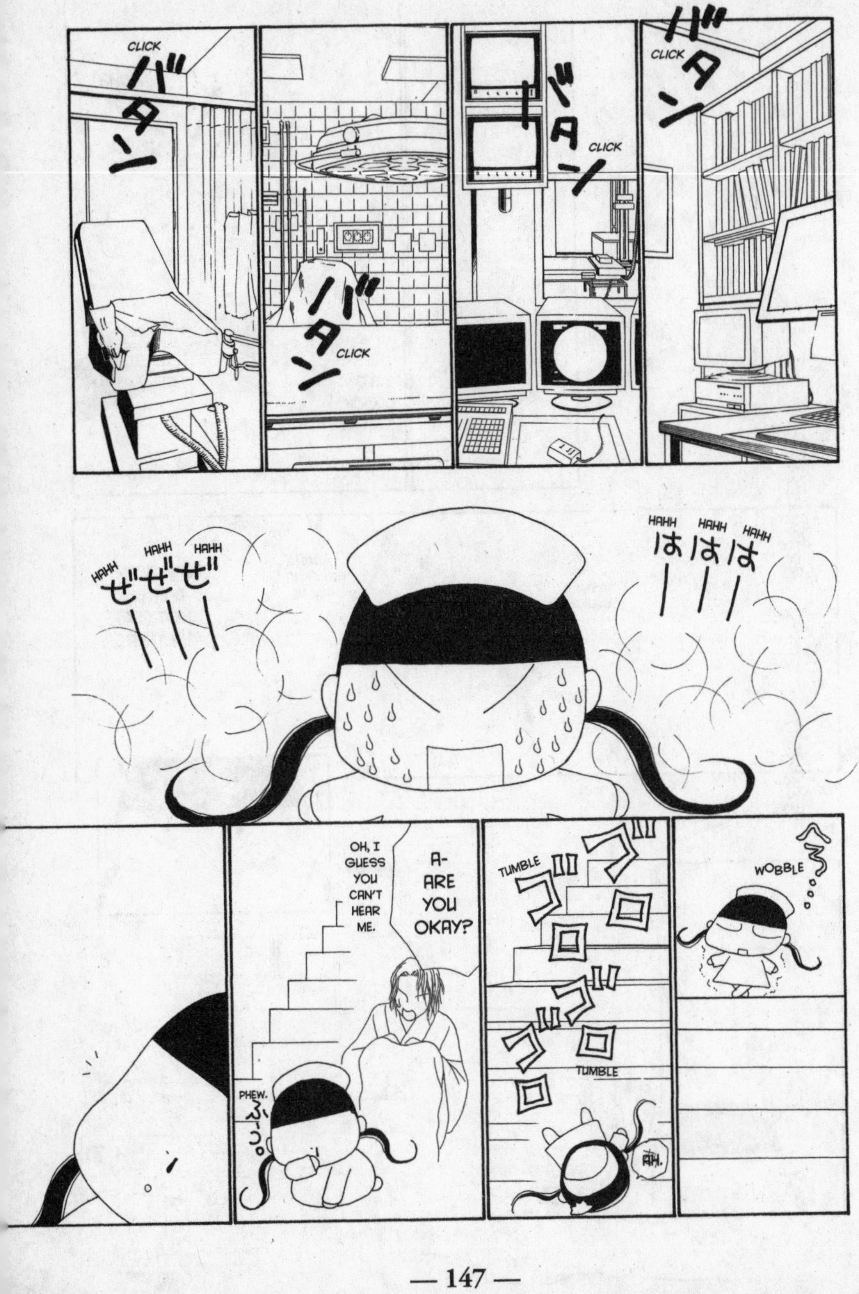
CLICK
バタン
CLICK
バターン
CLICK
バタン
CLICK
バタン
HAHH HAHH HAHH
ははは
HAHH HAHH HAHH
ぜぜぜ
WOBBLE
TUMBLE
TUMBLE
A- ARE YOU OKAY?
OH, I GUESS YOU CAN'T HEAR ME.
PHEW.
ふっ。

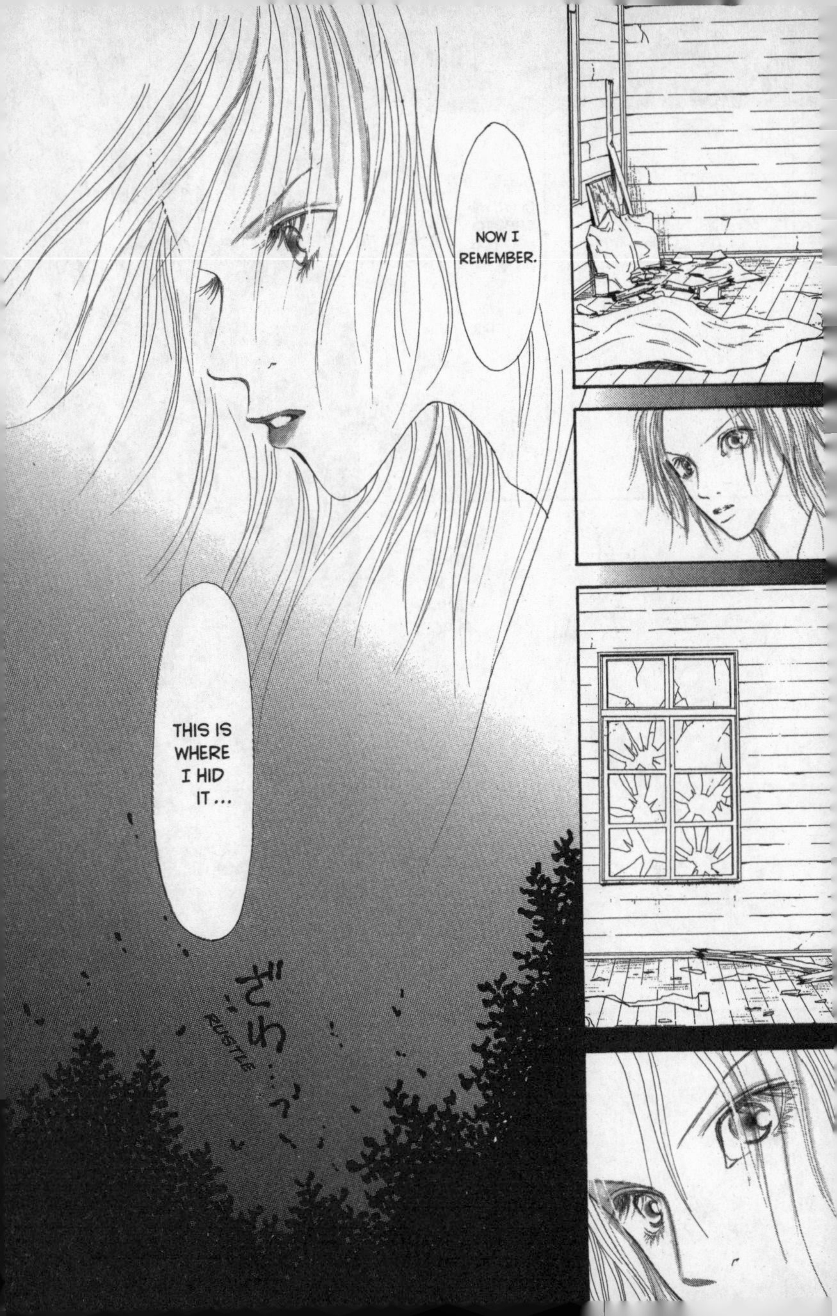
NOW I REMEMBER.
THIS IS WHERE I HID IT...
ざわ
RUSTLE

I DON'T KNOW IF I'LL LIVE THAT LONG.
QUIT TALKING NONSENSE! SOMEDAY YOU AND I WILL BE WORKING TOGETHER.
OKAY.
LET'S STAY TOGETHER FOREVER.
I'LL GIVE THIS TO HER TO-MORROW.
IT'D BE TOO EMBARRASSING IF SOMEONE FOUND IT, SO... I'LL JUST HIDE IT UP HERE.
THERE WE GO.
LIAR! YOU LIAR!
YOU SAID WE'D BE TOGETHER FOREVER!
YOU NEVER EVEN GAVE ME A LOVE LETTER!
YOU SAID YOU'D WRITE ONE FOR ME.
YOU PROMISED!

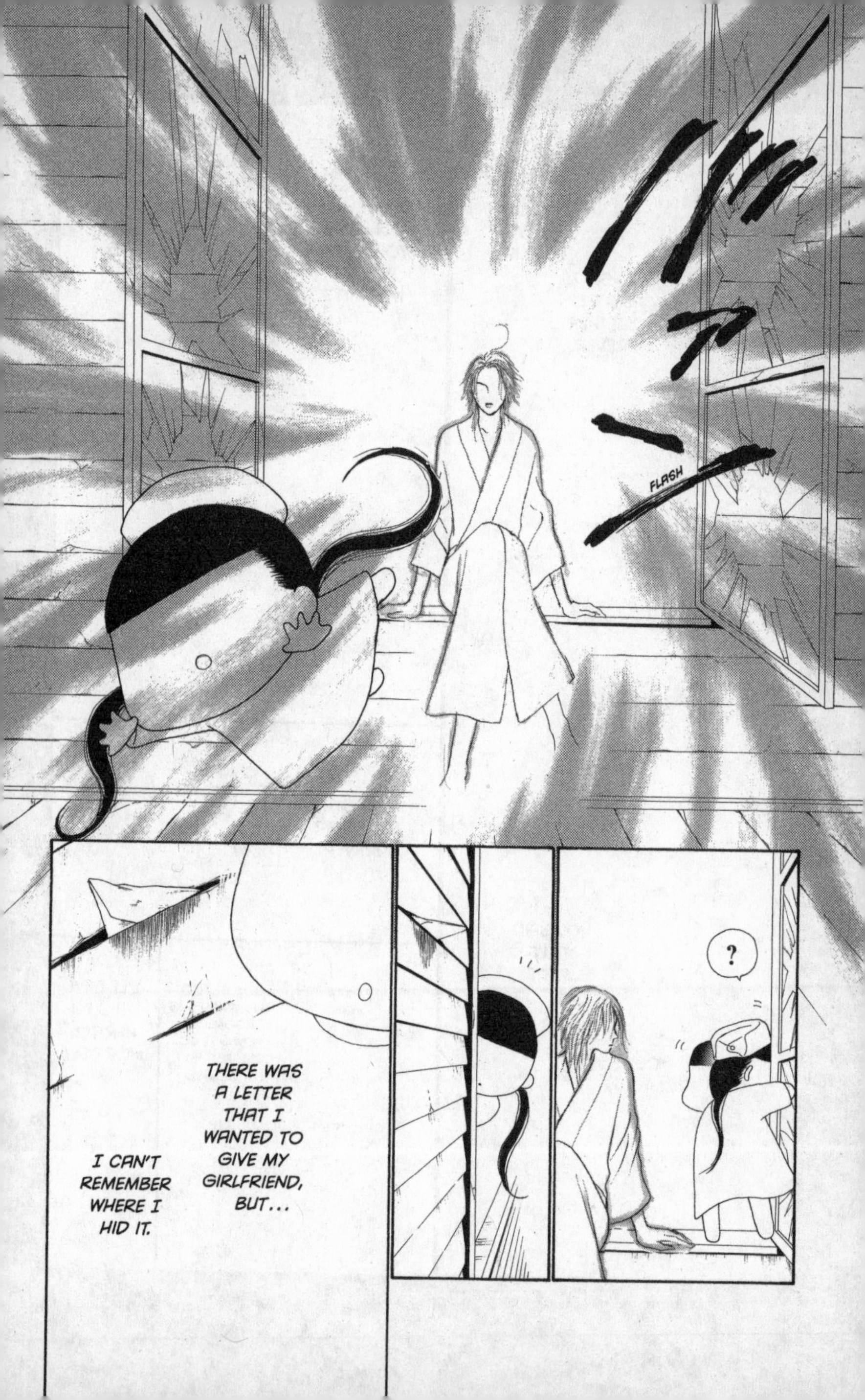
FLASH
?
THERE WAS A LETTER THAT I WANTED TO GIVE MY GIRLFRIEND, BUT...
I CAN'T REMEMBER WHERE I HID IT.

SLIP

ALL THIS TIME, I'D BEEN AVOIDING SEARCHING FOR IT!

SUNAKO!

I KNEW THAT IF I FOUND IT, I'D NEVER SEE KAYO-CHAN AGAIN...

I'D HAVE NO REASON TO LINGER HERE ANY LONGER...!

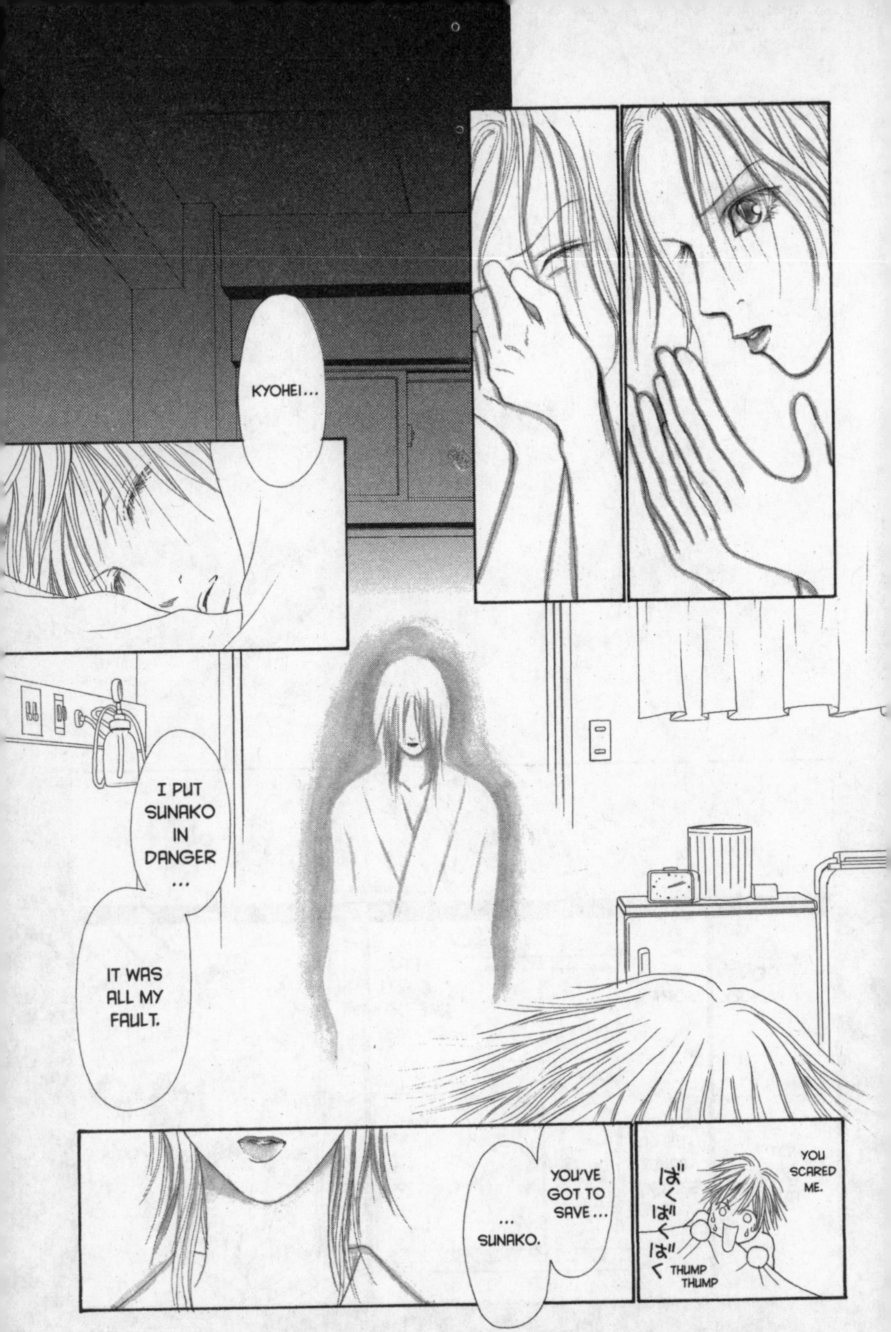
KYOHEI...
I PUT SUNAKO IN DANGER ...
IT WAS ALL MY FAULT.
YOU SCARED ME.
ばくばくばく
THUMP THUMP
YOU'VE GOT TO SAVE...
... SUNAKO.

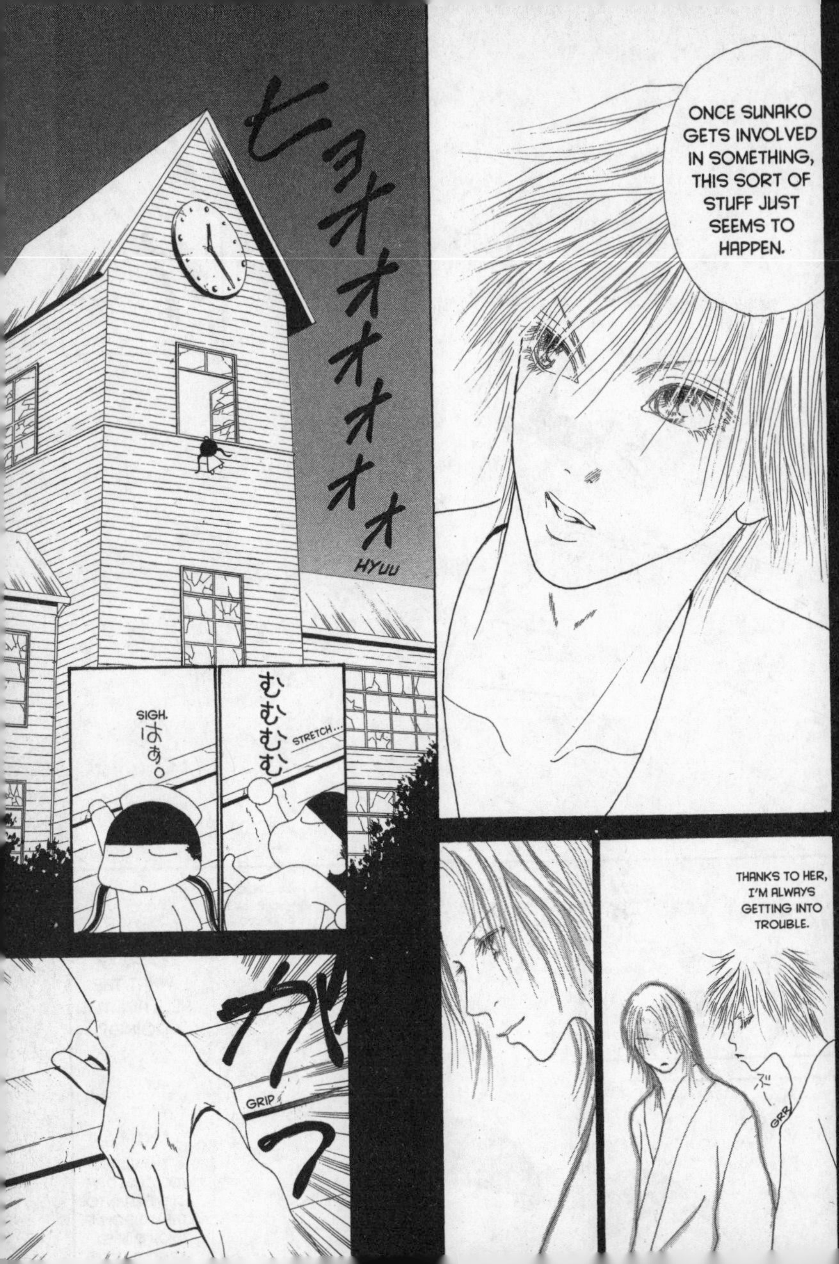
ONCE SUNAKO GETS INVOLVED IN SOMETHING, THIS SORT OF STUFF JUST SEEMS TO HAPPEN.
ヒョオオオオオオ
HYUU
むむむむ
STRETCH...
SIGH.
はぁ。
THANKS TO HER, I'M ALWAYS GETTING INTO TROUBLE.
GRR
GRIP

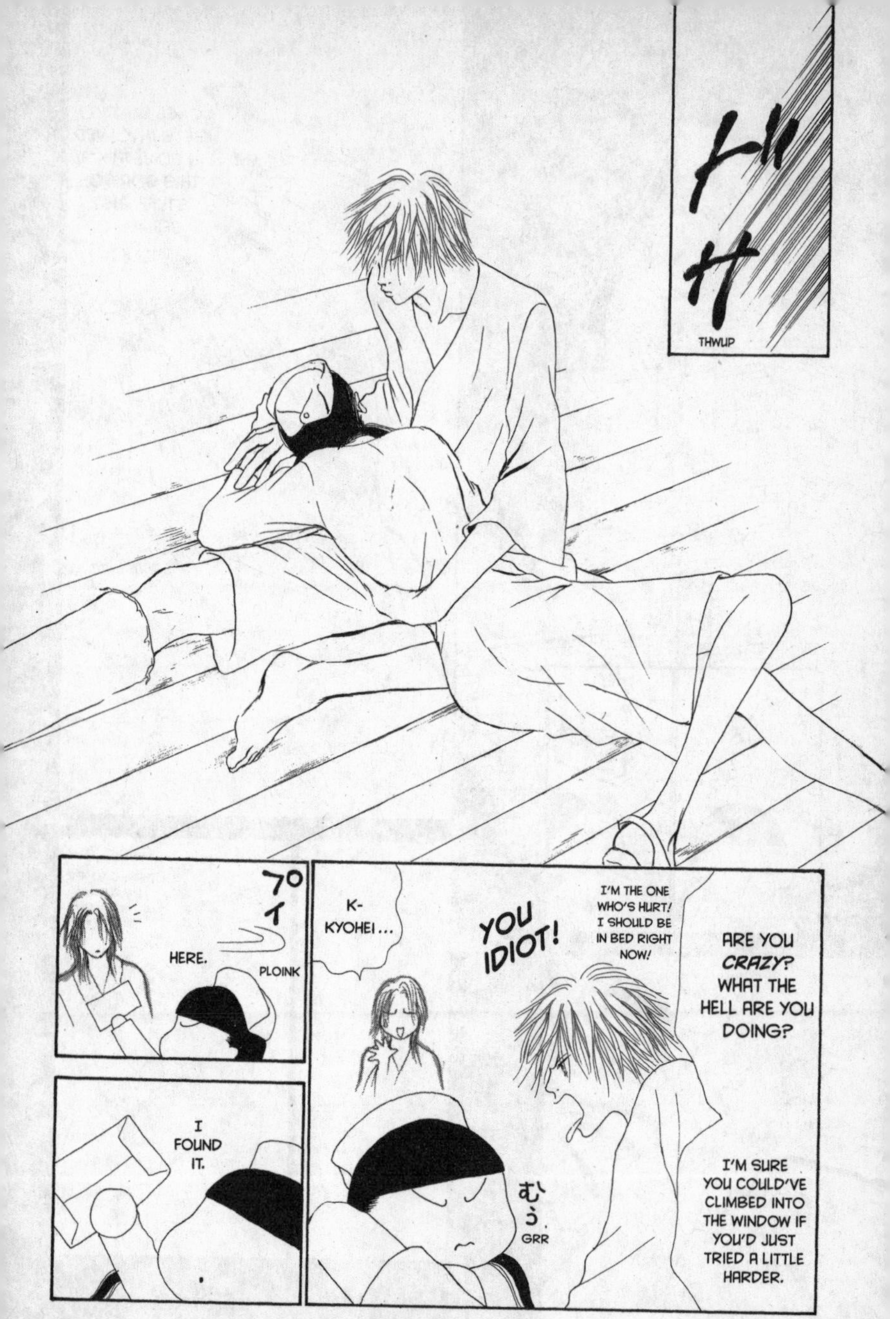
THWUP
ARE YOU *CRAZY*? WHAT THE HELL ARE YOU DOING?
I'M THE ONE WHO'S HURT! I SHOULD BE IN BED RIGHT NOW!
YOU IDIOT!
K-KYOHEI...
I'M SURE YOU COULD'VE CLIMBED INTO THE WINDOW IF YOU'D JUST TRIED A LITTLE HARDER.
むっ
GRR
プイ
PLOINK
HERE.
I FOUND IT.

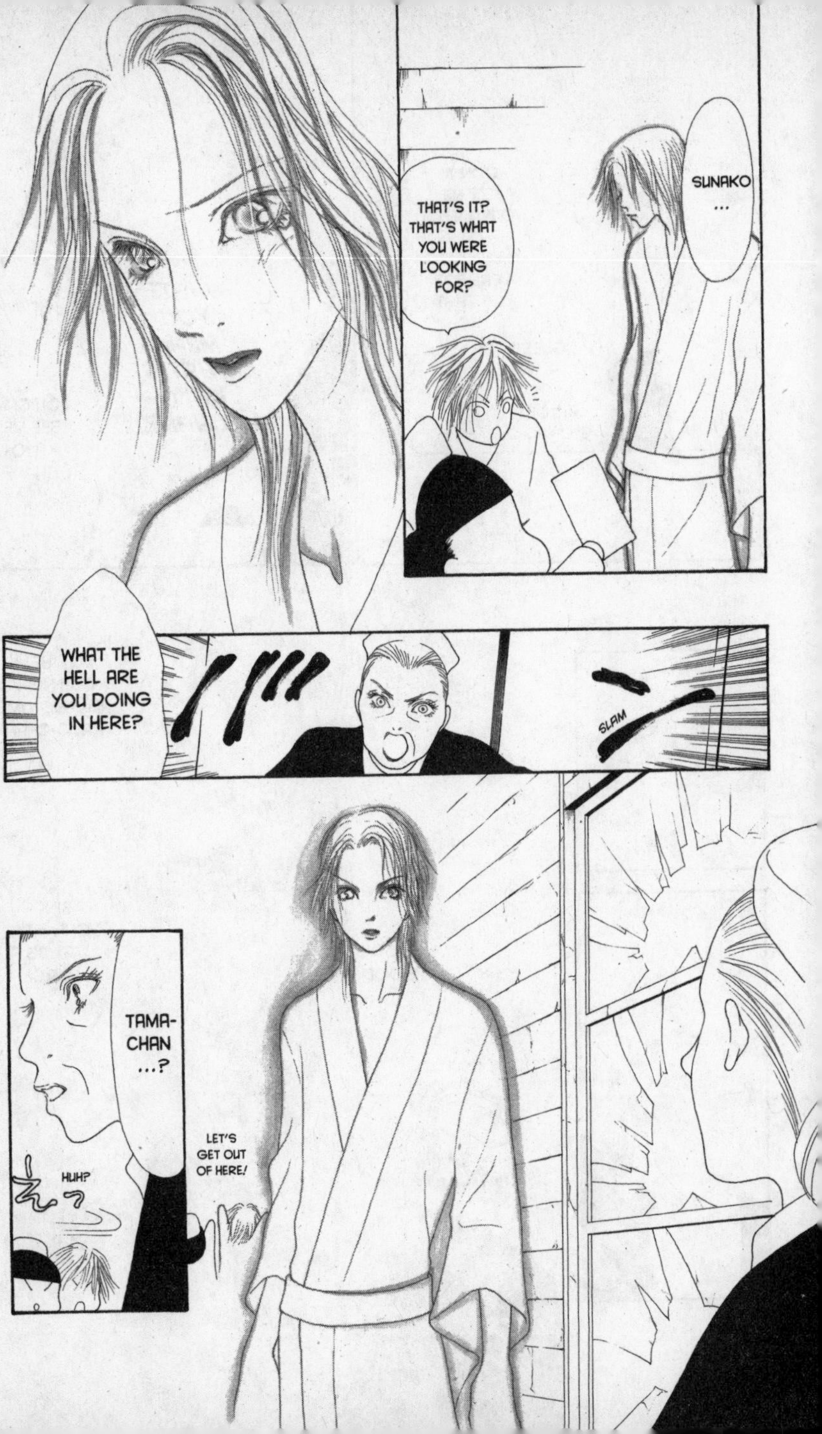

SUNAKO ...
THAT'S IT? THAT'S WHAT YOU WERE LOOKING FOR?
SLAM
WHAT THE HELL ARE YOU DOING IN HERE?
LET'S GET OUT OF HERE!
TAMA-CHAN ...?
HUH?

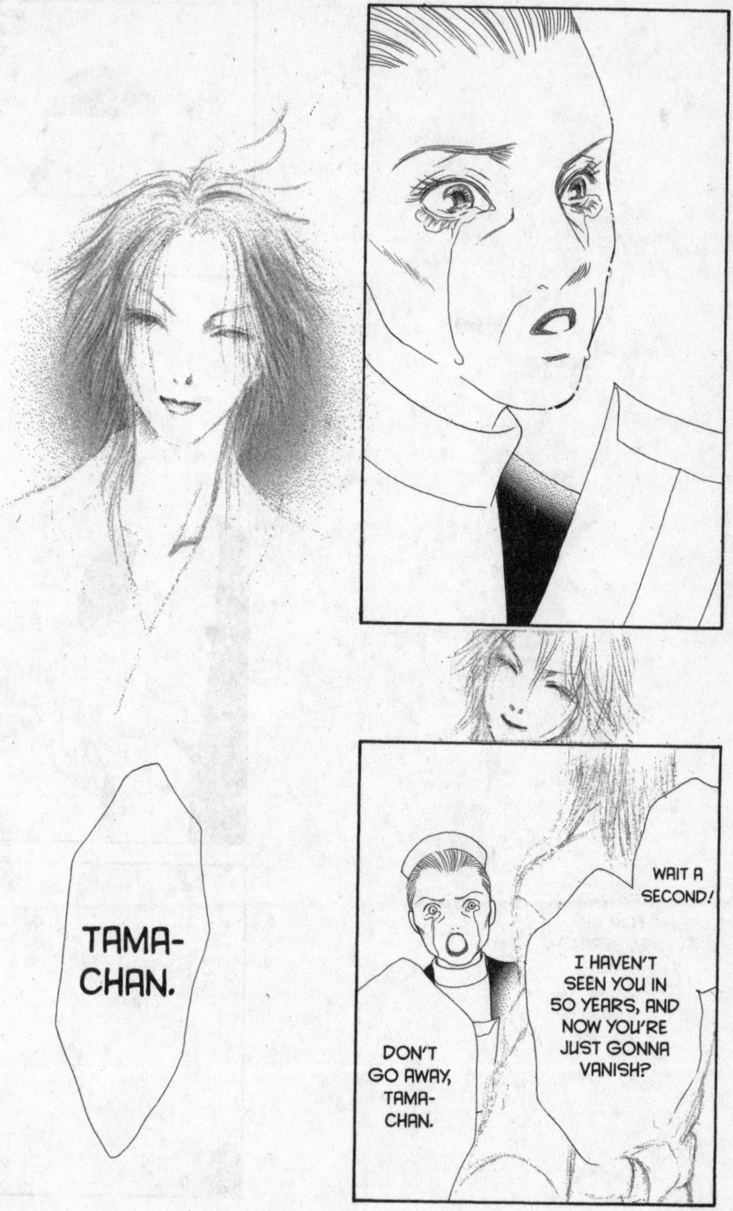
WAIT A SECOND!
I HAVEN'T SEEN YOU IN 50 YEARS, AND NOW YOU'RE JUST GONNA VANISH?
DON'T GO AWAY, TAMA-CHAN.
TAMA-CHAN.

THANK YOU SUNAKO. THANK YOU KYOHEI.

OH, FOR GOD'S SAKE...

ゴト……

THUD

SNIFF SNIFF SNIFF SNIFF

TAMA-CHAN...

CONTINUED IN WALLFLOWER BOOK 8

BACK IN AUGUST OF 2001... I WAS LUCKY ENOUGH TO GET A CHANCE TO TALK TO BANSAKU-KUN (THE BASS PLAYER) A LITTLE BIT BACKSTAGE (SEE BOOK 4), BUT THAT WAS IT. I HADN'T TALKED TO HIM SINCE. (I WENT TO TONS OF HIS CONCERTS SO MANY TIMES THOUGH...)

I'M SUCH A HUGE, HUGE FAN!

OVER A YEAR!

IT'S BEEN

OF COURSE! ♥

HHHH

BAN-CHAN GAVE ME **BACKSTAGE PASSES FOR THE BAROQUE CONCERT.**

WANNA GO?

ONE DAY BACK IN NOVEMBER...

I GOT A CALL FROM MASASHI TAKENAGA (SAMA), THE SINGER FROM THE BAND WRISK.

SO, I FINALLY MADE IT TO THE

BAROQUE
"PHEROMONE SHOWER" TOUR
AT ZEPP IN TOKYO ON NOVEMBER 29TH 2002!

APPARENTLY THEY SPELL THEIR NAME "BAROQUE" NOW.

THIS PASS IS VALID FOR FIVE PEOPLE.

TO WRISK-SAMA, VIP PASS FROM BANSAKU-BAROKKU

TAKENAGA-KUN (HE'S FRIENDS WITH BANSAKU-KUN. I ENVY HIM...)

YUJI (LOOKS A LITTLE BIT LIKE KIYOHARU.) WRISK'S ROADIE.

(LOOKS LIKE KIYOHARU)

YUKI-KUN. HE CANCELLED TWENTY MINUTES BEFORE THE SHOW.

BUTLER

I'D DO ANYTHING JUST TO SEE BANSAKU-KUN!

ME (I LOVE BANSAKU.) I LOVE KIYOHARU ♥ AS YOU ALREADY KNOW.

YEAH. ♥ I TOTALLY AGREE WITH YOU. ♥

BAN-CHAN WAS PRETTY COOL.

AND THEN THE SHOW FINALLY ENDED.

MELTING

AH...I REMEMBER WHEN I SAW KIYOHARU (SAMA) HERE. (I EVEN HAD THE SAME SEAT.)

I COULDN'T RESIST DANCING THAT TIME.

I CAN AT LEAST MOVE MY HANDS.

BLACK HOLE FILM...

IT WAS TOUGH FOR ME BECAUSE I COULDN'T DANCE DURING THE SHOW. I REALLY WANTED TO DANCE!

BUT I WAS AFRAID TO JOIN THE CROWD DOWNSTAIRS, BECAUSE THEY WERE SO ENERGETIC.

IN THIS TYPE OF SITUATION, YOU MUST BE VERY PATIENT AND WAIT FOR THE MEMBERS TO COME TALK TO YOU. OF COURSE THERE'S THE CHANCE THAT YOU MIGHT NOT GET TO TALK TO THEM AT ALL! (BANSAKU-KUN WAS TALKING TO YUUICHI-KUN FOR A LONG TIME.)

I GOT TO JOIN BAROQUE-SAN'S "BACKSTAGE AFTER PARTY." (IT TOOK PLACE INSIDE THE VENUE AFTER THE AUDIENCE HAD LEFT.)

I SPOTTED YUUICHI-KUN, CURRENTLY IN THE BAND I'LL (EX-NALSIST.)

AT THE CORRIDOR.

HEY! HOW'VE YOU BEEN?

HEY!

YU-YU-YUUICHI-KUN IS STANDING LESS THAN 1 METER FROM ME!

(TEXT MESSAGING) A FRIEND WHO'S ONE OF YUUICHI-KUN'S FANS.

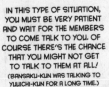

KYAA! KYAA! HE'S SO GORGEOUS! KYAA!

CALM DOWN.

WHOA! WHOA! IT'S BANSAKU-KUN! HE'S SO CLOSE! ♥♥♥

AND JUST THEN...!

I WAS BORED, SO I HUNG OUT WITH YUJI.

DON'T TURN YOUR HEAD, YUJI! I WANNA SEE YOUR FACE!

OKAY, OKAY.

OH, DO I? THANKS.

YOU LOOK LIKE BAN-CHAN FROM THIS SIDE.

WHOA. ♥

YOU LIKE KIYOHARU TOO. ♥

WHAT'S KIYOHARU'S PROBLEM? ALL HE DOES IS TALK TO YUUICHI.

HEY, YUJI.

MUMBLE

I WAS IN SUCH A BAD MOOD AFTER WAITING FOR SO LONG.

MUMBLE MUMBLE

PROBABLY REI-KUN'S FRIEND. HE WAS CUTE TOO.

STOP STARING.

STARING

HE WAS SO CUTE THAT I COULDN'T STOP STARING AT HIM.

OF COURSE HE DIDN'T LOOK AT ME AT ALL.

THANK YOU FOR COMING.

WE RAN INTO RYO-KUN, THE SINGER FROM BAROQUE!

AND THEN, AND THEN, AND THEN... ♥

HE LOOKS LIKE A CHARACTER IN A SHOJO MANGA. I BET HE'S CUTE.

SIGH

HE'S SO UNBELIEVABLY CUTE!

GORGEOUS GUYS LIKE HIM DO EXIST IN THIS WORLD, HUH...

REI-KUN IS SOOO CUTE!

HIS CLOTHES WERE REALLY COOL OFFSTAGE TOO.

ALL THE MEMBERS OF BAROQUE-SAN ARE VERY POLITE.

HE SAID HELLO TO ME EVEN THOUGH HE DIDN'T KNOW ME AT ALL. (ALSO KEIJI-KUN, YUJI-KUN AND AKIRA-KUN.)

BANSAKU-KUN LOOKS JUST LIKE A PRINCE. ♥

AH, HE'S SO GORGEOUS... ♥

HE HAS BEAUTIFUL HAIR, LONG LEGS AND ARMS, A GORGEOUS, TINY FACE, PRETTY EYES LIKE MARBLES AND SUCH SMOOTH, FLAWLESS SKIN!

HE HAD SUCH LONG, LONG EYELASHES. IT WAS ALMOST AS IF THEY WERE FAKE.

♥♥♥ SERIOUSLY, HE'S JUST LIKE A CHARACTER IN A SHOJO MANGA. ♥

THE THING THAT SURPRISED ME MOST WAS THAT...

HE SHOWED UP WITH HAIR EXTENSIONS... HE WAS WEARING THEM DURING THE SHOW.

HELLO.

GREAT SHOW!

BANSAKU-KUN FINALLY SHOWED UP! ♥♥♥

SQUIRT

HIS CLOTHES WERE REALLY CUTE OFF-STAGE.

HE'S HIP.

OH MY GOD... HIS WHOLE BODY LOOKS JUST LIKE A CHARACTER IN A SHOJO MANGA. (TAKENAGA-KUN IS KIND OF LIKE THAT TOO.)

SHE'S PROBABLY SAYING, "SORRY, IT'S SO BIG." AND...

"IT'S JUST A STUPID GIFT."

SO—

SO— IT-IT-IT'S—

WHAT'S THIS?

B-B-BIG...

IT'S SO TROPICAL...

↑ SUNAKO PRINT ALOHA SHIRT

IT-IT-IT-IT'S...

AH... UM...

UH... THANKS.

THE END

I WILL BE YOUR FAN FOREVER. ♥

I WAS BARELY ABLE TO SPEAK, SO TAKENAGA-KUN HAD TO BE MY TRANSLATOR.

"IT'S A PRESENT."

SHOCK

AH— AH-AH-

AHH!

I ATTEMPTED TO GIVE HIM A PRESENT (P)!

INSIDE— SUNAKO PRINT ALOHA SHIRT AND A KC CALENDAR. FOR HIM, IT'S PROBABLY JUST ANOTHER USELESS GIFT...

CONGRATULATIONS ON GETTING SIGNED WITH A MAJOR LABEL!

I WAS SO NERVOUS, I TOTALLY FORGOT TO TELL HIM IN PERSON, SO I MIGHT AS WELL TELL HIM NOW...

RECENT HAPPENINGS ①

THIS GUY WORKS AS AN ASSISTANT FOR KAZUTOSHI YAMANE, WHO'S A FRIEND OF MINE, AND ALSO A MANGA ARTIST (HIS MANGA IS IN GEKKAN JUMP), AND NOW HE WORKS FOR ME TOO. ♥

I HAVE BEEN BLESSED WITH THREE NEW *SUPER ASSISTANTS* STARTING WITH CHAPTER 29. ♥

YAMANE.

PEOPLE THINK HE RESEMBLES THE SINGER OF PSYCHO LE CÉMU.

YOU OWE ME ONE.

YOSHII

MY FRIENDS TOLD ME IN HIGH SCHOOL THAT I'D LOOK BETTER IN A GUY'S SCHOOL UNIFORM THAN I DO WEARING LOOSE SOCKS.

SHE'S CUTE AND MASCULINE.

I WOULD LOVE TO DRESS HER IN GIRLY CLOTHES... (AND WIGS).

APPARENTLY A LONG TIME AGO (?), SHE USED TO HANG OUT AT JINGUU BRIDGE IN COSPLAY. WOW. NOW SHE LIKES MELO-CORE MUSIC, AND HER TASTE IN MEN HAS COMPLETELY CHANGED. SHE'S NORMALLY A CALM PERSON, BUT HER PERSONALITY CHANGES WHEN IT COMES TO MANGA.

ARAKI-KUN.

YOU'RE CHOOSING YOUR ASSISTANTS BASED ON THEIR LOOKS, AREN'T YOU? ALL THE GIRLS ARE REALLY CUTE.

HE'S A PISCES AND HIS BLOOD TYPE IS AB. SAME AS MINE.

OUR NEGATIVE QUALITIES ARE VERY SIMILAR.

OR PICS OF THEM

HE'S A REALLY PURE, INNOCENT GUY WHO GETS ALL HAPPY WHEN HE SEES MY FRIENDS. I CAN'T BLAME HIM.... ALL OF MY FRIENDS ARE CUTE. ♥ HE'S A MANGA ARTIST, AND HE HELPS OUT ON HIS FREE TIME.

YOSHII AND ARAKI-KUN MAKE GOOD PARTNERS.

THANKS TO MY NEW ASSISTANTS, I WON'T CAUSE SO MUCH TROUBLE FOR THE OTHER KODANSHA COMICS MANGA ARTISTS ANYMORE! ♥ I HOPE WE CAN CONTINUE A GOOD WORKING RELATIONSHIP FOR A LONG TIME.

IS THERE ANYONE WHO CAN DRAW MOBU?

RIGHT!

I HAVE THE BEST ASSISTANTS IN THE WHOLE WORLD... THAT INCLUDES HANA-CHAN!

OH, WHAT'RE WE GONNA DO ABOUT MOBU?

*MOBU = PEOPLE IN THE BACKGROUND

THANK YOU FOR YOUR LETTERS. ♥

I WAS WONDERING WHY, AND THEN REALIZED THAT...

IN SOME OF THE LETTERS I'VE RECEIVED LATELY, PEOPLE HAVE BEEN WRITING THINGS LIKE "I'M AFRAID YOU WON'T LIKE ME BECAUSE I'M UGLY." AND "I'M SORRY THAT I'M UGLY."...

...WHEN I WROTE "I JUST HATE UGLY PEOPLE!" AT THE END OF THE BONUS PAGES IN BOOK 6.

HYAA!

...SOME PEOPLE HAD TAKEN IT PERSONALLY...

YOU POOR READERS HAVE NOTHING TO DO WITH THIS, AND I'M SORRY IF I'VE MADE YOU FEEL BAD.

I'VE HAD MANY NEGATIVE EXPERIENCES WITH UGLY PEOPLE. SOME PICKED ON ME (THE STORY IN BOOK 6 WASN'T THE ONLY TIME), STALKED ME, LIED TO ME AND SPREAD BAD RUMORS ABOUT ME (TOTALLY FALSE ONES) ETC.

ALL OF YOU WHO DID STUFF LIKE THAT TO ME IN THE PAST, YEAH I'M TALKING ABOUT YOU, ARE A BUNCH OF ASSHOLES!

I CAN TELL JUST FROM READING YOUR LETTERS. ALL OF YOUR PICTURES ARE CUTE TOO.

I'VE NEVER FELT ANYTHING BUT APPRECIATION AND LOVE TOWARD EVERYONE WHO ENJOYS MY MANGA. I LOVE YOU ALL! ♥

YOU GUYS ARE DEFINITELY NOT UGLY.

IN GUNMA

(I WAS IN SAPPORO FOR CHRISTMAS, AND SHIBUYA AND KABUKI-CHO FOR NEW YEAR'S. I WAS IN SHIBUYA RIGHT BEFORE THAT.)

YOU CAN'T SNOWBOARD IN THAT OUTFIT.

LEAVE ME ALONE!

I DON'T CARE!

YOU LOOK LIKE THE SUSPECT IN SOME MURDER MYSTERY.

YOU'RE WEARING ALL BLACK IN THE SNOW?

YOU'RE WEARING LEATHER SHOES IN THE SNOW?

...YOU WENT TO THE MOUNTAINS IN THAT OUTFIT?

SOME WENT SNOWBOARDING, AND THE REST WENT TO THE HOT SPRING.

WE SOAKED IN AN OUTDOOR HOT SPRING AS IT SNOWED. AWESOME! ♥

THE HOT SPRING WAS SO NICE.

I'M IN HEAVEN! ♥

MEGU-CHAN
SHE'S SO SEXY, EVEN FROM A FEMALE POINT OF VIEW. SHE'S CUTE TOO.

YUUKI   MARU-CHAN   MIHOKO

I DID BUY UNDERWEAR.

BY THE TIME I GOT USED TO THE GUYS COMPLAINING, WE HAD MADE IT BACK TO HACHIOJI. I DIDN'T FEEL LIKE GOING STRAIGHT HOME, SO...

WHY CAN'T THEY BE NICE LIKE THE GIRLS...

YOU LOOK LIKE THE SUSPECT IN SOME MURDER MYSTERY.

YOU WORE ALL BLACK TO GO TO A HOT SPRING?

YOU WORE LEATHER SHOES TO A HOT SPRING?

...YOU WENT TO A HOT SPRING IN THAT OUTFIT?

LEAVE ME ALONE!

HA, HA!

YOU WENT TO A HOT SPRING IN THAT OUTFIT?

I WENT TO VISIT MY FRIEND YUKO OGAWA WHO LIVES NEARBY.

...EVERYBODY KEPT REPEATING THE SAME THING OVER AND OVER.

HERE, I BROUGHT YOU BUCKWHEAT NOODLES. GO COOK THEM!

EARLY IN THE NEW YEAR...

PUFF PUFF

IT WAS JANUARY 2ND. I GOT A CALL FROM A FRIEND.

SO I LEFT THE HOUSE ALL DRESSED UP.

AND DESIGNER PERFUME TOO. ♥

AS LONG AS I'M GOING TO SEE ART, WHY NOT DRESS UP IN MY EXPENSIVE DESIGNER CLOTHES? ♥

I'M IN SHIBUYA RIGHT NOW. DO YOU WANNA GO TO A MUSEUM AND GET SOMETHING TO EAT? NORIKO'S HERE TOO.

MY FRIEND: MAA-CHAN. SHE'S A DESIGNER. SHE'S CUTE, AND MEN LOVE HER.

WE HUNG OUT IN HACHIOJI UNTIL THE NEXT MORNING, AND BELIEVE IT OR NOT...

I'LL GO! I'LL GO. I HAVEN'T BEEN TO HACHIOJI IN A LONG TIME.

I'M HAVING A FRIEND PICK ME UP TOMORROW MORNING, SO LET'S HANG OUT TOMORROW TOO!

LET'S GO TO HACHIOJI! MEGU'S GONNA BE THERE TOO.

I CALLED UP MY FRIEND AKIRA UESHIMA AND MADE HIM HANG OUT WITH US ALL NIGHT LONG.
I'M SLEEPY...
UH...SORRY.

NORICHI. SHE'S A HOUSEWIFE. SHE CAME TO VISIT FOR NEW YEAR'S FROM NAGOYA.

NORICHI WENT HOME.

BUT I HAVEN'T SLEPT AT ALL SINCE YESTERDAY...

AND THE NEXT THING I KNOW...

I DIDN'T BRING ANYTHING WITH ME...

A MINIVAN ARRIVED!

15 GUYS AND 8 GIRLS WERE SQUEEZED INTO THE CAR. (WE HAD ALL MET FOR THE FIRST TIME!) I ONLY KNEW MAA-CHAN AND MEGU-CHAN.

JUST LIKE THE TV SHOW "AINORI" (EXCEPT FOR NOBODY WAS TRYING TO HOOK UP).

THAT'S RIGHT! I ENDED UP IN THE SNOW ALL DRESSED UP IN MY EXPENSIVE DESIGNER CLOTHES...! ...IN THIS OUTFIT...

I-I CAN'T BELIEVE I'M IN THE SNOW

THEY TOOK ME TO THE SNOWY MOUNTAINS OF GUNMA. (I EVEN HAD TO STAY THERE FOR ONE NIGHT.)

LITTLE PURSE

LEATHER SHOES

VERY LONG SKIRT

...WAS I KIDNAPPED?

I WENT TO VISIT SOME FRIENDS OF MINE WITH KOTA-SAMA ON THE WAY BACK (?) FROM BAROQUE'S "ZEKKO KAMEN" TOUR. ♥

IN OSAKA

WE HAVEN'T GOTTEN USED TO IT YET, SINCE WE JUST MOVED IN.

HOW'S YOUR NEW HOUSE?

YUMMY UDON.

CHOMP CHOMP

がづっ

SAKAE.

SHE USED TO PARTICIPATE IN L'ARC-EN-CIEL'S COSPLAY GROUP NEAR JINGUU BRIDGE A FEW YEARS AGO.

THE HARDWORKING WIVES.

MATSUOKA PACHINKO PRO

YOU TOO.

ONE, TWO...

MATSUOKA FAMILY.

MATSUOKA, YOU LOOK OLDER NOW.

THE LAZY HUSBANDS.

I'VE BEEN FRIENDS WITH MATSUOKA FOR OVER TEN YEARS NOW. I'M HAPPY YOU FOUND A NICE GIRL.

WE ATE TAKOYAKI AND OKONOMIYAKI... ♥ ♥ AND WENT TO THE *ALICE AUAA* STORE.

HOW DO I LOOK? HOW DO I LOOK?

SHE'S NOT ALONE NOW!

I'VE NEVER SEEN THEIR CLOTHES IN TOKYO! KYAA!

がば
FWOOSH

IN NAGOYA

YUMMY CHICKEN.

KOTA-SAMA

I'M SLEEPY...

NORICHI.

HER HUSBAND, TORU.

YOUR HUSBAND LOOKS HANDSOME AS ALWAYS.

CHOMP CHOMP

がづっ

HARUTO. SLURP, SLURP.

HARUTO IS GUARANTEED TO BE GORGEOUS WHEN HE GROWS UP. BOTH OF HIS PARENTS ARE GOOD-LOOKING.

HAPPILY MARRIED COUPLE. ♥ ♥

HARU-CHAN.

HARU-CHAN. ♥

ANNAKA FAMILY

TOTAL LOVE BIRDS

MAA...

KOTA-SAMA IS A GIRL WHO LOOKS LIKE A PRETTY BOY.

WE HUNG OUT AND ATE TENMUSU... AND THEN I FOUND A *NA+H* STORE IN FRONT OF NAGOYA STATION! ♥ ♥ ♥

IT'S SO HARD TO FIND TENMUSU IN TOKYO! KYAA!

がば
FWOOSH

IT WAS SUCH A WONDERFUL TRIP (?)!

THE SHOWS WERE AWESOME ♥ AND THE FOOD WAS GREAT! ♥ AND I FINALLY BOUGHT THE CLOTHES I'D BEEN WANTING FOR SO LONG! ♥ ABOVE ALL, I GOT TO SEE MY OLD FRIENDS! ♥

ACTUALLY, I EVEN RAN INTO A FRIEND AT A VENUE IN NAGOYA (YUKA-CHAN WHO LIVES IN NAGOYA)! WHAT A SURPRISE!

I WAS SO HAPPY. ♥

AND...AS SOON AS I CAME BACK TO TOKYO, I WENT ON A SHOPPING SPREE AT JEAN PAUL GAULTIER IN OMOTESANDO AND H.NAOTO IN LAFORLET. AND THEN I WENT TO SEE BAROQUE'S "ZEKKO KAMEN" TOUR AGAIN, ONLY IN TOKYO THIS TIME....

I END UP DOING THE SAME THINGS, NO MATTER WHERE I AM.

THANKS TO KOSHIRO-KUN'S IMPRESSIVE SALES TECHNIQUE (?), I'VE BEEN BUYING A LOT OF CLOTHES FROM H.NAOTO IN LAFORLET LATELY....WE'VE BEEN FRIENDS FOR OVER TEN YEARS NOW.

THANKS FOR STICKING AROUND! ♥

I'VE FINALLY MOVED ... ALTHOUGH MY ROOM IS STILL MESSY.
I WASN'T CONFIDENT ENOUGH IN MY ABILITY TO TAKE CARE OF ANIMALS, SO I GAVE UP ON GETTING A PET. SNIFF ...
MY ROOM IS TRANSFORMING INTO A WEIRD PLACE WITH MY SANTA CHAIR, SKULL CHAIR, THIRTY DIFFERENT SKELETON ITEMS AND TWO TORSOS.
THAT'S RIGHT. I'M THE ONE WHO'S CHASING THE GUYS AWAY ... SIGH.

THANK YOU SO MUCH FOR YOUR LETTERS. ♥
YOU GUYS GIVE ME ENERGY ... THAT MAKES ME A MILLION TIMES STRONGER!
SORRY FOR MAKING YOU WORRY EVER SINCE I WROTE THAT I WAS "EMOTIONALLY IMBALANCED." THANKS FOR YOUR KINDNESS. I'M OKAY NOW ... PROBABLY ⟶ HEY!

I'M SORRY IT'S TAKING SO MUCH TIME TO WRITE YOU BACK.
I REALLY HOPE I CAN RESPOND SOMEDAY SOON ...!

SEE YOU ALL AGAIN IN BOOK 8! ♥

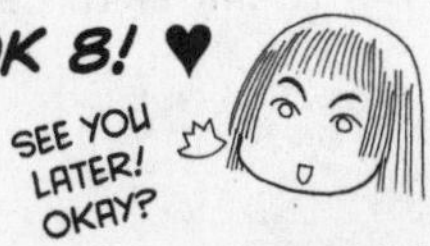
SEE YOU LATER! OKAY?

SPECIAL THANKS

HANA-CHAN,
ARAKI-KUN,
YOSHII.

AYUAYU WATANABE,
ATSUKO NAMBA,
IYU KOZAKURA.

MINE-SAMA,
SHIOZAWA-SAMA,
INO-SAMA,
EVERYONE IN THE EDITORIAL DEPARTMENT.

CREDITS FOR THE BONUS PAGES ...

MASASHI TAKENAGA-SAMA,
YUJI,
BAROQUE-SAMA

MA-CHAN, MEGU-CHAN,
NORICHI, KOTAKI-CHAN,
SAKAE, AN-CHAN,
TAKA MATSUOKA, YUKO NEO ...
WHAT DO YOU MEAN NEO?
KAI-CHAN, CHISATO-CHAN,
TORU-SAN, MAKO, KOSHIRO-KUN,
YUKA-CHAN AND HER FRIENDS,
EVERYONE WHO SENT ME LETTERS.

About the Creator

Tomoko Hayakawa was born on March 4.

Since her debut as a manga creator, Tomoko Hayakawa has worked on many shojo titles with the theme of romantic love—only to realize that she could write about other subjects as well. She decided to pack her newest story with the things she likes most, which led to her current, enormously popular series, *The Wallflower*.

Her favorite things are: Tim Burton's *The Nightmare Before Christmas*, Jean-Paul Gaultier, and samurai dramas on TV. Her hobbies are collecting items with skull designs and watching *bishonen* (beautiful boys). Her dream is to build a mansion like the one that the Addams family lives in. Her favorite pastime is to lie around at home with her cat, Ten (whose full name is Tennosuke).

Her zodiac sign is Pisces, and her blood group is AB.

Translation Notes

Japanese is a tricky language for most Westerners, and translation is often more art than science. For your edification and reading pleasure, here are notes on some of the places where we could have gone in a different direction in our translation of the work, or where a Japanese cultural reference is used.

Nosebleeds (page 27)

In Japan, nosebleeds are said to be caused by sudden sexual arousal. That's why Sunako often gets nosebleeds when she has a close encounter with one of the guys.

Rub-a-dub-dub (page 33)

Japanese families usually fill the bathtub once and share the same bath water. It's customary to wash your hair and body in the shower first before soaking in the tub. You never use soap in the tub itself.

Lone Wolf (page 51)

Ranmaru is imagining himself as the famous character in the popular TV series/manga *Kozure Ookami* (Lone Wolf and Cub). "Shito shito picchan" is part of the show's theme song. The series is about a samurai who travels with his baby.

しとしとぴっちゃん
しとぴっちゃん

shito shito pichhan shito picchan

...BE A FATHER...

BUT I'M KNOWN FOR MY INDEPENDENT LIFESTYLE, AND MY ABILITIES TO SEDUCE WOMEN.

SOME EVEN CALL ME "THE PRINCE OF THE WHITE ROSE." HOW CAN I POSSIBLY...

DAIGOROU.

PAPA!

*if you don't get this joke, go ask your mom.

A REAL IRON MAIDEN!

I'VE NEVER SEEN ONE BEFORE. ♥♥♥

AWWW.

Iron maiden (page 92)

The iron maiden, also known as the Virgin of Nuremberg, was a torture device used during the Middle Ages. The prisoner was shut inside and then pierced with numerous metal spikes.

Emperor Nero (page 92)

Nero was a Roman emperor from 54 A.D. to 68 A.D. Sunako-chan really knows her history.

THIS IS WHAT THEY USED TO EXECUTE PEOPLE BACK IN EMPEROR NERO'S TIME.

Dorifu (page 131)

Dorifu, or "The Drifters," is a famous comedy troupe.

Oden (page 138)

Oden is a tasty dish made up of various ingredients boiled in soup stock. Common ingredients include daikon radish, hardboiled eggs, *konyaku* (yam cake) and various types of fishcake. Oden food stalls are a common sight in urban areas.

Showa period (page 141)

The Showa period of Japanese history lasted from 1926—1989. The current period is called Heisei.

Loose Socks (page 170)

Loose socks are a type of white kneesock that schoolgirls wear with their uniforms.

Tenmusu (page 172)

An *onigiri* (rice ball) stuffed with tempura.

Takoyaki (page 172)

Takoyaki are octopus fritters. *Okonomiyaki* is a sort of pancake stuffed with meat and veggies.

Preview of Volume 8

We're pleased to present you a preview from Volume 8. This volume is available in English now!

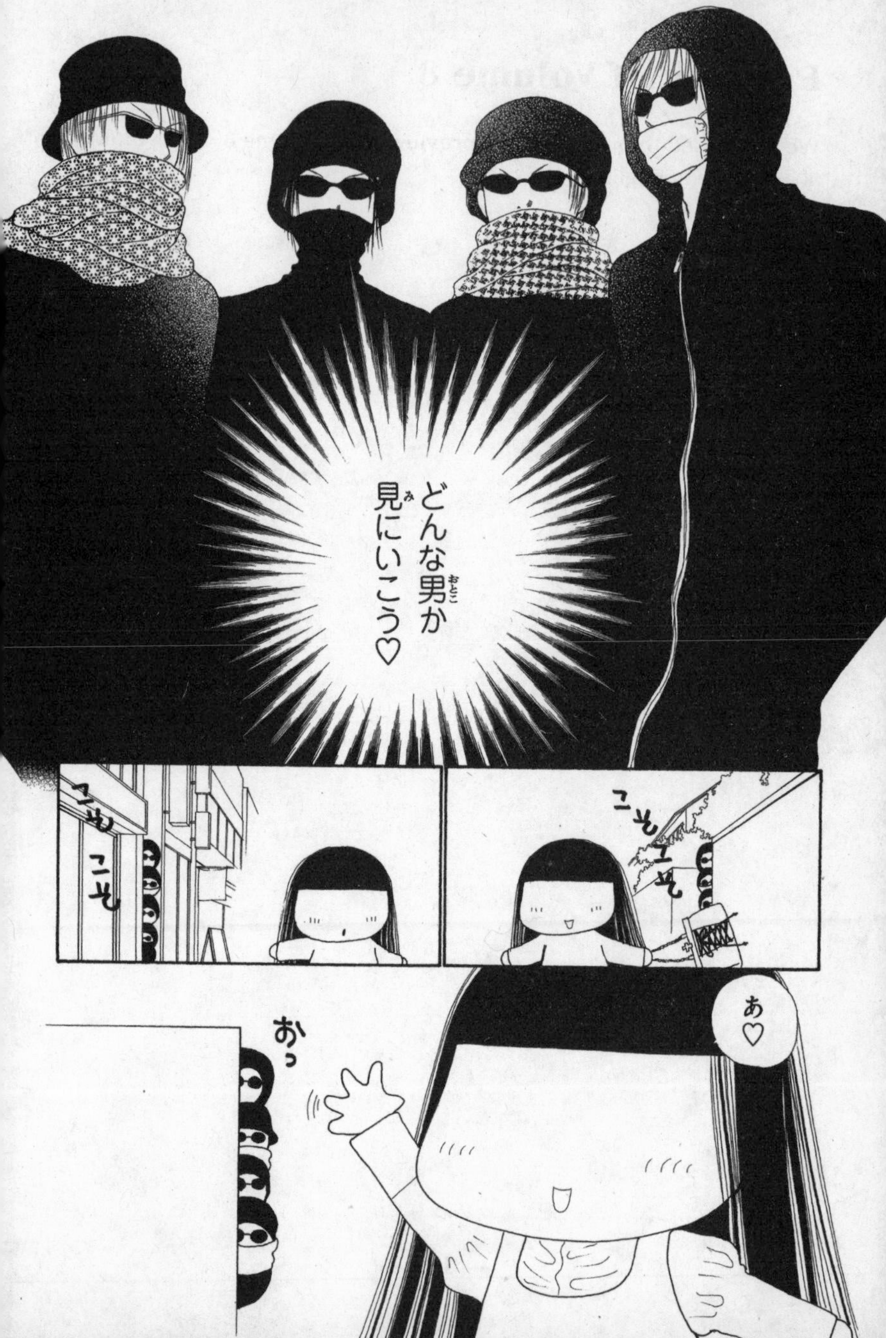
どんな男か
見にいこう♡
こそ
こそ
こそ
こそ
あ♡
おっ

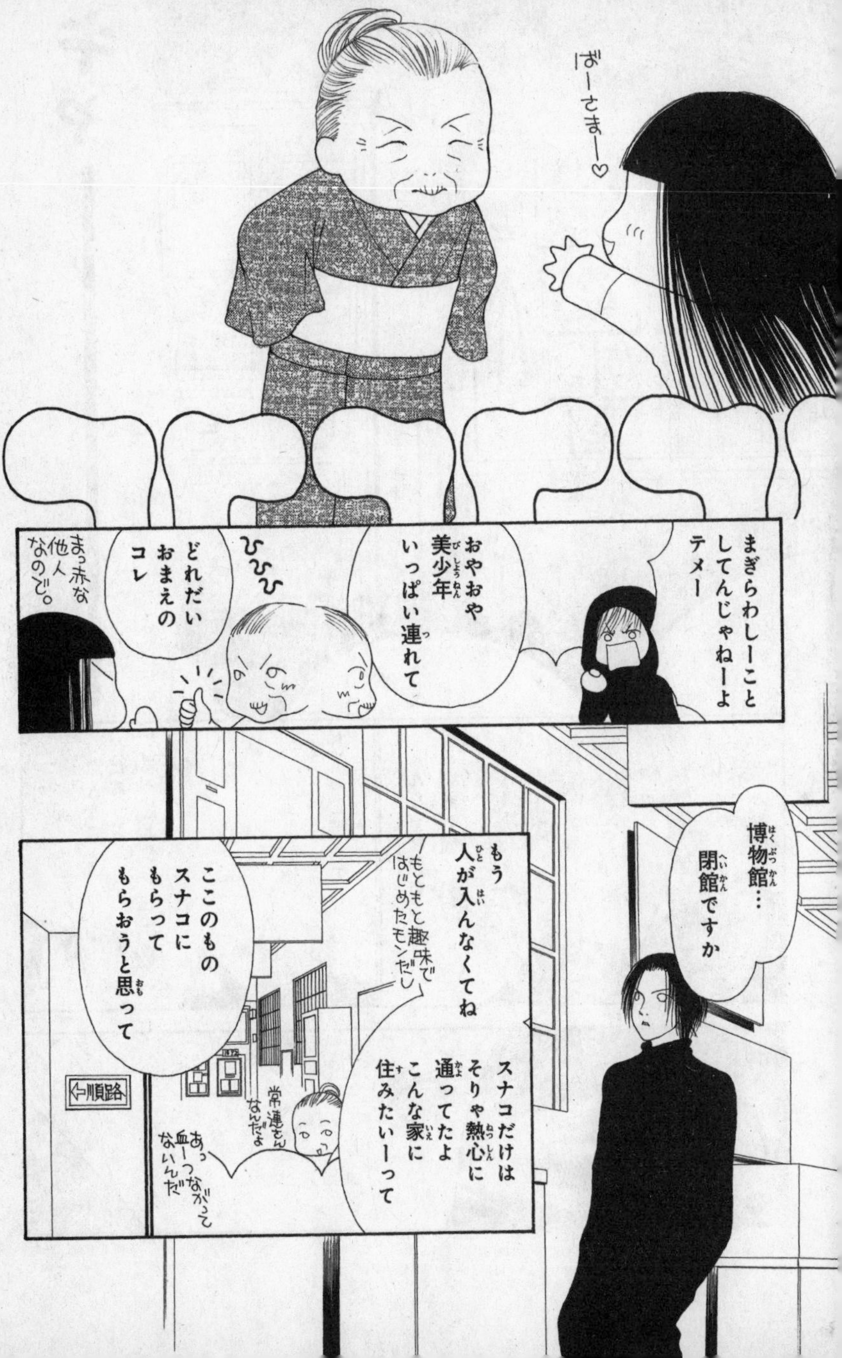
ばーさまー♡
まぎらわしーことしてんじゃねーよテメー
おやおや美少年いっぱい連れて
ひひひ
どれだいおまえのコレ
まっ赤な他人なので。
博物館…閉館ですか
もう人が入んなくてね
もともと趣味ではじめたモンだし
スナコだけはそりゃ熱心に通ってたよこんな家に住みたいーって
ここのものスナコにもらってもらおうと思って
⇦順路
常連さんなんだよ
あっ血一つながってないんだ

キャー

こ…
こんなこと
だろうと
思ったよ……

ちょっと待って!!

こんな気味悪いもの
あの家に置く気!?

ただですよ
いっぱいあんのに

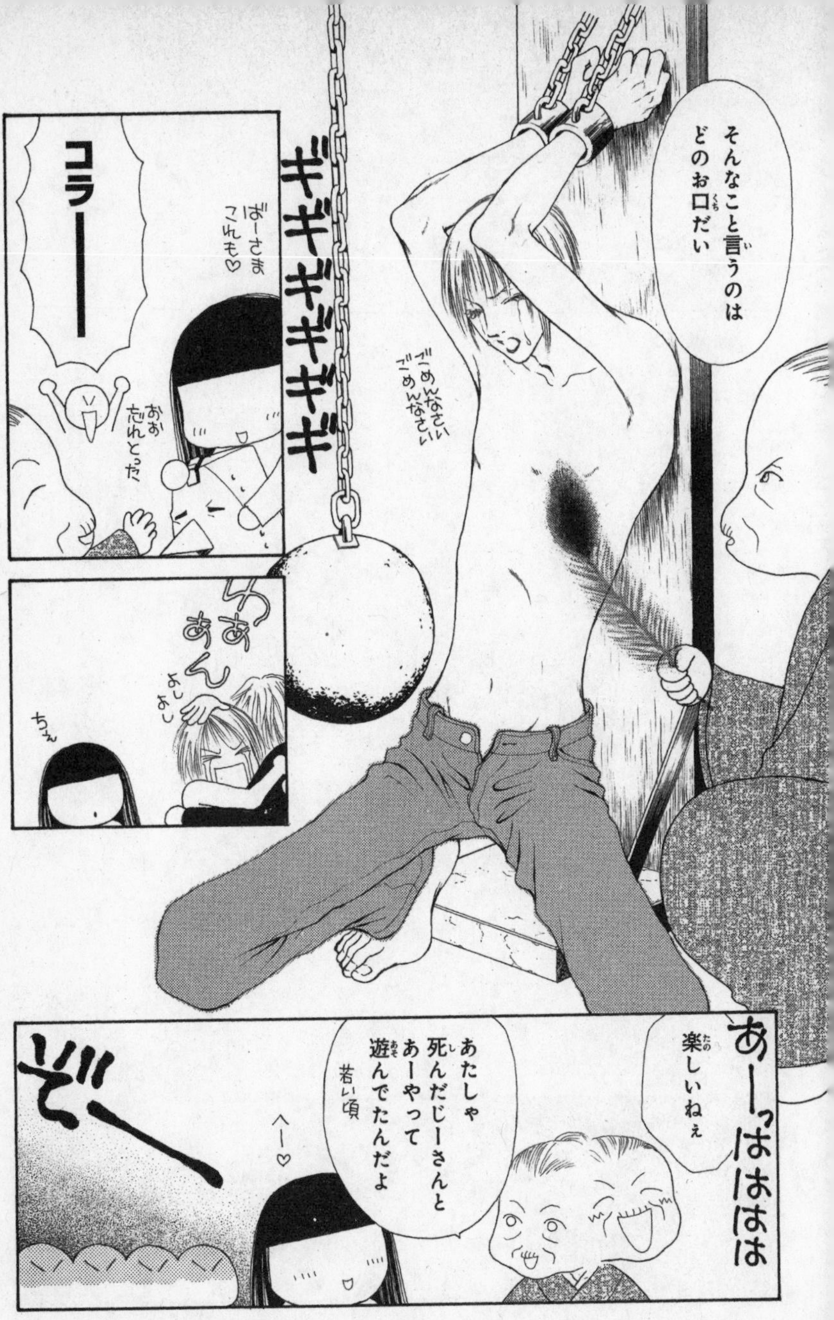
そんなこと言うのはどのお口だい
ごめんなさいごめんなさい
ギギギギギ
ばーさまこれも♡
コラーー
おお忘れとった
わああん
よしよし
ちーん
あーっははは
楽しいねぇ
あたしゃ死んだじーさんとあーやって遊んでたんだよ
若い頃
へー♡
ぞ〜